AGT-72

Language and Reality

Language and Reality

An Introduction to the Philosophy of Language

Michael Devitt and Kim Sterelny

A Bradford Book
The MIT Press
Cambridge, Massachusetts

This book was printed and bound in Great Britain

Library of Congress Cataloging in Publication Data
Devitt, Michael, 1938–
   Language and reality

   "A Bradford book."
   Bibliography: p.
   1. Languages—Philosophy.   I. Sterelny, Kim.
II. Title.
P106.D458   1987   401   86-20076
ISBN 0-262-04089-1 (hard)
ISBN 0-262-54046-0 (paper)

Contents

'**' indicates chapters and sections which are difficult and probably best ignored in an initial approach.

Preface

This book is an introduction to the philosophy of language. It is intended primarily, but not solely, as a textbook.

Our justification for writing a textbook is the usual one: dissatisfaction with the ones already available. We find some of these too discursive; some too long and encyclopaedic; some too difficult; some too wrong. Most important of all, none have the particular purpose and orientation of this book.

Introducing the philosophy of language is undoubtedly difficult. It is a field in which a hundred flowers, and many weeds, bloom. There is amazingly little agreement, even about basics. It is often not clear what problems a theory is trying to solve. It is often not clear whether theories are in competition and, if not, how they relate to each other. As a result, attempts in achieving the neutrality usually regarded as desirable in a textbook tend to founder; the student is presented with a bewildering *smorgasbord*.

We make no pretence at neutrality. A definite theoretical perspective pervades this book. The work of others is organized and placed relative to this perspective. We hope that this mode of presentation will help even those who reject the perspective. Aside from that, we think the perspective is an important one that has been decidedly under-represented in the philosophy of language.

Because of the role of this theoretical perspective we hope that this book will be of interest not only to students embarking on the philosophy of language but also to advanced ones and to professionals.

We have written on the philosophy of language before. Naturally enough, many of our earlier thoughts reappear in this book. However, writing it forced us to break new ground. We have developed our causal theory of natural kind terms. We have made our first serious attempt at theories of reference for artefactual kind terms like 'pencil' and socio-legal kind terms like 'bachelor'. We have worked hard to place the work of the transformational grammarians within our perspective.

We think that the book should be suitable for two slightly different courses. One course would be a beginning- or intermediate-level course aimed at students with possibly no more than a passing interest in the philosophy of language. Aside from students majoring in philosophy, we have in mind: literature students who have come across, for example, structuralist thought; linguistics students interested in semantics; anthropology students interested in linguistic relativity; and students in cognitive science interested in the problems of intentionality and linguistic competence.

The other course for which the book should be suitable would be a more traditional intermediate-level course for students with a committed interest in the philosophy of language. Passages in the book that are suitable for this course, but probably not for the other, appear between **s. These passages are difficult and are probably best ignored in an initial approach. (** before a chapter or section heading indicates that the whole chapter or section is in that category.)

We have used the following convention for quotation marks. To name an expression we either put it between single quotation marks or put it on display. To quote a passage we either put it between double quotation marks or put it on display. We also use double quotation marks for "shudder" or "scare" quotes. All quotation marks within quotation marks are single.

**Our perspective has four aspects. First, and most important, we are committed to *naturalism*. (a) We give the theory of language no special status: it is an empirical and conjectural theory like any other. (b) Our approach is physicalistic: we see people as nothing but complex parts of the physical world.

Naturalism has been particularly under-represented in thinking about language. It leads directly to what may be the most controversial parts of the book: our deflationary view of the significance of the study of language. In this century, theories of language have led to surprising and mysterious views of reality. Many thinkers in several fields have been led to forms of neo-Kantian relativism: Benjamin Lee Whorf in anthropology; Thomas Kuhn and Paul Feyerabend in the philosophy of science; Hilary Putnam in philosophy; the structuralists in just about everything. Michael Dummett's verificationist theory of language leads him into a different, but equally mysterious, anti-realism. "Ordinary language" and "conceptual analysis" philosophers identify the very subject of philosophy with the study of language. For Wittgenstein, philosophy was grammatical therapy. We stand opposed to all these pretentions for the study of language.

Second, our philosophy of mind is *functionalist*. It draws on such philosophers as Jerry Fodor, Daniel Dennett, William Lycan and Stephen Stich. We like to see our book as having a place in the exciting, and somewhat chaotic, inter-disciplinary field that has become known as *cognitive science*.

Third, we help ourselves to the insights of *transformational generative grammar*, whilst remaining sceptical of its claims about psychological reality.

Finally, we embrace *causal theories of reference* of the sort introduced by Saul Kripke, Keith Donnellan and Hilary Putnam. We are guided by Hartry Field in placing reference within the theory of language: reference is needed to explain truth.

Causal theories of reference have, of course, enjoyed quite a bit of attention and popularity in the philosophy of language. However, we do not think that the strength of the case for them has been fully appreciated, largely because they have not been set firmly in a naturalistic setting.

Quine's influence on our thinking is apparent throughout, not least in our naturalism. However, the book contains no systematic discussion of his views on language. In particular, we do not discuss his arguments for the indeterminacy of translation (though we think that the sceptical view of truth considered in chapter 9 is derived from Quine). Our excuse is that the arguments are just too difficult to be discussed helpfully in a book of this sort. Certainly, they are too difficult for us to discuss helpfully.**

We think it prudent to offer a few pre-emptive apologies. First, though we are confident that the programme we have endorsed *can* be carried out, certainly we have not demonstrated this. Still more certainly, we have not demonstrated it by doing it. These are early days for naturalistic philosophy in general and naturalistic philosophy of language in particular. So, though it is not surprising that its successes are fragmentary and partial, nonetheless those successes *are* fragmentary and partial. Second, the demands of clarity and our temperaments lead us to robust statements of our own views and their divergences from the views of others. Our responses to relativism and anti-realism are particularly vigorous. We do not mean to offend and hope we haven't. Finally, in the nature of things, reading guides cannot be comprehensive. We did our best to survey the literature in preparing the "suggested readings", but doubtless we have made many errors. All we can say to the disgruntled author of an omitted piece is that the omission may not have been deliberate.

The book was truly a joint production. In the beginning, there was the idea of a course along roughly the lines of the book. The idea was Sterelny's but it was for a course by Devitt. Reluctantly, Devitt adopted the idea. He gave the course in 1983, with the assistance of Sterelny. He wrote extensive notes. He was so pleased by this performance that he proposed a joint book to Sterelny. Sterelny wrote the first draft in 1984. Devitt used this for a repeat of the course in 1984 and began to write the second draft. He continued writing in 1985, and some version of the second draft was used for another repeat of the course. The final version of the book is the result of many amendments to the second draft by both of us – often, it seemed, far too many amendments.

The name proved difficult. We wanted '*Language, Mind and Everything*', for we enjoy mocking the pretensions of recent philosophy of language. However, we gave into the advice that jokey titles don't wear well and may not pay in Peoria. We settled for something more sober.

We are grateful to the following for written comments on early versions of parts of the book: John Bigelow, Fiona Cowie, Stephen Gaukroger, Peter Godfrey-Smith, Richard Hall, William Lycan, Ruth Millikan, Conall O'Conall, Philip Pettit, Stephen Stich, and David Stove. We are indebted to Elizabeth Gross for advice on structuralist literature. Finally we thank the following for their comments on the penultimate version: David Armstrong, David Braddon-Mitchell, John Bigelow, Fiona Cowie, and Peter Godfrey-Smith.

Michael Devitt
Kim Sterelny
June 1986

PART I

INTRODUCTION

1

Introduction

1.1 The philosophy of language

The philosophy of language raises issues both important and difficult.

The importance of language to human life is obvious. All human societies are language using, as are all their more or less normal members. Language acquisition is one of the few cognitive skills that is, near enough, both common and peculiar to humans. Some theorists have been led by this to see language as *the* most central characteristic of the human animal.

The obvious importance of language makes its study worthwhile, but does not prepare one for the ascendancy that this study has achieved in philosophy. Over the last century or so the philosophy of language has become the pivotal area of philosophy, particularly within the English-speaking tradition. Opinions about language have been thought to settle traditional philosophical problems in epistemology, metaphysics and ethics. The very nature of philosophy itself has been linked by many to the study of language. In our view, much of this goes too far: philosophy of language has become too big for its boots. We shall return to this often (parts IV and V).

The philosophy of language is certainly difficult. In part this is because of our closeness to language: we find it hard to get a proper perspective on it. In any case, there is a vigorous, wide-ranging and bewildering debate on foundational and conceptual issues in the philosophy of language. Many competing theories are on offer, yet it is often hard to see what these are theories *of*. What problems are they trying to solve? What counts as *evidence* for or against a theory? Are different theories really concerned with the same problems, so that they are really in competition? If not – and it often seems not – how do they relate to one another? Finally, the status of philosophical theories of language is obscure and controversial, as we shall begin to see in section 1.3.

You may wonder why language is studied *in philosophy* at all. Why is the study not left to linguistics which is, after all, "the science of language"? The three main branches of linguistics are phonology, concerned with *sounds*;

syntax, concerned with *grammatical structure*; and semantics, concerned with *meaning*. It is in semantics, or "the theory of meaning", that the theoretical and conceptual chaos mentioned above is most striking. There are also some similar problems in syntax. Philosophy is typically concerned with the most intractable and conceptually difficult parts of various disciplines. So it is not surprising that it is deeply concerned with semantics and has some concern with syntax. In contrast, it is not concerned with phonology at all.

Finally, a word of warning. What follows is not an auctioneer's catalogue of the theories and ideas in this controversial subject. It cannot therefore be either neutral or comprehensive. Our approach reflects our ideas of what is central and peripheral; of the main issues and of the blind and side alleys. The approach is not idiosyncratic, but it is not shared by all, or even most, philosophers.

1.2 What is the problem?

What are the main problems in the study of language? We can start answering this question by listing some of the most salient features of language.

1   A language is a system for communicating information between ourselves and others. The information may be about the social or physical environment, or it may be about ourselves.
2   Language serves other purposes of communication. It is used in non-informational and not purely informational social interactions: to greet, question, command, joke, offend, abuse, intimidate and so on.
3   Though the uses of language for communication are striking, its private uses should not be overlooked: we talk to ourselves; we write for our own future benefit. It may be that we often *think* in our language as well: we will return to this possibility (sections 7.2–7.3).
4   Implicitly, the above talk of language has been restricted to the "natural" languages of humans; for example, English or Swahili. Such languages are not our only communication systems; think of flag signals or "body language", for example. Nor are communication systems restricted to humans. Language (in our restricted sense) is, however, special in important ways.
    a   *Stimulus independence*. In most circumstances, as full a description as you like of a person's physical environment does not enable you to predict her next utterance. The contrast with animal communication systems, for example, is notable.
        Briefly, animal communication systems seem to be of two sorts. First, birds (and apparently non-human primates) have a fixed and

fairly small repertoire of distinct signals, each of which has a set function: flight call, alarm call and the like. A particular environment elicits the appropriate response. Human language does not consist of such a small fixed repertoire of predictable responses. Second, consider bees. A bee returning from a distant food source dances a message. The length of the dance and its pattern indicate the direction and distance of the food source. This remarkaby efficient system of communication differs from those of birds in having an unlimited number of signals: the length and the pattern are capable of infinite variations. Nevertheless, the bee's system is not flexible in the way human language is. Each response is environmentally fixed: if you know where the bee has been, and if you know the coding system, you can predict the pattern of the dance. In contrast, if a person comes from a food source – a good restaurant, for example – you cannot predict her words. Her food description – indeed, whether she talks about food at all – is stimulus-independent.

b   *Abstractness*. A sentence may abstract from many details of a situation, focussing on just one. Thus, 'Orson weighs 130 kg' tells you nothing about Orson other than his mass. Symbols in many other systems cannot be quite so abstract; a photograph or sketch of Orson will tell of many of his properties. Even the bee's dance cannot be silent on the distance of the food source while revealing its direction.

c   *Arbitrariness*. In general, linguistic symbols have no intrinsic or necessary connection with their referents. The inscription, 'Ronald Reagan', happens to refer to a certain president of the USA, yet it is in an importance sense arbitrary that it does so. That inscription could have been used to refer to Bob Hope; and Reagan could have been called 'Hopalong Cassidy'. This arbitrariness is nicely illustrated by the English logician, Charles Dodgson, better known as Lewis Carroll:

> "... – and that shows that there are three hundred and sixty-four days when you might get un–birthday presents –"
>
> "Certainly," said Alice.
>
> "And only *one* for birthday presents you know. There's glory for you!"
>
> "I don't know what you mean by 'glory'," Alice said.
>
> Humpty Dumpty smiled contemptuously. "Of course you don't know – till I tell you. I meant 'there's a nice knock–down argument for you!'"
>
> "But 'glory' doesn't mean 'a nice knock–down argument'," Alice objected.
>
> "When *I* use a word," Humpty Dumpty said, in rather a

scornful tone, "it means just what I choose it to mean – neither more nor less."

"The question is," said Alice, "whether you *can* make words mean so many different things."

"The question is," said Humpty Dumpty, "which is to be master – that's all." (Carroll 1962: 247)

What Humpty Dumpty is emphasizing is the arbitrariness of language. (This is not to say that Alice does not have a point too. This could be brought out using the distinction between speaker meaning and conventional meaning: section 7.4.)

d   *Medium independence*. Linguistic communication can be effected in speech, writing, braille, and so on. There seems to be no limit to the media we could use for, say, English. The birds and the bees are limited to one.

e   *Productivity*. The matching of each signal with its "meaning" is not something that we learn signal by signal (nor is it innately programmed into us signal by signal as are calls into birds). We learn the elements of signals – words – together with a recipe for making complete signals – sentences – out of the elements. Thus your knowledge of a few words and the constructions of English enables you to understand 'Andropov liquidated the Hungarians' and 'the Hungarians liquidated Andropov' even though you may never have come across these sentences before. (The bee's system has *some* productivity, but note how simple its generating recipe is.)

f   *Power*. One very special thing about language is its power and versatility. It can serve the many purposes of communication (1 and 2 above) and some private ones (3 above). It enables us to deal with the past and the future, the present and the absent. We talk of an enormous range of topics: of "tables, people, molecules, light rays, retinas, air waves, prime numbers, infinite classes, joy and sorrow, good and evil" (Quine 1966: 215). Contrast this with the bee's monomania.

It is clear that language gets its power from many of the other special features we have mentioned.

In sum, language is a uniquely powerful communication system that is stimulus – and medium-independent, abstract, arbitrary and productive. What is it about language that it gives it these salient features? What peculiar properties do linguistic symbols have that lead people to produce and respond to them the way they do? Our main problem is to describe and explain these properties which enable language to play its extraordinarily important role in people's lives. People can use the arbitrary symbol 'Thales' to convey information, or misinformation, about a Greek philosopher who has been dead for two millennia. How is this feat possible?

We shall follow custom and use the term 'meaning' as shorthand for the properties of language that concern us. So our main problem becomes that of explaining meaning.

Though explaining the meaning of linguistic symbols is the main problem, it is not the only one. A characteristic of these items – almost too obvious to mention – is that people *understand* them. It is because a person understands Swahili, it is because she is *linguistically competent* in Swahili, that she is able to participate in communication using Swahili. Because of that competence she produces and responds appropriately to Swahili sentences. What is it for a person to be competent in a language? Whereas the problem of meaning is concerned with a property of linguistic symbols, this problem is concerned with a property of people; more strictly, it is concerned with a property of minds. The two problems are clearly related: we can expect a theory of one to throw light on the other. However the problems are also clearly different. Yet, interestingly enough, we shall see (8.2, 8.7) that they are often conflated, with disastrous results for the study of language.

In part II, our focus will be on meaning and we will, so far as is possible, set aside issues to do with the mind's relation to language. However, it will prove impossible to ignore the issue of competence. In part III, the mind's relation to language is centre stage.

1.3 What is a theory of language?

We have mentioned a difficulty: there is obscurity and controversy over the status of theories of language (1.1). This issue of status is highly abstract: it requires a theory of theories of language, a "meta-theory". It would be nice to ignore the meta-theory and get on with the theory, but that is a luxury we cannot afford. We think that many mistakes in the theory of language arise from a mistaken meta-theory. Further, we think that these mistakes are often facilitated by a failure to be explicit about the meta-theory: once the implicit meta-theory is exposed, it can be seen to be implausible and unsupportable. So we shall start by laying our cards on the table. We shall return to this matter often in our criticism of other views.

Our approach to the problem of language is *naturalistic* in two respects. First, a theory of linguistic phenomena has just the same status as a theory of any other phenomena: it is empirical and conjectural. We are confronted with a mysterious and complex world and have developed theories to explain and render tractable these complexities: theories in physics, biology, the social sciences and the like. The theory of language is just another such theory; another part of our total theory of nature.

One can be misled into treating the theory of language differently by the fact that, at bottom, much of what it has to say at present is "common sense". People divide linguistic phenomena into sentences and words; they divide words into nouns, verbs, etc. They think that expressions are meaningful and have meanings. They think that words refer to parts of the world. They think that sentences express thoughts; that some are true and some false, but none are both; that some are questions and others commands; and so on. These gems of common sense, taken over by linguistics, may seem to have some special status. It is easy to succumb to the illusion that whereas science, especially its abstract and speculative branches like cosmology and particle physics, is conjectural, empirical and fallible, common sense is not. So, it is thought to be a *theory* that the earth and moon are linked by gravitational force, but a *fact* that sentences have meanings. This illusion is engendered by the familiarity of common sense.

Common sense is best seen as a mix of *folk theories* or, if talk of theories seems too pretentious here, *folk opinions*. These, like scientific theories, help people better understand and explain the phenomena that confront them. So the above gems are best seen as articulations of folk linguistics' response to features like 1–4 above (1.2). Folk theories differ from scientific ones in being immature: they are less precise, systematic and explicit; they lack a methodology for development. More seriously, they differ in being believed uncritically.

A glance at the past shows that folk theory has no special warrant. Much of early European folk geography, folk meteorology and folk medicine have been comprehensively rejected. We no longer think that the Earth is flat, nor that the winds are under the direction of supernatural agents. We no longer explain epilepsy as possession by spirits. Nevertheless, where a folk theory is working well, just as where a scientific theory is working well, it is *unlikely* to be wholly wrong. So, it is reasonable to suppose, for instance, that folk psychology, with its long history of fairly successful use (we have *quite* a good understanding of one another), has a lot of truth in it. Similarly, perhaps, folk linguistics. Nonetheless, even the best folk theories stand in need of revision and reconstruction.

Since theories of language have no special status, we face a problem of conciliation and integration. Our theory must fit in with the rest of our beliefs about people and the world. This brings us to the second respect in which our approach is naturalistic: it is *physicalistic*.

We think that people are best seen as part of the natural world. They are not special except in detail and complexity. (a) They are part of animate nature; part of the biological world. (b) The biological differs from the inanimate only in complexity: no vital essence distinguishes the living from the non-living. To be living is only to have a special, if complex, chemistry.

Physicalism is intrinsically plausible. It has excellent scientific support from evolutionary theory, biology and biochemistry. These sciences underscore the biochemical and physiological continuities between humans and the rest of nature. There are, we believe, no good arguments *against* this perspective.

Our theory of language must, therefore, be physicalistic. Any linguistic facts there are must be, ultimately, physical. Semantic notions like meaning, truth and reference can be used only if they can be explained in non-linguistic terms; they are not "primitive", not theoretically fundamental. Biologists were not satisfied to leave the notion of gene as primitive, they wanted to understand the mechanism by which inheritable characteristics are encoded in a cell. Their search led to the discovery of the structure of DNA. Similarly, we seek a deeper explanation of semantic notions. We might, for example, hope to explain them in psychological terms; then, hope to explain the psychological in neuro-anatomical and biochemical terms; then, explain those in physical and chemical terms.

Some think this hope is a vain one. In particular, the famous Harvard philosopher, W. V. Quine, doubts that we can explain a robust notion of meaning physicalistically. This leads him into semantic "eliminativism": the familiar notions of folk semantics have no place in a developed theory of humans and their languages. We are not eliminativist, but we accept his moral: if notions like meaning and truth cannot be explained in non-semantic, naturalistic terms, we should do without them in our theory of language.

We return to the defence of naturalism in part V.

**1.4 The menu

[Passages and references between **s are difficult and could well be ignored in an initial approach.]

We finish this chapter with a preview.

Part II is centred on the problem of meaning, on explaining those properties of linguistic symbols that enable them to play their distinctive role in our lives. In chapter 2 we argue that the core of a sentence's meaning is its truth conditions; that is, the property of a sentence which, together with the world, make it true or false. We suggest that the truth conditions of a sentence depend on the referential properties of its elements together with its syntactic structure. So, in chapters 3–5 we discuss reference and in chapter 6 we discuss structure.

We reject description theories of reference for basic terms like proper names and natural kind terms, urging causal theories instead. However, we find a place for description theories with some other terms. In discussing structure, we explain, and help ourselves to, the insights of transformational grammar.

In part III, our focus changes from symbols and their meaning to an intimately related but nonetheless distinct arena, the mind.

In chapter 7 we suggest that the relation between thought and language is somewhat symbiotic. On the other hand, thought is typically language-like in character. Indeed, we urge that most thoughts of the adult human *are* sentences of his public language in some kind of neural format. On the other hand, the development of that public language and the system of conventions it embodies must depend on the achievement of cognitive pioneers in having thoughts not then expressible in their public language.

Chapter 8 is devoted to the vexed and difficult problem of linguistic competence. We develop, to some extent, a view of competence, but the basic thrust of the chapter is critical. We reject certain intellectualist theories favoured by linguists and philosophers. We reject the view that the grammar being discovered by transformationalists is realized in each speaker. We doubt that any concepts, whether linguistic or not, are in any interesting sense innate.

Chapter 9 returns to the issue of truth, and confronts a recent development in theorizing about it. A number of contemporary philosophers have argued that the notion of truth is, in some way, theoretically redundant: we do not need it to explain anything. We describe this development and give our own justification for truth.

In chapter 10 we take a decidedly sceptical view of linguistic relativity: the view that (a) your general picture of the world is influenced and constrained by the language you speak, and (b) languages differ enough to produce incommensurable world views. We concede a little to this view but, in general, find it exciting only when false.

Part IV considers the relation between theories of language and the metaphysical doctrine of realism. Common-sense realism is the view that the ordinary furniture of our environment – cats, trees, stones, etc. – exist independently of us and our thoughts on the matter. Scientific realism takes a similar view of the objects of science. Many theorists have inferred anti-realist views from their favoured theories of language. In some usually ill-specified sense, the world is said to depend for its existence or nature on us.

We consider several of these theorists, taking a mostly critical view of their theories of language, and a very critical view of the metaphysical views they derive from them. However, our main point is that a realist metaphysics has more secure epistemic foundations than *any* theory of language. So, the appropriate strategy is to construct theories of language from that perspective, not to construct metaphysical views from the perspective of one's favoured theory of language. If a theory of language contradicts our best overall picture of the world, so much the worse for the theory.

In chapter 11 we consider the verificationism of the logical positivists and Michael Dummett. In chapter 12 we consider various forms of neo-Kantianism: the relativism of Benjamin Lee Whorf, according to which languages construct different realities; and, finally, the latest views of the former realist, Hilary

Putnam. Chapter 13 is devoted to structuralism. This movement, centred in France, is also committed to a relativistic neo-Kantianism.

The book ends, in part V, with a discussion of philosophy itself. Considerations about language have dominated much of twentieth-century, Anglo-American philosophy. In chapter 14 we recount that dominance, tentatively diagnose it, and reject it. Our stance is, as always naturalistic. In chapter 15 we reject another challenge to naturalistic philosophy: rational psychology. That approach takes our ordinary views of people and their language – folk psychology and folk linguistics – to be outside science; they are thought to supply knowledge of a different sort altogether.**

Suggested reading

1.2

Akmajian, Demers and Harnish 1979, part I, contains a good survey of animal communication.

1.3

Churchland 1979, *Scientific Realism and the Plasticity of Mind*, contains a vigorous defence of the possibility of massive revision of folk theory. He argues for eliminativism about the mind which, because of the links between mind and language to be explored later (part III), is closely related to semantic eliminativism. He summarizes his argument in his excellent introductory text, *Matter and Consciousness* (1984): 43–9.

Explanation of one set of facts in terms of another often involve quite complex relations between the two. See Fodor 1975, *The Language of Thought*: Introduction. See also Devitt 1984a, *Realism and Truth*: section 6.2.

Quine's classic assault on meaning and its relatives is, "Two dogmas of empiricism", in *From a Logical Point of View* (1961), reprinted in Rosenberg and Travis 1971, *Readings in the Philosophy of Language*. **This eliminativism was continued in *Word and Object* (1960) with his famous, but difficult, argument for the indeterminacy of translation: chapter 2.** The most readable account of his position is in *Philosophy of Logic* (1970): chapter 1. A sympathetic and interesting examination of Quine's views is to be found in Romanos 1983, *Quine and Analytic Philosophy*.

Just as linguistics should be naturalized so also should epistemology. The quotations from Quine in section 1.2 is from the opening paragraph of a marvellous essay arguing for a naturalized epistemology, "The scope and language of science" in *The Ways of Paradox* (1966).

1.4

There are a number of anthologies on philosophy of language, to which we shall often refer in the Suggested reading sections. Three general collections are, Rosenberg and Travis 1971, *Readings in the Philosophy of Language*; Steinberg and Jacobovits 1971, *Semantics*; and Davidson and Harman 1976, *The Logic of Grammar*. Also general in scope, but attempting a "state of the art" survey at the time of their publication are, Davidson and Harman 1972, *Semantics of Natural Language*; and Gunderson 1975, *Language, Mind and Knowledge*.

Schwartz 1977, *Naming, Necessity, and Natural Kinds*, is a good collection focussing on the problems of reference.

Block 1981, *Readings in the Philosophy of Psychology, Volume 2*, is an excellent collection on issues raised in part III. It is organised into parts, each of which has a helpful introduction. Searle 1971, *The Philosophy of Language*, is also helpful on part III issues.

Hacking 1975, *Why does Language Matter to Philosophy?*, is an historical overview of theories of meaning from Locke to Davidson.

PART II

MEANING

2

Truth and reference

2.1 Meaning and truth

Perhaps the favourite notion in folk linguistics is *meaning*. It is almost irresistible to start the explanation of language – such features as those listed in section 1.2 – by talking of the meaningfulness of language. We did not resist. We used 'meaning' as a blanket term to cover the special properties of linguistic symbols that enable them to play their striking role in people's lives (1.2). Of course, this talk of meaning does not really explain anything; it is little more than a convenient label for what needs explaining. From our naturalistic perspective (1.3), it would be particularly objectionable to rest content with this talk. So, what we need is "a theory of meaning".

However, first, a word of warning about the term 'meaning' (and cognates). Its popularity in linguistics is, in one respect, unfortunate. In its ordinary use the term is vague, perhaps even ambiguous. Certainly it has many applications that have nothing to do with language. Consider the following, for example: 'Aphrodite means to molest that Trojan'; 'Food must have no meaning for vegetarians': 'Rich police mean corruption'; 'He means well, but he's not too bright'. So, we should be careful about relying on intuitions that we would express using 'mean': they may not concern our problem. (See section 2.7 for more terminological warnings.)

To convey information, ask a question, issue a command, etc., one uses a sentence. The sentence is the basic unit of communication. A promising suggestion for explaining the meaning of indicative sentences is to focus on explaining *truth conditions*. For it seems that the core meaning of such a sentence is its truth conditions: its property of being true if a certain situation in the world obtains and not true if the situation does not. Thus it is central to the meaning of 'Bob likes the bottle' that it is true if and only if Bob really does like the bottle.

The centrality of truth conditions is supported by the folk linguistics. Though, 'Max, he's a wimp' and 'Max is a weakling' have a marked difference in conversational flavour, in an important sense they "have the same meaning". Further, anyone would judge those two sentences more alike in meaning than either is to 'Max, he's an animal'. Why? Because the first two sentences have the same truth conditions, whereas the third has different ones. This point can be illustrated in other ways. The main thing to preserve in translating one sentence into another is truth conditions. Moreover, two sentences that differ in truth value would not be found synonymous. If circumstances could make 'Many arrows didn't hit the target' true, while 'The target wasn't hit by many arrows' was false, the sentences cannot have the same meaning. (Test: do they have the same meaning? See section 6.5.)

Other parts of the phenomenon of language seem to support an interest in truth conditions and the notion of truth.

Inference is central to both language and thought. A consideration of inference provides further support for truth. Inference is a practice we engage in all the time, often without being aware of it. We frequently could not exploit our observational knowledge without it. Some inferential practices are good and some are not. What makes a practice good? The standard account is in terms of truth: inferential practices are good if they preserve truth; or, where the practices are suggestive (inductive) rather than demonstrative (deductive), if they tend to preserve truth. Given true premises, good inferences can be relied on to yield true conclusions. Bad inferences, or fallacies, lack this virtue. Consider the gambler's fallacy, for example: the gambler infers from his run of bad hands that the next one will be good; 'my luck must change'. This policy, known to lead to poverty, is bad because inferring counter-inductively fails to lead from truths to truths. Thus an interest in inference leads to an interest in truth.

Next, consider the use of language for communication, the first on our list of salient features (1.2). How does communication work? A likely answer is along the following lines.

People have an interest in controlling and manipulating the world to satisfy various needs. It is clear that cooperation, and hence language, play a crucial role in furthering that interest. Typically, it seems to play that role in the following way. A person has a belief – say, that spiders make perfect pets – and expresses it to a listener. He might do this by uttering the English sentence, 'Spiders make perfect pets'. How can the listener use this sound for his own purposes? First, he understands the sound: he assigns it the right truth conditions; in the present case, he takes it to be true if and only if spiders make perfect pets. Next, he takes the speaker to be sincere. So, he (rightly) takes the speaker to believe that spiders make perfect pets. Finally, he thinks the speaker reliable about such matters. So he will come to believe, or to be confirmed in his belief, that spiders do make perfect pets. He will behave accordingly. In this way people learn from each other about many matters of mutual interest: e.g. food, drink, shelter and, importantly, other people.

We think that the notion of truth conditions – or, as we shall often say briefly, the notion of truth – is central to explaining meaning. However, we must admit that the above considerations are very far from establishing this. Indeed, though it has seemed plausible to so many that truth is needed to explain meaning, it has recently become clear that it is very difficult to show why it is needed. We shall return to this deep and difficult matter in chapter 9. Meanwhile, we shall simply assume the need for truth. If truth is needed to explain meaning, then it in turn must be explained. We need a theory of truth.

2.2 Explaining truth conditions

A theory of truth must be *decompositional*: the truth conditions of a sentence must be a function of its constituents. Only thus can we explain one of the important properties that makes language special as a communication system: its productivity (1.2). We do not learn sentences individually: we learn elements plus the procedures for constructing sentences out of elements. If you understand 'Semiotics is fashionable' and you understand 'punk', then you understand 'Punk is fashionable'. If you understand 'deconstruction', you understand *any* sentence containing it provided that you understand the structure of the sentence and the other words in it. An indefinitely large number of those sentences are ones you have never come across; a likely example of such a sentence is, 'Deconstruction is as pretentious as it is worthless'.

The truth conditions of a sentence depend, therefore, on its syntactic structure together with the elements that fill that structure.

1 If we hold structure constant and vary the elements, truth conditions vary. The following sentences share the simplest English sentence structure, "one-place" predication, but are made true by very different situations in the world:

Reagan is wrinkled
Thatcher is tough
Andropov is dead.

2 Less obviously, if we hold the elements constant and vary structure, again truth conditions vary. This is illustrated most simply by changing word order in a "two-place" predication:

The USA nuked the USSR
The USSR nuked the USA.

However, there is a lot more to syntactic structure than word order. This is vividly demonstrated by structurally ambiguous sentences: sentences that have two (or more) distinct truth conditions even though the meaning of each element is held constant. Some examples:

Cheap wine and cider encourage annoying drunks
Modern realist movies are made by insulting crooks and producers
Dad is cooking.

The elements of sentences are words. What is it about a word that affects the truth conditions of sentences containing it? What part of its meaning plays this role? The obvious answer is its *reference*. Consider an example: a sentence with the simple structure of one-place predication. We can express the truth conditions of 'Reagan is wrinkled' in terms of reference as follows:

'Reagan is wrinkled' is true if and only if
    (a) there is some object that 'Reagan' designates and
    (b) 'wrinkled' applies to that object.

The sentence's property of being true if and only if Reagan is wrinkled is seen to depend, in part, on two distinct referential relations holding between parts of the sentence and objects: *designation*, holding between the name 'Reagan' and an object, Reagan; and *application*, holding between the predicate 'wrinkled' and many objects, wrinkled ones. The sentence's truth conditions depend also, of course, on the fact that it is a one-place predication. That determines that Reagan must be among the wrinkled objects for the sentence to be true.

We saw truth conditions as the core of sentence meaning (2.1). Our strategy now is to explain truth conditions partly in terms of the reference of words, and partly in terms of the structure of sentences which determine how truth conditions depend on reference. Given reference and structure, truth conditions are determined. So we will need a theory of reference and a theory of structure.

The approach to meaning that we have been outlining in this section and the last was started in the nineteenth century by the logician, Gottlob Frege (1952). At the same time, another very influential approach to meaning began as a result of the work of the linguist, Ferdinand de Saussure (1966): "structuralism". This approach differs most strikingly from Frege's in rejecting reference. We shall consider structuralism in chapter 13. Interestingly enough, both Frege and Saussure were relatively obscure in their own lifetimes.

We shall begin our discussion of theories of reference in the next chapter. Before that, we must consider some questions. What does the presence of non-indicative sentences in language show about our truth-conditional approach?

How can we explain the structure of the many sentences that are much more complicated than the simple predication used as our example? Is there more to word meaning than referential role? We shall take these in turn.

**2.3 Non-indicatives

One salient feature of language that we noted was that it serves communicative purposes other than that of conveying information (1.2). This fact has been illuminated by the work of J. L. Austin (1962a) and J. R. Searle (1969). They draw attention to such other "speech acts" as questions, requests and promises. Because of these, not all sentences are indicatives. The notion of truth conditions does not apply comfortably to any of these other uses of language.

Non-indicatives raise two questions about our truth–conditional approach to sentence meaning. Can that approach work for non-indicatives at all? Even if it can, do the truth conditions of a sentence, or some condition analogous to truth conditions, *exhaust* the sentence's meaning?

In answer to the first question, two ways have been suggested in which a theory of meaning for non-indicatives might be *modelled* on a theory of truth conditions.

First, it has been thought that while non-indicatives do not have truth conditions, at least some have analogous conditions. The view is that a theory of the *compliance conditions* of requests and imperatives would capture the core of their meaning. J. J. C. Smart is one who has recently argued this (1984). Many of our earlier remarks about assertions can then be transposed into remarks about requests. People would say that two requests have the same meaning, in an important sense, if they have the same compliance conditions; that is, if the same situation in the world has to be brought about to comply with them. On hearing the sound, "Befriend that spider", a person can use it for her purposes by first taking it to have been complied with if and only if she has befriended that spider. Next, if she takes the speaker to be sincere she will assume that the speaker wants her to befriend the spider. She will behave accordingly, taking account of her other attitudes, particularly towards the speaker and spiders. Compliance conditions must be explained in terms of the structure of the request and the elements that fill that structure, else we would have to learn them one at a time.

According to this suggestion, then, the core of a sentence's meaning is not, strictly, its property of being *true* if and only if a certain situation obtains, but rather its property of being *true, complied with, and so on*, if and only if a certain situation obtains. Its meaning is largely its truth conditions or other analogous conditions. And these conditions are all to be explained in terms of structure and reference along the lines we have sketched for indicatives.

Consider the bearing of this suggestion on our second question. It is clearly part of the meaning of a sentence that it has, say, compliance conditions not truth conditions. Yet, if the suggestion is correct, non-indicatives give no reason for doubting that the truth conditions, or analogous conditions, do exhaust the meaning of a sentence. For, that a sentence is an indicative and so has truth conditions, or an imperative and so has compliance conditions, is something determined by its structure.

Second, it has been thought that, despite appearances, non-indicatives can be true or false. This view has been defended in a number of different ways. One is through the technique of paraphrase. For example, some Scandinavian logicians have suggested that questions can be paraphrased as demands for knowledge (Aqvist 1965). Thus, 'Did Oswald kill Kennedy?' means 'Let it be the case that either I know Oswald killed Kennedy or I know that Oswald did not kill Kennedy'. In turn, demands can be given a truth-conditional analysis in so-called "deontic" logic. The idea is to identify a demand with a statement about what *ought* to be the case, that is to say, with an indicative.

A less direct approach to questions has been proposed by the American logicians, Belnap and Steel. Their proposal is to explain each question in terms of its possible answers. Thus the meaning of the question, 'Who is the ugliest president of the USA?' would be given by the disjunction of its possible answers. Since these answers are indicatives, the semantics of questions is given by atoms which are true or false. Derivatively, then, a *question* is true if it has a true answer, false otherwise ('When did you stop drinking your bathwater?' has no true answer for most of us).

It seems that this second suggestion would, unlike the first one, allow us to retain the idea that truth conditions, alone, exhaust sentence meaning. However, the suggestion does this by linking a sentence to the truth conditions of a paraphrase that is often intuitively very distant from the original sentence.

We find Smart's approach more natural and think that something like it must play some role in the theory of meaning. However, we have no need to adjudicate between the two suggestions. They are, after all, not incompatible: there are many different non-indicatives. So long as one of the suggestions is along the right lines, our interest in developing a theory of truth conditions is not parochial.

Some theorists have urged that there is a dimension of meaning beyond truth conditions. They have suggested that a theory of meaning must find room for a theory of the *pragmatics* of language use, a theory of the deployment of symbols in a social context.

J. L. Austin (1962a) distinguishes between the *locutionary* and *illocutionary* aspects of an utterance. The locutionary force of an utterance is, intuitively, its content. It is the condition that makes it true if an indicative, complied with if an imperative, and so on. The illocutionary force is what is done in making the utterance. It captures the "attitude" taken to the content in the utterance. The structure of an utterance may indicate its illocutionary force – as an imperative indicates a request – but it does not fully determine it. Thus, a given indicative sentence could be an assertion, an assumption, or a postulation. It could even be a threat: 'Unless there is a million dollars in the briefcase, the bomb will explode'.

One of the aims of pragmatics is to give a general account of illocutionary force; of the distinctions between requests, commands, and beggings; of the distinction between threats and warnings; and so on. These distinctions are, likely enough, in the beliefs and goals of the speaker. Someone who threatens believes that the content of the threat is undesired by its recipient. Similarly, with an assertion but not a hypothesis, the speaker intends the audience to see the utterance as an expression of his beliefs. We shall return to pragmatics briefly in part II, when our focus is on the mind's relation to language (7.4, 7.5, 8.8).

Some of the distinctions attended to in pragmatics clearly have a place in the theory of meaning. They are the ones captured in structure; for example, that between assertions and questions. Perhaps all the pragmatic distinctions have a place in a theory of meaning, in which case truth, and analogous, conditions do not exhaust sentence meaning. However, all the distinctions need not have a place. The theory of meaning is concerned with the properties of symbols that enable them to play their special role in people's lives. We can expect that some properties of symbols, though important enough for some purposes, will not be central enough to the phenomenon of language to warrant a place in the theory of meaning; a trivial example would be the length of a symbol. A non-trivial example might be the distinction in illocutionary force between an assertion and a threat.

Paul Grice's discussion of *conversational implicature* (1975) is concerned with other pragmatic linguistic phenomena. We think, as does he, that these are not appropriately covered by the theory of meaning.

Grice claims that a pervasive feature of language is that people say one thing but imply much more. He does not have in mind irony or metaphor; the "literal" meaning of the utterance is *part* of its overall conversational load. Here are two typical examples.

1 Two thieves are in a warehouse. They hear a siren in the distance. One turns to the other and says, 'That is not an ambulance'. They depart in haste. What the thief said *means* no more than that the noise was no ambulance. No irony. No metaphor. No special code. He *implied* more, of course: that they should split.
2 A nobleman and his lackey are together in one of the rooms of the official residence. The nobleman says, 'It's rather cold for April'. The lackey closes

the window and lights the fire. Again, what is conversationally implied outruns what is said.

In sum, we think that some but not all of the concerns of the theory of pragmatics should be dealt with in the theory of meaning.**

2.4 Explaining structure

In section 2.2, we illustrated how truth conditions can be explained in terms of reference and structure. However, the example, 'Reagan is wrinkled', has such a simple structure that it could give a grossly misleading impression of the difficulties of our task. In particular, many sentences contain elements that are quite unlike 'Reagan' and 'wrinkled' and yet which play crucial roles in determining truth conditions. Consider the following passage:

> ". . . And I haven't sent the two Messengers, either. They're both gone to the town. Just look along the road, and tell me if you can see either of them."
>
> "I see nobody on the road," said Alice.
>
> "I only wish *I* had such eyes." the King remarked in a fretful tone. "To be able to see Nobody! And at that distance too! Why, it's as much as *I* can do to see real people, by this light!"
>
> . . .
>
> "Who did you pass on the road?" the King went on, holding out his hand to the Messenger for some hay.
>
> "Nobody," said the Messenger.
>
> "Quite right," said the King: "this young lady saw him too. So of course Nobody walks slower than you."
>
> "I do my best," the Messenger said in a sullen tone. "I'm sure nobody walks much faster than I do!"
>
> "He can't do that," said the King, "or else he'd have been here first . . ."
> (Carroll 1962: 258–61)

'Nobody' is not a name nor any other kind of definite singular term (=, roughly, a term that purports to refer to just one object), it is a "quantifier". Its important effect on truth conditions cannot be captured by treating it, as the King does, as if it had a referent.

Many other examples make the same point. The following one is beloved by writers of logic books:

Every man loves some woman.

This sentence is ambiguous between every man loving some woman or other, and some woman being universally loved by men. There is no parallel ambiguity in the following sentence:

Max loves Alphonse.

The moral is that the ambiguity of the first sentence cannot be understood by treating 'every man' and 'some woman' as if they were names.

Since the work of Frege, and especially since Alfred Tarski's pioneering 1931 paper, "The concept of truth in formalized languages' (in Tarski 1956), generations of logicians have been beavering away, attempting to construct compositional theories of truth for a range of different types of sentences. For instance, some have attempted to give truth conditions for sentences like 'It's possible to be an honest politician'. These are *modal* sentences, employing the concepts of necessity or possibility. Some have tried to handle tensed sentences. Much of this work is complex, difficult and technical. All of it depends to some extent on modern logic. We shall, therefore, spare you an exposition of these results.

Despite the many advances that have been made in laying bare the structure of natural language sentences, and thus in showing how their truth conditions depend on reference, the task is far from finished. We see it as seriously incomplete in the following three ways.

First, there are many complexities which still resist, fully or partly, logicians' tools. Consider the quantifiers, for example. While Frege and Tarski developed explanations of the quantifiers 'at least one', 'all', 'none' (and several related ones), nobody has tamed those like 'most', 'many' and 'a few'.

** Secondly, we think that many apparently successful explanations must be regarded as incomplete because they make use of the notion of "possible worlds". Saul Kripke (1959) was an early and influential deployer of this notion to explain modal sentences. Necessity was seen as truth in all possible worlds; possibility, as truth in some possible world. Subsequently, the notion has been used for other kinds of sentences. For example, it has been used for subjunctive conditionals like 'If today had not been pension day, Granny would have been sober'. (This sort of conditional is often called "counterfactual" because it implies the falsity of the indicative form of its antecedent; in this case, implying that it is pension day.) It has also been used on epistemic ascriptions like 'Thatcher believes that God is an Englishwoman'. The objection to all these explanations is that they leave us with a notion in our semantic theory that badly needs explaining: the notion of possible worlds.

Many possible-worlds semanticists seem surprisingly unconcerned by this problem. Some acknowledge it, but shuffle their feet in response. Some others offer reductions: possibe worlds are really sets of sentences, or whatever. We do not find any of these reductions satisfactory. For one thing, the reductions are often to entities no more acceptable than possible worlds themselves: non-physical objects of various kinds. Other suggestions look circular, from our point of view at least. One cannot *both* invoke possible worlds to explain the semantic properties of sentences *and* explain a possible world as a set of semantically interpreted sentences. Finally, the various attempts to "explain away" possible worlds suffer from a variety of technical problems.

David Lewis (1973, 1986) confronts the problem of possible worlds squarely. He scorns any shamefaced attempt to identify these worlds with entities usually found more acceptable. He thinks that they are perfectly respectable entities as they stand. He is committed to the genuine existence of a countless infinity of parallel universes among which ours is picked out as special only in being the one that is actual-for-us. This is some elephant to swallow without blinking. We shall return to it in section 2.6.**

Thirdly, these categories of quantified sentences, modal sentences, and the like, typically do not, in the first instance, apply to the sentences of natural languages. They apply rather to formulae in the formal languages of logic. These languages have been specially invented to represent what seem to be the underlying structures or "logical forms" of the sentences of natural languages. They are, therefore, simpler than natural ones. They are also much better behaved than natural ones: they are explicit rather than elliptical; they are unambiguous; they bar monsters like 'This sentence is false'; and so on. So, the theories of formal languages must somehow be brought to bear on their true targets by linking the logical formulae to the sentences that are their natural language counterparts. For instance, the quantified formulae,

$$(x)(\text{Man } x \rightarrow (Ey)(\text{Woman } y \ \& \ \text{Loves } xy))$$

(read: For any x, if x is a man then there is a y such that y is a woman and x loves y), and

$$(Ey)(\text{Woman } y \ \& \ (x)(\text{Man } x \rightarrow \text{Loves } xy))$$

(read: There is a y such that y is a woman and, for any x, if x is a man then x loves y) are mapped onto the earlier

Every man loves some woman

each capturing one of its meanings.

('x' and 'y' in the above formulae function like cross-referential, or "anaphoric", pronouns. Logicians call such symbols "variables". The difference between the two formulae is described as a difference in the "scope" of the quantifiers: in the first, the "existential" quantifier '(Ey)', reading "there is a y", is inside the scope of the "universal" quantifier '(x)', reading "for any x"; in the second, the reverse is the case.)

This further task of relating all natural language sentences to logical formulae is necessary if those sentences are to be made amenable to truth-theoretic semantics. The task is very difficult. The great hope for solving it lies with the movement in linguistics started by Noam Chomsky in the 1950s, "transformational generative grammar". The transformational approach has made great advances in understanding the syntactic structures of natural languages. It distinguishes between the deep structure and surface structure of a sentence. Some of those influenced by Chomsky – the "generative semanticists" – identify logical formulae like the above with deep structures. The transformational rules then pair the logical formulae with the natural language sentences. Others, including Chomsky himself, have a more complicated view of the relation between syntax and meaning. We shall consider these matters in Chapter 6.

In sum, it is certainly true that a vast amount of work remains to be done to explain the bearing of syntactic structure on truth conditions.

2.5 Are referential roles enough?

Is there more to word meaning than referential role? For example, is there more to the meanings of 'Thatcher' and 'snow' than their roles of referring to Thatcher and snow, respectively?

The discussion of non-indicatives (2.3) has raised doubts about the slogan that has, in effect, been guiding our discussion: "the meaning of a sentence is its truth conditions". Further doubts are raised by the dicussion to follow. Indeed, we shall see that, under one interpretation, the slogan is clearly false (2.6).

We shall start with a simple case, proper names. Have we told the full story of a name's meaning when we specify its bearer? That seemed to be the view of Mill:

> proper names are not connotative: they denote the individuals who are called by them; but they do not indicate or imply any attributes as belonging to those individuals. (Mill 1961: 20)

We shall call the view that the meaning of a name is exhausted by its role of designating its bearer, the "Millian View" (though it is not obvious that Mill himself subscribed to it). The view is plausible and simple. Nonetheless, it has been almost unanimously rejected. In this section we shall see why.

Identity statements

On a Millian view, it is easy enough to explain the difference in meaning between the following:

> Everest is snow-covered
> Annapurna is snow-covered.

The meaning of a name is its role of designating a certain object. 'Everest' and 'Annapurna' designate different objects and so differ in meaning. Identity statements show that this cannot be the whole story.

Compare the following statements, both of which are true:

> Everest is Everest
> Everest is Gaurisanker.

The difference between them is striking. There have been various attempts at characterizing the difference. Some have claimed that the first sentence is "analytic" (truth dependent only on meaning) whilst the second is "synthetic" (truth dependent partly on the world). But others are dubious of the notion of analyticity. Some have claimed that the first is necessary whilst the second is only contingent. But Saul Kripke has argued (1980) – we think plausibly – that both sentences are necessary. However, we do not have to resort to analyticity or necessity to capture the very different roles these sentences play in people's lives (and hence their different meanings; 1.2, 2.1): they are epistemically and cognitively so different. Knowledge of logic is sufficient to establish the first, for it is an instance of the logical law that everything is self-identical. In contrast, the second is an important piece of geographical knowledge: it is the discovery that a certain mountain known to the Tibetans is one and the same as a mountain known to the Nepalese.

The Millian view is clearly in trouble with identity statements. If the meaning of a name were simply its role of designating a certain object, then 'Everest' and 'Gaurisanker' would have the same meaning because they designate the same object. And if they had the same meaning, then so would the two identity statements above because the only difference between them is in those names. We have seen that the sentences do differ in meaning. So the names must differ in meaning also; the Millian view is wrong.

Existence statements

Consider next the following statements:

James Bond does not exist
Reagan exists.

These singular existence statements pose a further problem for the Millian view of names. How could a negative existence statement like the first one be meaningful? It would not be meaningful if it had nonsense syllables where a term should be. Yet, since it is *true*, there is nothing for 'James Bond' to designate, and hence, on the Millian view, that name should be just nonsense syllables. The view leads to the paradoxical conclusion that if a negative existence statement is true then it is meaningless. The positive statements pose a problem too. They become tautologous: if they are meaningful then they are true, for their contained name must have a bearer to be meaningful. Once again we see that the meaning of a name must involve something other than its referent.

Empty names

A closely related problem is posed by "empty" names. An empty name is one without a referent; 'James Bond' is an example. Empty names occur in many perfectly meaningful statements (other than existential ones); for example:

James Bond is disgustingly successful.

How could such a statement be meaningful on a view that can give no meaning to a name that does not designate?

Experience suggests that many will be tempted by one of two responses. First, "'James Bond' may not designate a real man but it does designate a fictional man". This response is encouraged by our ordinary way of talking about fiction. Nevertheless, it is quite unacceptable. A fictional man is no sort of man at all, just as a toy tiger is no sort of tiger. We are attempting to give a scientific theory of language. There is no place in science for talk of the non-existent. To think otherwise is to show "a failure of that feeling for reality which ought to be preserved even in the most abstract studies" (Russell 1919: 169). The explanation of the meaning of empty names must link them to reality.

The second tempting response is as follows. "'James Bond' may not designate a flesh and blood man but it does designate something: an idea, perhaps, or a concept." Now whatever the merits of this response – and we think they are few – it is beside the present point. Think back to the simple example that introduced our talk of reference (2.2): 'Reagan is wrinkled'. This sentence is made true by a wrinkled Reagan, which is a situation in the external world not in the world of ideas. And the referential relation which we are using to help explain these truth conditions, and which we called 'designation', is a relation between 'Reagan' and Reagan, a flesh and blood part of that external world not an idea in someone's mind. Whatever relation there may be between 'Reagan' and a Reagan-like idea is not, in this sense, designation. On the Millian view, designation exhausts a name's meaning. And the problem for that view is that 'James Bond' does not designate anything.

In saying this, we are not claiming that you *could not* designate an idea if you wanted to. Of course you could, and we just did with 'Reagan-idea'. We could even designate the idea of James Bond:

> The idea of James Bond is disgustingly successful: it made Fleming millions.

The point is simply that, on our usage, neither 'Reagan' nor 'James Bond' do designate ideas.

The second response amounts to a proposal to use the word 'designate' in a different way. We have seen that the proposed usage would be irrelevant to the Millian view and at odds with the truth-conditional approach to meaning. Nevertheless, perhaps it should be adopted anyway. That is to say, perhaps it is language's relation to ideas rather than the world that is central to the explanation of meaning. We think not. Our task is to explain the special role of language in our lives. A cursory glance at our earlier description of this role (1.2) shows how much it involves the world of bread, wine, shelter, other people, etc. An explanation of meaning that ignores this world in favour of ideas is very implausible. Note, for example, that the earlier existence statements are not concerned with the existence of ideas but with that of people. *An explanation of meaning must somehow relate language to the external world*. (We return to this when discussing the structuralists in chapter 13.)

Opacity

From the sentences

> Falwell persecutes Bob Dylan
> Bob Dylan is Robert Zimmerman

we may infer

> Falwell persecutes Robert Zimmerman.

In true sentences like the first one we can substitute for any singular term a co-designational term and be sure of preserving truth; the rule of "substitutivity of identity" applies; the sentences are "extensional" or "transparent". In contrast, from the sentences

Falwell believes Bob Dylan destroyed the moral fibre of America
Bob Dylan is Robert Zimmerman

we may not always infer

Falwell believes Robert Zimmerman destroyed the moral fibre of America.

Falwell may be unaware that Robert Zimmerman is none other than the dreaded Bob Dylan, with the result that the latter sentence is false. The rule of substitutivity may not apply to names in contexts like this. The sentences are then "non-extensional" ("intensional", spelt, notice, with an 's') or "opaque".

Opaque contexts are troublesome and intriguing. Attempts to deal with them have built a small industry within the philosophy of language. They are too hard for more than a passing mention in this book. They get such a mention here because they pose another problem for the Millian view of names. If all there were to the meaning of 'Bob Dylan' was its role of designating Dylan, then we could *always* substitute for it the co-designational name 'Robert Zimmerman' without change of meaning. Yet we have just seen that this substitution into an opaque context does change meaning, for it may change a true sentence into a false one. Once again, there must be something other than reference to the meaning of name.

Our discussion in this section has been all about names. Names seem more connotation-free than most terms. So it is not surprising that the meaning of terms other than names also goes beyond reference.

Consider cases of identities only. First, take two statements involving another sort of singular term, definite descriptions. (A definite description is usually formed in English by placing the definite article, 'the', in front of a general term. In contrast, an indefinite description has an indefinite article, 'a' or 'an', before a general term. A general term is one that usually admits a plural ending and can apply to each severally of any number of objects; e.g. 'cat'.)

The morning star is the morning star
The morning star is the evening star.

What we said of identity statements involving names applies equally here. The first sentence is a boring triviality; the second, a significant discovery. The definite descriptions 'the morning star' and 'the evening star' cannot have the same meaning even though they have the same referent. Their meaning is not simply their referential role.

Next, take two statements involving general terms:

Cordates are cordates
Cordates are renates.

Only the second sentence is news: it tells us that the same creatures that have hearts have kidneys. The meanings of the general terms 'cordate' and 'renate' are different and hence not given by their referential roles.

2.6 Enter senses

Faced with the phenomena described above, semanticists have devised two strategies. First, our theory can be enriched by accepting that there is indeed more to the meaning of a term than its referential role. This was the strategy of Frege and of many who have followed him. The usual idea is to supplement reference (sometimes called "extension") with "sense" (sometimes called "intension"): each term has a sense and, normally, a referent. Co-referential terms may differ in meaning because they differ in sense. Empty terms are abnormal in lacking a referent, but differ from nonsense syllables in still having a sense.

The second strategy is to enrich ontology (our view of the sorts of things that exist). This is the strategy of the earlier-mentioned possible-worlds semanticists, in particular of David Lewis (2.4). Much earlier it was the strategy of Meinong. The strategy accepts an ontology of possible worlds. As well as this universe, there is a countless infinity of alternative universes. Somewhere in this thicket, anything that could exist does exist; anything that could happen does happen. That is what it means to say that something is possible, on this view. This vast ontology enables Lewis to say that apparently co-referential terms are not really co-referential. Though 'the first female Prime Minister of Great Britain' and 'the person who led Great Britain into the Falklands War' both designate the same entity *around here*, they do not do so in all possible worlds. Though 'James Bond' designates nothing in this world, there are many other possible worlds where it does designate something. On this view, many uses of 'exist' are rather like 'here'. To say that James Bond does not exist is just to say that he is not local; from the perspective of people elswhere he does exist. It is not that a notion of reference is insufficient to capture the meaning of names and other terms. It is rather that the notion of reference we have employed is too parochial. A more cosmopolitan notion is called for.

This strategy has an internal problem. Saul Kripke has argued that a proper name is a "rigid" designator: it "designates the same object" "in every possible world" (1980: 40). If so, the strategy fails to explain the differences we have noted in the meaning of identity statements. If Kripke is right, 'Everest' and 'Gaurisanker' designate the same object not just in this world but in every possible world. So we still cannot explain the difference noted in terms of the referential roles of the names: they have the same referential roles. We are left with one of the main problems of the last section.

We find Kripke's modal intuitions plausible, but doubt that they can bear much weight. Our objection to the possible-worlds strategy is more global. It has already been indicated: we find the claim that there literally exist non-actual possible worlds *simply incredible*. Resting our case with this remark would place us among the philosophers who respond to Lewis' views with an "incredulous stare", with which he claims, reasonably enough, it is hard to argue (1973: 86).

** Lewis concedes that his ontology does violence to common sense, but he thinks that its virtues outweigh this drawback. For it has explanatory value outside the theory of reference; most famously, in the explanation of modality. Some things that did not happen could have happened. Germany might have won World War II. America might have lost the War of Independence. These are grand-scale unactualized possibilities. There are myriad small-scale ones: you might not have read this book; Rebecca might not have popped the question; and so on. Lewis takes this talk to be all about possible worlds. To say that such and such is possible – to say that it might have happened – is to say that it *did* happen somewhere else: it happened in some other possible world. It is true that Germany might have won because there is some unfortunate world where it did win.

Modality is perhaps the most appealing place to make use of possible worlds, but Lewis uses them elsewhere as well: to explain causation and counterfactuals ('If today had not been pension day, Granny would have been sober').

What are we to say to this list of virtues? Can we do better than our stare? We think so, though the details of our response depend on just how we take the commitment to possible worlds. We might take the commitment to be essentially semantic: possible worlds are entities that function only to provide truth conditions for troublesome sentences; sentences containing modal notions, causality and the like. We cannot accept possible worlds for this role, because doing so would violate the naturalistic approach we endorsed in section 1.3. We would be committed to entities with no non-semantic justification. We would also be committed to non-natural relations: someone using the name 'Reagan' would be in a relation not just to our Reagan, but also to entities in other possible worlds. These are entities to which we stand in no causal relation: possible worlds are causally segregated from one another. Indeed, there would be no naturalistic relation between us and denizens in this soup of possibilia; no relation employed outside semantics. So on this construal of the commitment to possible worlds, semantic theory would be *sui generis*. The idea that language is special is to be resisted; it is just another natural phenomenon, albeit one especially characteristic of us.

We do not think Lewis understands his proposal in this way. He takes himself to be explaining features of a reality we should believe in for reasons that are quite independent of language. Among these are modal features: the many ways that things could have been. True, the apparatus of possible worlds does yield a neat account of the semantics of various sentences, but only because it provides a plausible explanation of the facts the sentences report.

To deal with this view of possible worlds, we need to deploy our naturalistic predilections in a different way. We think that *explanations* must be given in naturalistic, typically causal, terms. We explain events and processes by appeal to the causal order of the world. We explain some feature of that order – say the characteristic chemical property of valency, a property partially determining the way elements combine – by appeal to deeper features of that order: the structure of the electron shells of the atoms of those elements. Explanation appeals to the order and structure of our world. Lewis's possible-world explanations do not have this characteristic. Facts about our world are explained in terms of the goings on in worlds that cannot affect our world at all. There are *no* transworld causal relations. The point is not just that these explanations are too high-priced. We do not think that they are explanations at all.**

We endorse the first strategy: terms have senses. So we need a theory of sense. There is an important constraint on that theory: it must relate sense to reference. We cannot introduce a notion of sense just to give meaning to empty terms and to distinguish co-referential ones. If its introduction is not to be hopelessly *ad hoc*, it must do some other theoretical work. The major work must concern reference.

The classical idea is that sense *determines* reference; in Frege's terminology, the sense contains "the mode of presentation" of the object (1952: 57). It is in virtue of its sense that a term refers to whatever it does, or that it fails to refer. So, we might hypothesize that the sense of a term *is* its meaning; there is nothing more to its role in our lives than its sense.

Our concern so far has been with meaning, a property of linguistic symbols. A characteristic of these symbols, which we have briefly mentioned, is that people *understand* them (1.2). Understanding a language – being *competent* in it – is a property of human minds (and perhaps of some other minds), and so will be mostly discussed in part III (chapter 8). However, it is appropriate to introduce it now because the positing of senses has led philosophers into a certain theory of understanding. They start by saying that understanding a term is "grasping its sense". Combine this with the classical idea that sense determines reference and it is tempting to say, further, that anyone who does grasp the term's sense is in a position to *tell* what it refers to: she *knows* what it refers to; she has a *criterion of identification*. So, for example, someone who understands 'Spiderfingers Lonergan' is in the position to identify the well-known mobster. Most who subscribe to the classical idea have succumbed to this temptation.

The classical idea has intuitive and theoretical appeal. It gives sense the appropriate theoretical work. Further, we have already established the need for a theory of reference (2.2). If sense determines reference then a theory of sense, together with an account of that determination, will fulfil that need. It will tell us in virtue of what 'truck' refers to trucks and not, for example, chairs. It will tell us in virtue of what 'Reagan' refers to Reagan and not, for example, Thatcher. Contrariwise, we may hope that a theory of reference will give us a theory of sense; that the aspects of reality we have to call on to explain reference are all that we need for sense.

In the next chapter we examine a theory of reference for one of the simplest categories of terms, proper names. The theory is, briefly, that names abbreviate descriptions.

The discussion in this chapter has been guided by the slogan, "the meaning of a sentence is its truth conditions". The consideration of non-indicatives in section 2.3 showed that this slogan may be oversimplified; truth conditions may not exhaust meanings. Our dismissal of the Millian view and introduction of senses brings out another inadequacy of the slogan: it does not distinguish between two different theses. Our initial thesis was that *explaining* meaning is *explaining* truth conditions (2.1). However, there is another, probably more popular, thesis: *giving* meaning is *giving* truth conditions. Much of the talk associated with the slogan, including ours in this chapter, is ambiguous between these two theses. The dismissal of the Millian view undermines the second thesis but not the first.

If our concern is simply to give the truth conditions of a sentence, then the only property of any contained word that is relevant is its referent. Since there is more to the word's meaning than its role of referring to that referent, namely its sense, and since all aspects of its meaning must be relevant to the sentence's meaning, there must be more to giving the sentence's meaning than giving its truth conditions.

We think that the slogan should be interpreted as the first thesis. Ignoring the problem of non-indicatives, the explanation of a sentence's meaning is the explanation of its property of having certain truth conditions. In this explanation, the sense of a word is important. For, though we can give the reference of a word, and hence its contribution to the sentence's truth conditions, without mentioning its sense, we cannot explain its reference without doing so.

2.7 Terminological warnings; use and mention

We have adopted a range of terminology: 'meaning', 'truth', 'refer', 'designate', 'sense', and so on. There is more to come. These terms are taken over from ordinary language; they are part of folk linguistics (1.3). It is important not to presume that our technical uses of these terms are the same as their ordinary uses. Indeed, it is most unlikely that they will be the same. We have already sounded a warning by pointing to the vagueness of the ordinary term 'meaning' (2.1) and to the limitations on our use of 'designate' (2.5). Much the same goes for many other terms. When we take one into our theory, we usually give it a meaning that is related to its ordinary one, but different from that meaning in being more precise. There is nothing peculiar about this practice. Many technical scientific terms started out in life as ordinary ones; think of the physical term 'mass', for example.

This warning has a corollary. One should be on the lookout for different technical usages among semanticists. Sometimes these variations are relatively systematic within cultures or sub-cultures. For example, British philosophers tend to use 'refer' for the referential properties of *singular* terms only, whereas American philosophers tend to use it for the properties of *all* terms. We follow the latter practice; thus designation and application are both modes of reference for us. Though sometimes one usage of a semantic term is more common than another, there is no question of one being *right*. Sensitivity to variations of usage is important to avoid disagreements that are not substantive but merely verbal.

These points may seem straightforward enough, but they are not without controversy. The "ordinary language" school of philosophy took the philosophy of language to *be* the study of the ordinary use of semantic terms. So sensitivity to ordinary usage is all that is required. The test of a theory is whether it accords "with what we would ordinarily say". There is no place for technical terms (except perhaps ones that are *defined* in ordinary terms). Our discussion in section 1.3 implies the rejection of this "ordinary language" view. We shall criticize it directly in chapter 14.

Throughout our discussion, we have been careful to put a name inside single quotation marks when we want to talk about it - to *mention* it -rather than *use* it to talk about its bearer. This care about "the distinction between use and mention" may seem rather pedantic, yet it is very important in the philosophy of langue. Elsewhere, it is hardly worth the fuss because the difference between the referent of a name when used and when mentioned is so obvious; nobody would confuse the person Thatcher with the name 'Thatcher' (or so one would think, yet many myths, religions, superstitions, and sayings are riddled with such confusions). As a result people are ordinarily rather casual about putting quotation marks around a name when they mean to mention it. However, in the philosophy of language we are talking *about names* (and other expressions). To do this we have to use the names of names. The difference between the referent of such a name when used and when mentioned is not obvious at all. Indeed, many philosophical works have been vitiated by a failure to distinguish use and mention.

No philosopher has done more to emphasize the importance of care with this distinction than W. V. Quine. The following example of care is taken from him and should be studied as an exercise.

> 'Boston is populous' is about Boston and contains 'Boston'; "'Boston' is disyllabic" is about 'Boston' and contains "Boston". "Boston" designates 'Boston', which in turn designates Boston. To mention Boston we use 'Boston' or a synonym, and to mention 'Boston' we use "Boston" or a synonym. "Boston" contains six letters and just one pair of quotation marks; 'Boston' contains six letters and no quotation marks; and Boston contains some 800,000 people. (Quine 1940: 24)

Putting an expression between quotation marks is not the only device that can be used to mention it: the expression can be put on display. We have made extensive use of this device. A few pages back, for example, we concluded section 2.5 with a discussion of the identity statements 'Cordates are cordates' and 'Cordates are renates', both of which were put on display.

Putting an expression on display or between quotation marks does not always indicate that it is being mentioned not used. It is often the sign, not surprisingly, that the expression is being taken from someone else and quoted. Quotation marks also have the role of "shudder" or "scare" quotes. This indicates that the author, while using the expression, is distancing himself from its full meaning. In this book, we always use single quotation marks to indicate that an expression is being mentioned. We shall reserve double quotation marks for quotation and scare quotes.

Suggested reading

2.2

For Frege's approach to language, see several essays reprinted in *The Philosophical Writings of Gottlob Frege* (1952), particularly the first seven or so pages of his 1892 paper "On sense and reference", also reprinted in Davidson and Harman 1976, *The Logic of Grammar*. For a nice introduction, see Currie 1982, *Frege, an Introduction to his Philosophy*.

The view that a truth-conditional approach to language requires a substantive theory of reference is not uncontroversial. In a classic article that guides our approach, "Tarski's theory of truth", Hartry Field (1972) pointed out that Tarski himself was content with a trivial theory of reference. Both Donald Davidson in "Reality without reference", first published in 1977 and reprinted in Davidson 1984, and John McDowell in "Physicalism and primitive denotation: Field on Tarski" (1978), argue that a theory of reference is not needed. We find these arguments obscure and unconvincing: see chapter 15; also, Devitt 1981a, *Designation*: sections 4.8–4.9; 1984a, *Realism and Truth*: section 10.1–10.6. The articles by Field, Davidson and McDowell are all reprinted in Platts 1980, *Reference, Truth and Reality*.

The view that truth consists in "correspondence to the facts" has been traditionally known as the *correspondence theory* of truth. In attempting to explain truth in terms of reference and structure, we are offering a correspondence theory. For more on this, see Devitt 1984a: 26–7.

For a careful and systematic exposition of the view that a theory of meaning is a theory of truth, see Lycan 1984, *Logical Form in Natural Language*. He is more sympathetic than we are to Davidson's formulation of these issues.

2.3

Smart outlines his theory of compliance conditions simply and readably in *Ethics, Persuasion and Truth* (1984). The Scandinavian line on non-indicatives was first presented in Aqvist 1965, *A New Approach to the Logical Theory of Interrogatives*, part I. The more general Scandinavian line is summarized in Follesdal and Hilpinen 1981, "Deontic logic: an introduction". Belnap has defended his views on questions in a number of places, but most recently in Belnap and Steel 1976, *The Logic of Questions and Answers*. All these works except Smart's are technical and difficult.

Two classic, non-technical, works in pragmatics, emphasizing the importance of non-indicative uses of language, are Austin 1962a, *How to do Things with Words* and Searle 1969, *Speech Acts*. See also the first three papers in Searle 1971, *The Philosophy of Language*, and part 7 of Rosenberg and Travis 1971, *Readings in the Philosophy of Language*.

For Grice's theory of conversational implicature, see "Logic and conversation" (1975), reprinted in Davidson and Harman 1976, *The Logic of Grammar*. For a clear and thorough exposition of Grice's notion, see Walker 1975, "Conversational implicatures". For a criticism of some aspects of this theory, see Sterelny 1982, "Against conversational implicature".**

2.4

** Tarski's famous definition of truth was in "The concept of truth in formalized languages", reprinted in Tarski 1956. This is a long and difficult article.** A good exposition of its main ideas can be found in Quine 1970, *Philosophy of Logic*: chapter 3; see also Field 1972.

**   More complex languages – including adverbs, tenses, pronouns and the like – are treated in Lewis 1972, "General semantics", in Davidson and Harman 1972, *Semantics of Natural Language*, and reprinted in Lewis 1983, *Philosophical Papers: Volume I*. See also Dowty, Wall and Peters 1981, *Introduction to Montague Semantics*.

The most accessible of Kripke's works on modal logic is, "Semantical considerations on modal logic" (1962), reprinted in Linsky 1971, *Reference and Modality*. For Lewis' views on counterfactuals and possible worlds, see *Counterfactuals* (1973). Jaakko Hintikka pioneered the application of possible worlds semantics to epistemic contexts: *Knowledge and Belief* (1962). A clear introduction to the utility of talk of possible worlds in semantic theory and logic is provided by Bradley and Schwartz 1979, *Possible Worlds*. They illustrate the metaphysical coyness that is endemic among those who talk about possible worlds: they do not come clean on the status of possible worlds. The technical problems alluded to in our text are pointed out by Lewis and Lycan (see suggestions for section 2.6).

Quine is a famous sceptic not only about possible worlds but about modal notions in general: see "Reference and modality" in *From a Logical Point of View* (1961), reprinted in Linsky 1971; "Necessary truth" and "Three grades of modal involvement" in *Ways of Paradox* (1966).**

Donald Davidson was the first to take an optimistic view of the task of applying Tarski to natural language in his 1967 essay, "Truth and meaning", reprinted in Davidson1984 and in Rosenberg and Travis 1971.

2.5

The classical account of the problem posed by identity statements is given in the first two pages of Frege's, "On sense and reference", reprinted in Frege 1952 and in Davidson and Harman 1976. The problem has seemed intractable to many and has developed a vast literature: Shwayder 1956, Wiggins 1965, and Linsky 1963 are some typical examples.

The problem of existence statements for the Millian view is nicely brought out by Russell in his 1918 paper, "The philosophy of logical atomism", reprinted in *Logic and Knowledge* (1956): 233, 241. The view that empty names refer to fictional entities can be found in Cartwright 1960, "Negative existentials", reprinted in Caton 1963, *Philosophy and Ordinary Language*; and in Crittenden 1966, "Fictional existence". Quine considers and rejects the view that an empty name refers to an idea in his classic paper, "On what there is", in *From a Logical Point of View* (1961).

**   The difficult matter of opaque contexts is discussed by Frege in the above-mentioned article. The contemporary problem has been best posed by Quine; see particularly, "Quantifiers and propositional attitudes", reprinted by Quine 1966, in Linsky 1971, and in Davidson and Harman 1976. Kaplan 1969,

"Quantifying in", in Davidson and Hintikka 1969, *Words and Objections*, in Linsky 1971, and in Davidson and Harman 1976, is another classic on the subject.**

2.6

The strategy of introducing senses is also to be found in Frege's article.

Kripke introduced the idea of names as rigid designators in a 1972 paper, later reprinted with a preface as the book *Naming and Necessity* (1980): 48. This very influential work plays an important role in our book.

** For the possible-worlds strategy, see the suggestions for sections 2.4 above. Plantinga 1974, *The Nature of Necessity*, chapters 6–8, provide an interesting defence of commitment to possible worlds. A good review of the literature is to be found in Lycan 1979, "The trouble with possible worlds" in Loux 1979, *The Possible and The Actual*. .

A comparison of Kripke's writings on modal logic with *Naming and Necessity* suggests that even he is coy about possible worlds.

Lewis defends his position in *On the Plurality of Worlds* (1986). He argues that his position is coherent and plausible, and that attempts to purchase the advantage of possible worlds at a smaller ontological price cannot succeed.**

2.7

The quotation from Quine is drawn from section 4 of *Mathematical Logic* (1940); the section is called "Use versus mention" and is a very nice discussion of the issue.

3

Description theories of reference: names

3.1 The classical description theory

According to the classical description theories of Gottlob Frege and Bertrand Russell, the sense of a name is given by a definite description associated with the name; its sense is the sense of that description. So names can be treated as abbreviated descriptions. Consider the following example taken from Frege (1952: 58n). Given what is commonly believed about Aristotle, we might suppose that the definite description associated with 'Aristotle' is 'the pupil of Plato and teacher of Alexander the Great'. If so, that description expresses the sense of 'Aristotle'.

Sense is supposed to determine reference, so this theory of sense, together with an account of that determination, should supply the theory of reference (2.6). And so it does. In virtue of what does a name designate its bearer? It does so because the definite description which expresses its sense *denotes* that bearer. This reduces our original problem of explaining reference for names to that of explaining reference for definite descriptions. In virtue of what does a definite description denote a certain object? Nevertheless, we have made progress because we had that problem anyway; two problems have been reduced to one. Further we have the beginnings of an answer to the problem for descriptions. Briefly, the definite description 'the F' denotes x if and only if 'F' applies to x and to nothing else; for example, 'the author of *Word and Object*' denotes Quine because 'author of *Word and Object*' applies only to Quine. This is Russell's famous "theory of descriptions". The theory is only the beginnings of an answer because it pushes us back to another problem: that of explaining reference for the general terms that fill the place of 'F'. In virtue of what does a general term apply to an object? But once again we have made progress, because this is also a problem we had anyway. (Interestingly enough, this other problem did not strike enthusiasts for the description theory of names. We shall return to this in sections 3.3 and 4.2.) In sum, the description theory, together with Russell's theory of descriptions, reduces three problems of reference to one: the problems for names, definite descriptions and general terms are reduced to the problem for general terms.

The description theory supplies a theory of sense and thereby a theory of reference. There seems to be nothing else to the meaning of a name than its sense and reference (2.6). So the description theory is a complete theory of meaning for names.

We have an interest not only in meaning, but also in understanding. What is it to be in a position to use a name properly – to understand a name? It is to "grasp its sense". What is that? The description theory has a simple answer: to grasp a name's sense is to associate it with the appropriate description. Combine this with the above theory of reference and we get an important and appealing conclusion; the competent speaker can *identify* the name's bearer. Someone who understands 'Spiderfingers Lonergan' must associate with it a description that picks out the mobster. In other words, she must know identifying facts about him. Thus the classical description theory gave in to the temptation mentioned in section 2.6.

Consider next how the classical description theory handles the various issues that led us to introduce senses (2.5).

The identity statement

Everest is Gaurisanker

is informative. How does the theory account for that? The names in this statement have different senses in virtue of being associated with different descriptions: 'Everest' is associated with, say, 'the distant tall mountain seen from Tibet'; 'Gaurisanker' with, say, 'the distant tall mountain seen from Nepal'. These descriptions have different senses in virtue of having elements with different senses: 'Tibet' in the first, 'Nepal' in the second. That is why the statement is informative.

The theory is equally successful with singular existence statements containing names. These are seen as equivalent to statements containing definite descriptions; that is, like 'The F exists' if positive, and like 'The F does not exist' if negative. The former is true if and only if the definite description denotes; the latter, if and only if it does not denote. With the help of Russell's theory of descriptions, once again, we can give the necessary further explanation: 'the F' denotes if and only if there exists one and only one thing that 'F' applies to. So, the negative statement is true if the general term fails to apply uniquely. Such failure does not render the statement meaningless and thus does not lead to paradox. Similarly, there is nothing tautological about a true positive statement: even if it were false, it would be meaningful.

Appearances of empty names in other contexts are also treated readily. A name is empty because its associated description fails to denote. But the description, and hence the name, still has a sense. Its sense depends partly on its structure – that of a definite description – and partly on the sense of its contained general term. Neither of these are affected by its failure to denote.

The problem of opacity is not so easy. The description theory explains why substituting one name for another with the same referent changes the *meaning* of a sentence: see above on identity statements. However, it does not explain why the substitution can change the *truth value*. There is no obvious reason why the two sentences,

Monique believes that the author of *Syntactic Structures* is a great linguist
The author of *Syntactic Structures* is the most influential contemporary anarchist writer,

fail to entail

Monique believes that the most influential contemporary anarchist writer is a great linguist.

The failure of the rule of substitutivity of identity is just as puzzling for definite descriptions as for names, and so treating names as abbreviated descriptions does not help with it. Differences in sense that do not lead to differences in reference should be irrelevant to truth conditions.

Frege proposed an ingenious solution. However, we must pass over this in silence in accordance with our policy of treating opacity lightly (2.5).

Despite these virtues, the classical description theory is open to serious objection.

1   People often associate many definite descriptions with a name. *We* do with 'Aristotle'; apart from that mentioned, we associated 'the systematizer of syllogistic logic', 'the author of *The Nichomachean Ethics*', and so on. Which of these gives the sense of the name? Which one is so important that if it fails to denote, even if all the others do, the name is empty? It is implausible to think that any one description has that much importance.

2   Suppose there is a definite description that has this important role for one user of a name. It seems most unlikely that the same description will have that role for all users. With a name like 'Aristotle' we would expect to find many different descriptions playing that role in the speech community. So 'Aristotle', even when used to refer to that famous Greek philosopher, would be many-ways ambiguous. (Frege accepted this consequence of his theory, regarding the ambiguity as an imperfection of ordinary language; 1952: 58n.) We get a converse of the earlier problems of identity statements; we must explain why 'Aristotle is Aristotle' is *un*informative. Given the

many senses of 'Aristotle', it should usually be as informative as 'Everest is Gaurisanker'.

3 Suppose that the description which gives the sense of 'Aristotle' is the one we took from Frege. Now consider,

(a) Aristotle taught Alexander the Great

According to the description theory it abbreviates

(b) The pupil of Plato and teacher of Alexander the Great taught Alexander the Great.

So it should seem trivial in just the same way that

(c) Bachelors are unmarried

is trivial. Yet it does not. Some philosophers attempt to explain the triviality of (c) by saying tht it is necessarily true, known *a priori* (known "independently of experience"), or analytic. Whatever the merits of these explanations, they do not seem to apply to (a); it seems contingent, *a posteriori* (empirical), and synthetic. Similarly, according to the theory,

Aristotle never taught anyone

should be contradictory in just the same way as

That bachelor is married

is contradictory.

** Saul Kripke has introduced the term 'rigid designator' to capture the difference between names and definite descriptions that we have just indicated (1980: 48–9). A name, unlike a description, is rigid in that it designates the same object in every possible world (2.6). Thus, in another possible world (a) might have been false (and so is not necessarily true) because the person *we* refer to by 'Aristotle' – Aristotle himself – might have had a different teaching career. In contrast, (b) is necessarily true because in other possible worlds its truth depends not on the properties of the person we refer to by 'the pupil of Plato and teacher of Alexander the Great' – again Aristotle himself – but on the properties of whatever object satisfies that description in that world. And to satisfy that description an object must, of course, have taught Alexander the Great.

(For those, like us, who do not think there are, literally, any possible worlds beyond the actual one, this talk of possible worlds must be seen as a picturesque way of saying what might have been so: 2.6)**

In sum, it seems that names do not abbreviate descriptions in the simple way specified by the classical description theory.

3.2 The modern description theory

The implausibilities of the classical theory led to the modern theory, often called the "cluster" theory. The earliest sign of this theory seems to have been in a typically enigmatic remark by Ludwig Wittgenstein (1953: section 79). However, the most influential exponents of the theory were Peter Strawson and John Searle. Instead of tying a name tightly to one definite description, as the classical theory does, the modern theory ties it loosely to many. This cluster of descriptions expresses the sense of the name and determines its reference; the name refers to the object, if any, that *most*, but not necessarily all, of those descriptions denote. The theory can be made more sophisticated still by allowing some descriptions to have greater weight in the vote than others. Thus, in the cluster associated with 'Aristotle', doubtless 'the systematizer of syllogistic logic' weighs more heavily than 'the son of the court physician to Amyntas II'.

Where does the modern theory stand on understanding? The straightforward view, taking understanding as "grasping the sense", requires the association with the name of the appropriate cluster of descriptions. So once again the competent speaker of 'Spiderfingers Lonergan' is in a position to *identify* the mobster: he is the unique object that satisfies most of the cluster she associates with the name.

** However, it is often not clear what view modern theorists have of understanding. Sometimes this suggestion seems to be that it is sufficient for the understander to associate at least one of the cluster with the name; or, perhaps even associate some identifying description that is not in the cluster. This would be to combine a classical theory of understanding with a modern theory of sense. It would leave the connection between understanding and sense (and hence reference) unexplained and mysterious. For this reason, we shall ignore this suggestion.**

The modern theory may seem to answer the objections to the classical theory (3.1) as follows. It avoids 1 by not requiring that we pick, in an apparently arbitrary manner, one of the many descriptions a person associates with a name to bear the burden of reference; the cluster of descriptions bears the burden. The problem of ambiguity posed by 2 is removed because the many descriptions associated with the name by the speech community can all be accommodated in the cluster. The absence of triviality indicated in 3 becomes explicable. The sense of a name does not require that all the descriptions in the cluster denote the bearer. So we should not expect 'Aristotle taught Alexander the Great' to seem trivial, necessary, *a priori*, or analytic in the way 'Bachelors are unmarried' does. Even though, say, 'the pupil of Plato and teacher of Alexander the Great' is in the cluster for 'Aristotle', it is not trivial to be told that Aristotle taught Alexander, for that description might have been one of the minority that did not denote Aristotle.

However, the success of the modern theory in answering these objections is far from complete. The theory is open to an objection very like 1. Presumably, not every decription associated with a name, however incidental, is to be included in the cluster. So the modern theory is committed to selecting some descriptions that *define* the name and rejecting others that express *merely accidental* properties of its bearer. The theory faces an awkward cut-off problem. It is not easy to produce a principled method of selection. The modern theorist will either be pushed backwards towards the classical theory, or forwards to an implausible holism in which every associated description is included in the defining cluster (so every change in belief about the bearer changes the meaning of the name).

The answer to 2 is unsatisfactory. It seems most unlikely that a principled method of selecting the cluster for a name will select the same cluster for all users: people vary in their beliefs about an object and in their views of which beliefs are central, which incidental. So the name 'Aristotle' would still be many-ways ambiguous.

More seriously, a complex analogue of problem 3 arises. Though it is not trivial to ascribe any one property to Aristotle, it should seem trivial to ascribe to him *most of the group* of properties picked out by the cluster of descriptions associated with his name. A sentence like

Aristotle had most of the following properties: born in Stagira, pupil of Plato, author of the *Nichomachean Ethics*, systematizer of syllogistic logic, teacher of Alexander the Great . . .

should seem necessary, *a priori*, and analytic. Yet it does not seem so.

** Kripke has made the point as follows (1980: 61-3). The name 'Aristotle' is a rigid designator (3.1). So, in another possible world it will designate the same person, namely Aristotle, that it designates in this world. In that world, that person might have had *none* of the properties mentioned in the cluster: he might have been born after his parents left Stagira; he might have been stillborn; he might never have met Alexander; and so on. The result is that the displayed sentence is far from trivial: it expresses an entirely contingent and empirical fact about Aristotle, discerned from the study of history, and open to revision in the face of further discovery.

We find this objection persuasive, but many others do not. For example, John Searle, one of the founders of the modern theory, had this to say:

> it is a necessary fact that Aristotle has the logical sum, inclusive disjunction, of properties commonly attributed to him: any individual not having some of these properties could not be Aristotle. (1958: 160)

In this passage Searle grasped the nettle of necessity long before Kripke presented it to cluster theorists. The problem is that Kripke's objection rests on modal intuitions that many do not share.

Furthermore, there is a way of avoiding most of this objection, as Kripke points out. We have been taking the description theory as a theory of sense, and hence of meaning: descriptions express the sense of a name; the name is synonymous with the descriptions. It is because of this that the theory is committed to the necessary truth of statements that do not seem necessary; for example, it is because *being the teacher of Alexander the Great* is part of the meaning of 'Aristotle', on the classical view, that 'Aristotle taught Alexander the Great' should be necessary on that view. Suppose we took the theory not as a theory of sense but *only* as a theory of reference: the name refers to whatever is picked out by the associated descriptions. This can be combined with the assumption that a name is a rigid designator and then the theory will not generate unwanted necessities. 'Aristotle' refers in any world to an object that is the same as the one picked out by the cluster we associate with the name in this world. Since there is no problem in that object having different properties in another possible world, there is no problem in the earlier sentence about Aristotle being contingent.

This manoeuvre does not avoid the objection entirely: it leaves some knowledge as inappropriately *a priori*. People who understand a name would still, presumably, have to know which cluster fixes its reference. So mere understanding of the name 'Aristotle' would suffice for knowledge of the displayed sentence; it would suffice for a whole lot of *contingent* knowledge about Aristotle. In brief, the manoeuvre results in that strange beast, the contingent *a priori*.

Aside from that, the manoeuvre is no help with the problems of selection and ambiguity. Worst of all, it leaves us with a seriously incomplete theory. If a cluster of descriptions does not give the sense of a name, what does? Senses were introduced to solve various problems – for example that of identity statements – which showed there was more to the meaning of a name than its role of designating its bearer (2.6). We still need senses for those purposes and so we still need a theory of sense. Furthermore, the theory we need must somehow relate the sense of a name to the description that determines its referent. The great advantage of the theory before this manoeuvre was that the cluster that fixed the referent also expressed the sense.**

Finally, note that though the cluster theory does well with the stimulus independence, arbitrariness, and medium independence of language, it does not do so with the abstractness of language. 'Orson weighs 130 kg' seems to be concerned with only one thing about Orson. According to the cluster theory, it is concerned with all the high points of his nature and history.

The difficulties we have raised so far for the description theory, whether classical or modern, are serious but not catastrophic. They should shake one's faith in the theory but, in the absence of an alternative, perhaps not lead one to abandon it. However, Kripke has developed another line of argument which is catastrophic for description theories. It does not rest on modal intuitions.

3.3 Names and knowledge

Kripke's argument is aimed at the central idea of all description theories **(even those that are only theories of reference)**: that the reference of a name is determined by the descriptions the speaker associates with the name. This idea leads, as we have already indicated (3.1, 3.2), to the view that the competent speaker must know identifying facts about the referent. Until recently this view was regarded as almost a truism in the philosophy of language. ("*How else* could a speaker's act of reference pick out a particular object?'). Kripke showed that the view was false. So the associated descriptions do not determine reference. So they do not express the sense which determines reference.

A more precise statement of the central idea is as follows:

> For any name token '*a*' and object *x*, '*a*' designates *x* if and only if *x* is denoted by a weighted most of the definite descriptions associated with '*a*' by the speaker.

This is general enough to cover all description theories. Classical theories assign a weight other than zero to only one description. Holistic modern theories assign such weights to all the associated descriptions. The more plausible modern theories assign them to the non-incidental descriptions.

What is it for a speaker to "associate" a definite description, say 'the *F*', with '*a*'? It is for him to have a belief he would express, '*a* is the *F*'. What is it for that description to "denote" *x*? It is for '*F*' to apply to *x* and to nothing else (3.1). It follows from the central idea, therefore, that the speaker must have a belief about the bearer of any name he successfully uses that is *true* and would not be true of anything else. There is no reason to withhold the term 'knowledge' from this true belief: the speaker knows identifying facts about the bearer. So we arrive at the "truism" that Kripke rejected.

Kripke showed that it is neither necessary nor sufficient for a name to designate an object that the speaker associates with the name identifying knowledge of the object. As a result, he showed that understanding a name – being able to use it properly – does not consist in the having of such knowledge (cf. the temptation mentioned in 2.6 and 3.1).

Identifying knowledge is not necessary

Consider the name 'Cicero'. Many people have heard of Cicero and can refer to him by that name. Do they have the identifying knowledge required by description theories? Our situation is probably typical. We associate with 'Cicero' the descriptions 'is Tully' and 'the denouncer of Catiline'. That near enough exhausts our knowledge of Cicero. The problem for description theories is that though these associated descriptions do indeed identify Cicero they are not *appropriate*: for they contain names. Descriptions must then be found for these names. We can do no better for 'Tully' than 'is Cicero' and, of course, 'the denouncer of Catiline', and no better for 'Catiline' than 'the person denounced by Cicero'. We can identify the referent of each name in terms of the others but have no independent way of identifying the referent of any. Our efforts to comply with the demands of description theories lead us in an obvious circle. Nor is the problem one of our special ignorance. Even those with a good deal of classical knowledge may find it difficult to produce a *name-free* identifying description of Cicero.

'Einstein' is a name on everyone's lips. How many could identify its bearer? It is common to associate 'the discoverer of the Theory of Relativity' with the name. But that will do the job only if the Theory of Relativity is identified independently of Einstein. Few of us could manage that.

What these two examples show is that description theories require people who appear to refer successfully with names to have beliefs they do not in fact have: they are too *ignorant*. The theories also face a problem of *error*: they seriously underestimate the number of *false* beliefs people have.

Public opinion polls and the like show that people are often quite mistaken about famous and historical figures. They think, for example, that Einstein invented the atomic bomb, or that Columbus was the first person to think that the world was round. Often the only non-trivial belief that they hold about someone is false. Yet when they use the names for such people they still succeed in referring to them; their assertion, "A city in Ohio was named after Columbus" is a truth about Columbus not a falsehood about some ancient Greek.

The role of false belief can be explored through examples of Wittgenstein and Kripke. Wittgenstein's example concerns Moses. Suppose that we discovered that nobody satisfied the descriptions normally associated with 'Moses': 'the man who led the Israelites out of Egypt', 'the man who as a child was taken out of the Nile by Pharaoh's daughter', etc. We would probably conclude that there was no Moses; that 'Moses' was an empty name designating nothing. And so we should conclude according to description theories. These theories miss an alternative possibility, as Kripke's speculations about Jonah demonstrate.

It is unlikely that the biblical story of Jonah is true of any actual man; unlikely even that substantial parts of it, particularly the parts about the big fish, are. Does it follow that 'Jonah' is an empty name? It does not: Jonah *might have been a real person about whom a legend has grown*. Imagine we discover that the facts were as follows. There *was* a person called 'Jonah' who lived a fairly ordinary life. The only unusual thing about his life was the superstitious regard his fellows held him in: they tended to tell peculiar stories about him. After his death these stories blossomed into the biblical story of Jonah; all the truths about Jonah (except trivial ones like being a man) were forgotten.

In the situation imagined, our uses of 'Jonah' designate the man around whom the legend grew. Earlier predications using the name, such as those in the Bible, are mostly false because that man lacked the ascribed properties. Present predications, reflecting the deflation of the legend, will be true.

Description theories cannot accommodate these claims. These theories must conclude that the imagined discovery shows that 'Jonah', in its earlier uses, was an empty name. None of the earlier predications, not even the trivial ones like being a man, can be true. We have not replaced a false theory about Jonah with a true one about him: until the discovery, we had no theory *about him* at all. Note that it is *not possible*, on the description theory, for an earlier scholar to speculate, or find evidence, that Jonah was a certain ordinary man that he, the scholar, has tracked down. Such speculations, such evidence, cannot be *about Jonah* because they deny the descriptions on which our use of the name depends. These consequences of description theories are not plausible.

The possibility that the Jonah case raises is not fanciful. For instance, it precisely parallels scholarly speculation about King Arthur: that the Arthurian legends grew around a real, though less colourful, figure.

We conclude that the kind of knowledge attributed to us by description theories is not necessary. We can use a name to designate an object even when we are ignorant of the object. We can do it even when our error about the object is massive.

Identifying knowledge is not sufficient

Suppose that a person intent on misleading his audience launches into a narrative without making it clear that he is story-telling. Alternatively, to avoid deliberate deception, suppose the person tells something that is in fact a vivid dream but which he, deluded as he is, thinks is true. The audience believes the narrative and later passes it on to others. It turns out that there are people, not known to the narrator, who fit the descriptions of his characters. *Must* we say that the narrator (and thence his audience) was talking about those people? We *might*, especially if the parallels were both striking and unexpected: some might even see it as a case of extrasensory perception. There is an alternative: we might dismiss the parallelism as a matter of chance. Despite the fact that the narrator's descriptions fit those people, he did not refer to them.

The examples of Einstein and Columbus also illustrate the insufficiency of identifying knowledge. The person who associates with 'Einstein' the description, 'the inventor of the atomic bomb', does not designate Oppenheimer; the person who associates 'Columbus' with the description, 'the first person to think that the world was round', does not designate some ancient Greek.

Consider finally Kripke's famous example of Gödel. Most people with some knowledge of logic know that Gödel first proved the incompleteness of arithmetic. Suppose that this proof had really been discovered by Schmidt, a student of Gödel, and had been stolen by Gödel. Schmidt, naturally depressed and disillusioned by this turn of events, dies. Gödel goes on to undeserved fame and Princeton. Now consider the many who associate with 'Gödel' only the description 'the discoverer of the incompleteness of arithmetic'. In this counter-factual situation the description they associate denotes Schmidt. Does their use of 'Gödel' then designate Schmidt? Surely not. If Kripke's slander were correct, their assertion of 'Gödel discovered the incompleteness of arithmetic' would be a false staement about Gödel, not a true one about Schmidt.

These examples show that even where descriptions that identify an object are associated by a speaker with a name, the name may not refer to that individual. Identifying knowledge is no more sufficient for reference than it is necessary.

3.4. Reference borrowing

We have written so far as if everyone has to stand on his own in determining reference for a name: each person has to provide identifying descriptions that signal the bearer's famous achievements, or most distinctive personal or physical characteristics. But perhaps we can borrow our reference from others. There are some who could satisfactorily identify Cicero and Einstein. Maybe they can carry the rest of us. This is an important suggestion, which we shall later adopt, but it does not save description theories.

Strawson explicitly adopts reference borrowing (1959: 182n). The form it takes for Strawson is the form it must take for a description theory: the association of a definite description that refers to another person's reference. (John Bigelow has ingeniously suggested to us a fall-back position for the description theorist on reference borrowing: borrowing from one's younger self. We shall leave it to the reader to adapt the argument to this position.) Suppose that yesterday Alice heard George talking with enthusiasm of someone called 'Joshua'. She does not know Joshua from Adam, but she rightly thinks that George does. So Alice's gossip today can meet the requirements of description theories: she associates with 'Joshua' the identifying description, 'the person George was referring to yesterday by 'Joshua''. This is only satisfactory, of course, because Alice can support her use of 'George' with an appropriate description, and because George can identify Joshua. Borrowing can go further: Alice talks to Ruth, Ruth to Sebastian, and so on. Each person designates Joshua in virtue of associating with his name a description that refers to the previous person in the chain.

The idea of a reference chain is well taken, but even this version of the description theory requires knowledge where there may be none. First, the borrower must remember at least one other user of the name, and remember that user not merely by name: an identifying description must be provided. This may, of course, send the borrower off on further reference borrowing whch in turn requires further knowledge. Second, the reference *lender* must be able either to identify the referent on her own, or remember where she borrowed the name from. And so on. There is a danger of circularity here: Sebastian depends on Ruth, Ruth depends on Alice, and Alice, forgetting all about George, comes to depend on Sebastian. Someone in the chain must be able to go it alone. Aside from this problem of circularity, it is unlikely that the required knowledge is present for most users of a name; we naturally *forget* most of this information. We forget where we got a name from. Or we remember but can't identify the person satisfactorily. Or we identify her, but she is no better off than we are: she cannot identify the bearer. Reference borrowing is some help to description theories but not *enough* help.

There is a final refinement of description theories that we need to consider. Would it not be sufficient for the speaker to be able to *recognize* the bearer of the name? Instead of describing the bearer, he can pick her out in a line-up. This is not a great departure from the spirit of description theories. Indeed Strawson contemplates something like this in allowing that descriptions may contain demonstrative elements (1959: 182n). For, to pick someone out in a line-up is equivalent to associating her with the description, 'that person', pointing at the person in question.

Description theories of this kind are more plausible yet. In particular, the refinement increases the value of reference borrowing: the lenders are often people we could recognize but not describe. Nevertheless, the theories still require more knowledge than we often have. There are limitations on the number of objects most of us could successfully point out. We could manage it for our friends, many of our acquaintances, and some of our famous contemporaries. However, we can but dimly call to mind many we can name. We certainly cannot identify historical figures like Cicero this way.

Finally, neither this refinement nor reference borrowing is any help with the problem of error. The reference lender may be misdescribed or misidentified. Or *he* may be mistaken: he has false information about the bearer or would pick out the wrong person in a line-up.

3.5 Rejecting description theories

We think that description theories of names are wrong not merely in details but in fundamentals. The whole programme is mistaken. Of course, we do not claim to have *demonstrated* this: there are a few knockdown arguments in philosophy. So, moves can still be made to continue the programme; for example, by denying the evidence ("The ignorant do *not* designate Einstein"). We won't follow these lines of thought further. Instead, we aim to undermine the description theories in two further respects. First, we shall emphasize their essential limitations in the rest of this chapter. Second, we shall develop an alternative in the next few chapters.

Even were we to set aside the fact that a description theory requires speakers to have more knowledge than they actually have, the theory is essentially incomplete. A description theory of names explains the referential properties of one category of term, names, by appeal to those of another, definite descriptions: on the classical theory, '*a*' designates x in virtue of being associated with 'the F' which denotes x; designation is explained in terms of denotation. The referential properties of descriptions are explained, in turn, by appeal to those of general terms: 'the F' denotes x in virtue of the fact that 'F' applies to x and nothing else; denotation is explained in terms of application (3.1). What account of general terms is on offer? In virtue of what does 'F' apply to Fs? Perhaps a description theory of *some* general terms would be satisfactory: words like 'bachelor', 'judge' and 'murderer' may seem definable. This process cannot, however, go on for ever: there must be some terms whose referential properties are not parasitic on others. Otherwise, language as a whole is cut loose from the world. Description theories, which explain one part of language in terms of another, can give no clues as to how, ultimately, language is referentially linked to reality. These theories pass the referential buck. But the buck must stop somewhere.

Strangely enough the essential incompleteness of description theories of reference was not noticed until recently. It is still ignored by most writers on reference.

A famous science-fiction fantasy, invented by Hilary Putnam to refute description theories of natural kind terms (1975: 223-7), helps to bring out this incompleteness (and shows again that identifying knowledge is not necessary). Imagine that somewhere in the universe there is a planet, Twin Earth. Twin Earth, as its name suggests, is very like Earth. In particular, each Earthling has a *doppelgänger* on Twin Earth who is molecule for molecule the same as the Earthling. Consequently, many Twin Earthlings speak a language that seems like English. Indeed it is phonologically and syntactically the same as English. Is it semantically the same too? It cannot be if we deem it to include the proper names that Twin Earthlings use, because it is not referentially the same. When an Earthling uses a name in English, he refers to an object on Earth. When his *doppelgänger* uses what is apparently the same name, he refers to an object on Twin Earth. Friend Oscar declares his voting intentions: "I'll vote for Reagan; we need a dangerous president for a dangerous world". He is talking about our local Earthly Reagan. Twin Oscar produces an utterance that sounds the same, but he is not referring to Reagan; he has never heard of Reagan nor of any other Earthling. He has his own problems with Twin Reagan in Twin USA.

What does this show? It shows that reference, and hence meaning, does not depend solely on the association of some words with other words, for all those associations are the same in Twin English as in English. Further, there is no internal state of the speaker that determines the reference, and hence the meaning, of his words, for Oscar and his twin are alike internally. No association of descriptions or mental images will make Oscar's words refer to Reagan rather than Twin Reagan. No state of Oscar's brain will do the job. As Putnam put it, "'meanings' just ain't in the *head*" (1975: 227). We must look for some relation that language and mind have to things outside themslves to explain meaning.

Indeed, *how could* meanings be in the head? Meaning depends on reference and reference relates a person and his words to something outside him. To suppose that something internal to an object is sufficient to determine its relation to a particular object external to it is to suppose that it has a truly magical power. A person no more has this power over the relation of reference than he has it over the relation of kicking, teaching, being taller than, or being the father of.

(Twin-Earth fantasies appeal to philosophers, but not to many others, as Stephen Stich has emphasized; 1983: 62n. If you are one of the others, try to invent a less outlandish example that makes the same point.)

For all this, there are some important truths in the description theory. The idea that we must know something about an entity in order to refer to it by name is appealing. We shall return to it (4.4). The idea of reference borrowing is especially important. It highlights what Hilary Putnam calls "the linguistic division of labour" (1975: 27–8). Our ability to use our language is, in part, a social capacity. It depends on our interactions with others in a community of varying interests, capacities and expertise. Putnam made the point about general terms: our capacity to talk about chromosomes, microchips and curved spacetime, despite our ignorance of these things, is a result of our social links to others whose acquaintance with them is more intimate. The same is true of names: a person often succeeds in designating an object only in virtue of being at the end of reference chains running through her linguistic community to the object. However, our view of the nature of those links is very different from that of the description theorist.

Suggested reading

3.1

Frege's theory of names is briefly introduced in the 1892 paper, "On sense and reference" (1952: 57–8). **Most of this paper is devoted to Frege's ingenious solution to the difficult problem of opaque contexts.** For more on his view of names, see his much later (1918) "The thought", reprinted in Klemke 1968, *Essays on Frege*.

Russell's theory of names appears in several works first published between 1910 and 1920. The simplest statement is probably, *The Problems of Philosophy* (1967) chapter 5. See also, "Knowledge by acquaintance and knowledge by description", in *Mysticism and Logic* (1957); and "The philosophy of logical atomism", in *Logic and Knowledge* (1956). Russell distinguished ordinary proper names from "logically proper names". His description theory applies to the ordinary ones. He had a Millian theory of the logically proper ones. They behave the way he thought names *ought* to behave. They stand in a relationship of the utmost intimacy to their bearers. They immediately and directly focus attention on an object and that is all they do. Only 'this', which we would not normally call a proper name at all, seems to qualify as a logically proper name. The reader must avoid being misled by the fact that Russell often writes as if ordinary names were logically proper. He does this to get familiar examples.

Russell's theory of descriptions first appeared in his famous 1905 paper, "On denoting", reprinted in Russell 1956 and in Davidson and Harman 1976.

For a later Russellian reaction to the problem of identity statements, see Fitch 1949, "The problem of the morning star and the evening star".

3.2

For Searle's theory of names, see "Proper names" (1958), reprinted in Caton 1963, *Philosophy and Ordinary Language*, and in Rosenberg and Travis 1971, *Readings in the Philosophy of Language*. See also his *Speech Acts* (1969: 162–74), reprinted as "The problem of proper names" in Steinberg and Jakobovits 1971, *Semantics*. For Strawson's theory, see *Individuals* (1959: 180–3, 190–4). A cluster theory is also to be found in Wilson 1959, "Substances without substrata".

The suggestion that the understander need not know the whole cluster seems to be present in Strawson. Evans 1973, "The causal theory of names", pp. 193–4, reprinted in Schwartz 1977, *Naming, Necessity, and Natural Kinds*, takes Strawson in this way.

** For Kripke's discussion of the modal consequences of description theories, rigid designation, and the distinction between theories of meaning and theories of reference, see *Naming and Necessity* (1980), particularly: 3–15, 48–78; also, "Identity and necessity" (1971), reprinted in Schwartz 1977. Dummett 1973, *Frege*, pp. 111–35, is a vigorous response to Kripke. See also Linsky 1977, *Names and Descriptions*, chapters 3–4. The ramifications of Kripke's lines of argument are thoroughly explored in Salmon 1982, *Reference and Essence*.**

3.3–3.4

For Kripke's non-modal argument against description theories see *Naming and Necessity* (1980: 79–91). A similar line of argument is to be found in Donnellan 1972, "Proper names and identifying descriptions". See Kroon 1982, "The problem of 'Jonah': How *not* to argue for the causal theory of reference", for a criticism of one Kripkean argument.

The following defences of description theories in the face of Kripke's argument seem to threaten circularity: Loar 1976, "The semantics of singular terms"; McDowell 1977, "On the sense and reference of a proper name"; Schiffer 1978, "The basis of reference". On the problems of circularity, see Kripke 1980: 160–2; also Devitt 1981a, *Designation*: pp. 21–3.

For a recent defence of description theories, see Bach 1981, "What's in a name?"

3.5

An example of an influential philosopher who seems to miss the incompleteness of description theories is John Searle; see his *Intentionality* (1983a), particularly chapter 9.

4

A causal theory of reference: names

4.1 A causal theory

The basic idea of causal theories of reference, due particularly to Kripke (1980), is that a term refers to whatever is causally linked to it in a certain way, a way that does not require speakers to have identifying knowledge of the referent. The causal links relate speakers to the world and to each other.

We start with the simplest case, proper names. How is a person able to use 'Einstein' to designate a physicist he has never met and whose theories he does not grasp? This problem divides in two.

1   How do we explain the introduction into the language of 'Einstein' as a name for Einstein? We need to explain how people were first able to use that noise to designate a certain individual. This requires a theory of *reference fixing*. Our theory of reference fixing looks to the causal *grounding* of a name in an object.
2   How do we account for the social transmission of the name 'Einstein' within the linguistic community? Most of us had nothing to do with the introduction of the name but can use it to designate Einstein because we have gained the name from others. To explain this we need a theory of *reference borrowing*. We shall offer a causal theory of this also.

The basic idea of the causal theory of grounding is as follows. The name is introduced *ostensively* at a formal or informal dubbing. This dubbing is in the presence of the object that will from then on be the bearer of the name. The event is perceived by the dubber and probably others. To perceive something is to be causally affected by it. As a result of this causal action, a witness to the dubbing, if of suitable linguistic sophistication, will gain an ability to use the name to designate the object. Any use of the name exercising that ability designates the object in virtue of the use's causal link to the object: ostension of the object prompted the thoughts which led to the use of the name. In short, those present at the dubbing acquire a semantic ability that is causally grounded in the object.

The basic idea of the causal theory of reference borrowing is as follows. People not at the dubbing acquire the semantic ability from those at the dubbing. This acquisition is also a causal, indeed perceptual, process. The name is used in conversation. Hearers of the conversation, if of suitable linguistic sophistication, can gain the ability to use the name to designate the object. The exercise of that ability will designate the object in virtue of a causal chain linking the object, those at its dubbing, and the user, through the conversation.

A name not only has a reference (usually), it has sense (2.6). If the causal theory is to emulate the description theory in accounting for both (3.1), we must give a theory of sense. We earlier expressed the hope that a theory of reference will supply a theory of sense (2.6). And so it turns out. We identify the sense of a name with the type of causal chain linking uses of the name to its bearer. The aspects of reality we have to call on to explain reference are all we need for sense. The reference of a name is determined by the appropriate causal chains and, in virtue of that, by its sense. The chains yield what Frege would call, "the mode of presentation" of the object (2.6). So Frege was right in thinking that there was more to a name's meaning than its referent, but wrong in thinking that the extra was expressed by a definite description. The causal theory, like the description theory, is a complete theory of meaning for names.

With the description theory of reference went a theory of understanding, a theory of what it is to be competent with a name (3.1). Such a theory is also implicit in the above introduction to the causal theory. When we talk of an ability to use a name gained at a dubbing or in conversation, we are talking of competence. This ability consists, largely, in thoughts – beliefs, desires, hopes, and the like – prompted by perception of the object at its dubbing or by conversation about it. Our view of this competence will be set out in more detail later (8.8) after we have discussed thoughts (chapter 7).

So the picture is this. At a dubbing, a name is introduced by grounding it in an object. There is a causal chain linking the ability gained at the dubbing to the object. In virtue of that link, the reference of the name is fixed as the object. Exercising the ability by using the name adds new links to the causal chain: it leads to others having abilities dependent on the original ability. Thus, we can use 'Einstein' to designate Einstein because we are causally linked to him by a chain running through our linguistic community to someone present at his dubbing.

Let us illustrate this picture. The typical name is of a humble object and so we take as our example the name of Devitt's late cat: 'Nana'. Two people were present at her dubbing. There was no elaborate ceremony: one said, "Let's call her 'Nana' after Zola's courtesan", and the other agreed. This simple suggestion, agreed to, was enough. Each person saw and felt the cat, saw the other person, and heard his or her words. Each person was sophisticated enough to know what was going on. The cat occupied a unique place in this complex causal interaction. In virtue of that place she was named 'Nana'. In virtue of that place the abilities the two gained were ones to designate Nana.

A few minutes later, the name was used for the first time: "Nana is hungry". That first use designated Nana. It did so because that name token was produced by an ability created by the dubbing in which Nana played that unique role. Underlying the token is a causal chain grounded in Nana.

The two dubbers did not keep the name to themselves. They introduce others to the cat: "This is Nana". They told others of her name: "Our cat is called 'Nana'". They used the name in conversation: "I must get home to feed Nana". Those who heard and understood these utterances gained abilities to designate Nana by her name; they borrowed their reference from the dubbers. When they went on to use the name there were causal chains underlying those uses that stretched back to Nana via the ability of the reference lender. From those uses still others gained abilities underlying which were similar chains. Such chains are "designating chains", or, briefly, "d-chains". So, underlying a name is a network of d-chains.

4.2 Virtues of the causal theory

The theory developed so far is oversimplified in various ways, but we can see already that it has many attractive features. First, it shares with description theories the capacity to account for the following special features of natural language (1.2): stimulus independence; arbitrariness; medium independence. A name is stimulus independent in that the causal chain on which its use depends does not require the presence of the object. It is arbitrary and medium-independent in that any symbol in any medium can be placed in the appropriate causal relation to the object. However, unlike description theories (3.2), it can also account for the apparent abstractness of proper names: as Mill observed, names do not "imply any attributes as belonging to" the object (2.5).

Second, the causal theory avoids the problems of description theories. Since a name does not abbreviate a cluster of definite descriptions, there is no problem selecting which descriptions are in the cluster for a person (cf. 1 in 3.1–3.2); nor, avoiding unwanted ambiguities arising from cluster differences between people (cf. 2); nor, coping with surprising trivialities, necessities, analyticities and *a priorities* (cf. 3). The connection between naming and knowing is cut (cf. 3.3–3.4): we do not require that name users be able to identify bearers; we offer a very different view of competence with a name. People designate Catiline despite their ignorance of him; they designate Jonah despite their errors about him. They do this by borrowing their reference from others who in turn borrow theirs, and so on, right back to those who named the objects. None of these borrowers needs to be able to identify his lender. No lender needs to be an expert about the object. Ignorance and error are no bars to reference.

Third, the theory can solve the problem of identity statements. This was one of the problems that led to the introduction of senses (2.5–2.6) and thus encouraged description theories in the first place (3.1). That our theory can solve this problem may seem surprising, for our theory is rather similar in spirit to the Millian view, as our agreement with the above Millian observation indicates. However, we disagree with the Millian view in a way that is important to the problem of identity statements. There *is* more to the meaning of a name than its role of designating a particular object: a name has a sense. We identify this sense with the type of d-chain that makes up the network for the name.

The problem is to explain the striking difference between

Everest is Everest
Everest is Gaurisanker.

The second sentence is informative in a way that the first is not. Why? Because the causal network underlying 'Everest' is not that underlying 'Gaurisanker'. Hence to state the second sentence the speaker needs two semantic abilities; he needs access to two distinct causal networks, albeit ones that are grounded in the one object. These networks are partly in the speaker's mind, and are distinct there. So the names are not synonymous for the speaker. To know that Everest is Gaurisanker he must, on the basis of geographical evidence, relate the two abilities. There is nothing trivial about that knowledge. In contrast, the knowledge that Everest is Everest requires access to only one causal network together with a belief in the law of identity; to assert the first sentence is to exercise an ability with 'Everest' twice in airing a commitment to the triviality that everything is self-identical.

What about the other problems that led to senses? Existence statements and empty names require further developments, which we will give briefly in the next section. Opacity is difficult and cannot be handled here. However, we can indicate the lines of our solution. The sentence

Falwell believes Bob Dylan destroyed the moral fibre of America

depends for its truth not simply on the referent of 'Bob Dylan' but also on the mode of presentation of the referent. In this respect our solution follows Frege. However, our view of that mode differs from Frege's as we have noted (4.1). The above sentence can be true only if Falwell's belief involves the appropriate causal network.

Fourth, consider a problem that we have so far ignored: that posed by the *ambi-*

guity of names. Proper names typically have more than one bearer. What determines which bearer is designated by a particular use of such a name? This problem can be put clearly in terms of a helpful distinction between *types* and *tokens*.

Tokens are datable, placeable parts of the physical world. Thus, Nana and her successor, Lulu, are cat tokens. The obvious examples of word tokens are inscriptions on a page or sounds in the air. Types, on the other hand, are kinds of tokens. Any token can be grouped into many different types. Thus, Nana and Lulu are tokens of the type *cat*, *female*, *pet of Devitt*, and so on. And, prior to this sentence, this paragraph contains two tokens of the inscription type 'Nana' and eleven of the inscription type *four-lettered*. Inscription types and sound types are identifiable by their overt physical characteristics and so we might call them "physical" types. Word tokens are also grouped semantically. Suppose that an inscription type 'Liebknecht' is used in a book on German history to refer to two different people, father and son; the type is *ambiguous*. Sometimes we will group the tokens that refer to the father in one type and those that refer to the son in another. We thus get "semantic" types. Tokens that are in different media cannot be of the same physical type but may be of the same semantic type; for natural languages are medium-independent. A spoken and written token of 'Liebknecht' might supply an example of tokens of the same semantic type from different media.

We can now put the problem of ambiguity as follows. What settles which semantic type a given token of an ambiguous physical type belongs to? In virtue of what does a token of 'Liebknecht' have one referent rather than the other?

Intuitively, the semantic type is determined by *what the speaker had in mind* in producing the token. So the matter is settled by some facts about the speaker's psychology. What facts precisely? Description theories say that it is the speaker's association of descriptions with the name token that counts. So, a token of 'Liebknecht' designated the father not the son because the speaker associated descriptions with it that denote the father not the son. We have seen that this kite will not fly. Our causal theory gives a different answer: it is the ability exercised in producing the token that counts. So 'Liebknecht' designated the father because it was caused by an ability which is grounded in the father.

Our solution to the problem of ambiguity, like that of description theories, is speaker-based. We do not overlook the importance of the linguistic and non-linguistic *context* of an utterance but see all aspects of it, aside from the relevant parts of the causal history, as having only evidential significance. The context guides an audience in removing ambiguity; it supplies evidence of what the speaker has in mind and hence evidence of the semantic reality, but it is not that reality.

Some philosophers have thought differently: they have given a context-based solution according to which the context determines the semantic type of a token. We can see that this solution is wrong by considering an example that is most favourable to it: the sound type, 'Newton', which is used to designate both a famous physicist and an Australian golfer who recently lost an arm. These bearers of the name are as different as could be. If context disambiguates, it will do so unequivocally here. Suppose someone says, "The unit force, a newton, is named after Newton". Suppose this takes place in a science classroom. Indeed, let every contextual feature point towards Isaac. According to the context-based view, these features are not merely very good evidence that 'Newton' here designates Isaac but determine that it does so. Yet it may still designate Jack. The speaker may be joking; or he may think that the golfer mooonlights in physics; or whatever. No piling up of contextual detail makes it impossible for 'Newton' to designate the golfer.

Fifth, and perhaps most important of all, the causal theory promises an explanation of the *ultimate* links between language and the world. Furthermore, the explanation in terms of causation seems agreeably naturalistic (1.3). In rejecting description theories, we pointed out that they cannot explain the ultimate links (3.5): they make the reference of some words dependent on that of others, and thus leave reference *internal* to the language. We need an explanation of the *external* relation that the whole system of words bears to the world. We emphasized this with the help of Putnam's Twin-Earth fantasy. The causal theory we have offered in this chapter makes the reference of names dependent on an external relation. When Oscar declares, "I'll vote for Reagan; we need a dangerous president for a dangerous world", he refers to our Earthly Reagan not Twin Reagan. Why? Because his words stand in a certain causal relation to the Earthly Reagan. If Oscar has any causal relation to Twin Reagan, it is a very different one that is irrelevant to reference.

Return to our solution to the problem of ambiguity. The reference of a speaker's token of 'Liebknecht', who he "has in mind", is determined by his psychological states *together with* the way those states are causally embedded in the environment. For, the token refers to the object which grounds the ability exercised in producing the token.

4.3 Developing the theory

It is scarcely possible to exaggerate the extent to which the theory proposed so far is in need of supplementation. We have already mentioned the problems of exist-ence statements, empty names, and opacity (4.2) and will say something about the first two in this section. We shall also discuss *multiple grounding*, an elaboration of the causal theory that is important for handling many problems. In the next section, we shall consider whether any knowledge of the object is required for reference. Other matters must be set aside, most notably the following.

1   What are abilities to designate? What goes on when we borrow reference? What kind of perceptual link to an object is required for grounding? We need to discover the social and linguistic preconditions of learning and introducing names. We shall throw some light on these questions in part III when considering the relation of mind to language. However, we shall not throw much. Partly this is because this book is not the appropriate place to attempt to do so, but largely it is because we are unable to do so. We, and we think others, simply do not know enough about the cognitive areas of the mind to answer these questions.

2   Our theory so far is concerned only with names. What of other terms? We need a theory of reference for all terms. Are they all to be treated causally like names, or are some to be handled by a description theory or some other theory of reference? How far can the causal theory be extended? We shall consider these questions in the next chapter.

Empty names

The causal theory distinguishes empty names from nonsense syllables, for even an empty name has an underlying causal network. What makes it empty is that its network is not properly grounded in an object. This can come about in two different ways.

First, a name may be introduced as a result of a false posit: a person wrongly thinks that an entity exists. Suppose that Zappa, perhaps after indulgence in strange chemicals, hallucinates an extra-terrestrial visitor. Zappa attempts to name this visitor 'Tilda'. Since there is nothing there, he does not really name anything, of course; his attempt at grounding fails. But he tells people about his experience, believing it real, and a network grows in just the way it would have had 'Tilda' named a real visitor.

Second, and much more common, a name may be introduced in what is explicitly or implicitly a work of fiction: a story, novel, film, etc. Suppose that Zappa is not hallucinating but rather is bent on cashing in on the general fascination with science fiction. He writes a novel about an extra-terrestrial named 'Tilda'. Out of his imaginative act a network for the name grows up that is not grounded in an object. How does it do so? Why does it do so? These are interesting questions which must be left to another time.

Existence statements

Our account of singular existence statements follows straightforwardly from this. The sceptics who respond to Zappa's alleged encounter with an extra-terrestrial by claiming,

Tilda does not exist,

will be saying something which is both meaningful and true. It is meaningful because the name has an underlying causal network. It is true because its network is not grounded in an object. On the other hand, the gullible who claim,

Tilda exists,

will be saying something which is both meaningful and false.

Reference change and multiple grounding

The theory sketched so far makes simple reference change impossible, for the reference of a name is immutably fixed at a dubbing. So the theory's account of language change is deficient. We have shown how additions to the language occur through dubbings. It is clear how a name dies out: people cease to add new links to its network by using the name. However, there is no explanation of how the reference of a name can change.

Gareth Evans (1973) has emphasized the importance of such an explanation with a number of nice examples. Here is an adaptation of one of them. Twins A and B are born and dubbed 'Shane' and 'Dawn' respectively. After the ceremony, the twins are somehow mixed up: everyone calls A 'Dawn' and B 'Shane'. The mistake is never discovered: the twins grow up, and grow apart, with each invariably "misnamed". Twin A turns out to be fiery, aggressive and physical, quite unlike twin B who is mild, self-effacing and intellectual. What do we say of the boringly many utterances, 'Dawn is fierce' and 'Shane is mild'? Our simple version of the causal theory gives the wrong result: twin B was dubbed 'Dawn' and B is not fierce. Hence all those 'Dawn is fierce' tokens should be false. Yet they are surely not false. We want to say that all the years of calling A 'Dawn' and B 'Shane' have resulted in these *being* their names. The names have changed their references since the dubbings.

A more sophisticated causal theory is called for. Its central idea is that a name is typically *multiply* grounded in its bearer. In our original sketch, the reference of a name was fixed at a dubbing. All subsequent uses of the name were parasitic on that dubbing; all d-chains trace back to that one grounding. What this account misses is that many uses of a name are relevantly similar to a dubbing. They are similar in that they involve the application of the name to the object in a direct perceptual confrontation with it. The social ceremony of introduction provides the most obvious examples: someone says, "This is Nana", pointing to the beast in question. Remarks prompted by observation of an object may provide others: observing Nana's behaviour, someone says, "Nana is skittish tonight". Such uses of a name ground it in its bearer just as effectively as does a dubbing. As a result it becomes multiply grounded. The dubbing does not bear all the burden of linking a name to the world.

Return to the twins and the problem of reference change. The name 'Dawn' was grounded in B at the dubbing, but from then on always grounded in A. The initial grounding in B pales into insignificance when compared with these thousands of groundings in A. So 'Dawn' now designates B.

Evans gives an actual case of reference change: the name 'Madagascar'. For us it is the name of a large African island. However, it (or something like it) was originally the name of a portion of the African mainland. The change took place because of a misunderstanding by Marco Polo. Our account of the change is as follows. Before Marco Polo all groundings of 'Madagascar' were in the portion of the mainland and so that was what the name designated. For some time after his mistake there was doubtless a good deal of confusion, with those influenced by him grounding the name in the island and those influenced by the locals grounding it in the mainland. However, Marco Polo's mistake led finally to a systematic pattern of groundings in the island. The d-chains underlying our uses go back to those groundings. So those uses designate the island.

What about the period of confusion? What did the name refer to then? There would have been no serious problem if those influenced by Marco Polo and those influenced by the locals did not mingle. Marco Polo's mistake would then have quickly led to 'Madagascar' having a new meaning and reference whilst its old meaning and reference lived on with the locals. The name would have become ambiguous. However, it is more likely that the two groups did mingle. So, for a period, each use of the name would have underlying it some d-chains grounded in the mainland and some others grounded in the island. In these circumstances, there is no fact of the matter which object the name designated; reference is simply indeterminate. What we need is a new semantic notion: *partial* designation. We can then say that though the name did not designate either object, it partially designated both. Notions of partial reference are very useful in handling cases of confusion. However, this is not the place to discuss such refinements.

4.4 The *qua*-problem

In rejecting description theories of names and urging our causal theory, we have insisted that a person can use a name successfully without having identifying knowledge of its bearer. The causal theory inclines us to go further: the person need not have any knowledge of the bearer; the beliefs he has about it may all be false. Is this going too far?

Some philosophers have thought that the user of a name must know, at least, *what kind* of object its bearer is (e.g. Geach 1962: chapter 2). Yet when we consider the way a person can borrow reference, this does not seem plausible. She can pick up a name on a very slender basis, wrongly inferring all sorts of things about its bearer. Perhaps it names a university yet she believes it to name a person, a cat or a river. She is linked into the causal network for the name and so there seems to be no good reason to deny that she uses the name to designate the university.

However, when we consider groundings, the rejection of any knowledge requirement on reference for names begins to seem too extreme. Two features of a grounding suggest this.

1   Think once more of a grounding of 'Nana'. The name was grounded in Nana in virtue of perceptual contact with her. But that contact is not with *all* of Nana, either temporally or spatially. Temporally, the contact in any one grounding is only with her for a brief period of her life, with a "time-slice" of Nana. On the strength of such contacts, Nana, the sum of many time-slices sighted and unsighted, is the referent of 'Nana'. Spatially, the contact is only with an undetached part of her, perhaps a relatively small part of her face (she may be peering around a corner). In virtue of what was the grounding in the whole Nana not in a time-slice or undetached part of her?

   The question is not to be airily dismissed on the assumption that names do, as a matter of fact, always designate "whole objects". Even if this were so, it would surely be possible to name temporal or spatial parts of objects. So there must be something about our practice which makes it the case that our names designate whole objects. In any case, we often do name parts. Sickeningly coy examples are to be found in *Lady Chatterly's Lover*. Think also of 'Sydney' which is the name of part of Australia. Temporal examples do not leap to mind so readily. 'The Terror' naming a part of the French Revolution is one example. And we might name a tadpole without thereby naming the frog it turns into.

2   Think next of a situation where the would-be grounder is very wrong about what he is perceiving. It is not a cat but a mongoose, a robot, a bush, a shadow, or an illusion (like Zappa's extra-terrestrial: 4.3). At some point in this sequence, the grounder's error becomes so great that the attempted grounding fails, and hence uses of the name arising out of the attempt fail of reference. Yet there will always be *some* cause of the perceptual experience. In virtue of what is the name not grounded in that cause?

Consideration of 1 shows that there must be something about the mental state of the grounder that makes it the case that the name is grounded in the cause of the perceptual experience *qua whole object*. It is unhelpful to say that it is the grounder's intention that makes it so. In virtue of what did the grounder intend the whole object? It seems that the grounder must, at some level, "think of" the cause of his experience under some general categorial term like 'animal' or 'material object'. It is because he does so that the grounding is in Nana and not in a temporal and spatial part of her.

This immediately yields an answer to our question in 2. The grounding will fail if the cause of the perceptual experience does not fit the general categorial terms used to conceptualize it.

It seems then that our causal theory of names cannot be a "pure-causal" theory. It must be a "descriptive-causal" theory: a name is associated, consciously or unconsciously, with a description in a grounding. A descriptive element has entered into the characterization of a d-chain. Does the association of a description with the name amount to knowledge (assuming the grounding is successful)? Does the grounder have to know that Nana is an animal, material object, or whatever? Knowledge may be involved here, but we shall leave discussion of question until later (5.5, 14.4).

Clearly, we have moved some distance back toward the description theories rejected earlier (3.3-3.4). However, the extent of the move should not be exaggerated. First, the association of a general categorial term certainly does not amount to *identifying* knowledge of the object. Second, our move is a modification of the causal theory of grounding. The causal theory of reference borrowing remains unchanged; borrowers do not have to associate the correct categorial term.

The move away from a pure-causal theory of names has a price, as we shall see (5.3).

In this chapter we have introduced our causal theory of names. This serves as a model for causal theories of reference. We must now turn to developing such theories for other terms. The plausibility of the Millian intuition that names lack connotation suggests that names are semantically unusual. So even if a causal theory is right for them, it may not be right for others. Consideration of other terms leads to a modification of our theory of names (5.6).

Suggested reading

4.1

Causal theories of names originated with Kripke 1980, *Naming and Necessity*: 91-7; and with Donnellan 1972, "Proper names and identifying descriptions", which appeared with the original version of Kripke's work in Davidson and Harman 1972, *Semantics of Natural Language*. For a fuller development of the ideas in this section, see Devitt 1981a, *Designation*: sections 2.1-2.3.

4.2

For more on the handling of identity statements, see Devitt 1981a: section 5.5. It is important to note that our theory is not strictly Millian. Some critics of Kripke thought that the causal theory allowed no meaning to a name beyond its bearer: it was a theory of "direct reference"; see Loar 1976, "The semantics of singular terms", for an example and Devitt 1980a, "Brian Loar on singular terms", for a response.

** Our causal theory is applied to the problems of opacity in Devitt 1981a: chapters 8–10; 1984b, "Thoughts and their ascription". These show that epistemic contexts can be handled without recourse to possible worlds.**

For more on the ambiguity of names see Devitt 1981a: sections 1.4, 2.4. **See Lewis 1972, "General semantics", in Davidson and Harman 1972, reprinted in Lewis 1983, for an example of a context-based approach to ambiguity.**

4.3

For a little more on abilities to designate, reference borrowing and groundings, see Devitt 1981a: sections 5.1–5.3.

For a lot more on empty names and existence statements, see Devitt 1981a: chapter 6. Donnellan 1974, "Speaking of nothing", reprinted in Schwartz 1977, *Naming, Necessity, and Natural Kinds*, also discusses these topics from a causal perspective.

For some nice examples of reference change and confusion, see Evans 1973, "The causal theory of names", reprinted in Schwartz 1977. For more on the multiple grounding and the solution to these problems, see Devitt 1981a: sections 2.8, 5.4. The notion of partial reference was introduced in Field 1973, "Theory change and the indeterminacy of reference".

The following are critical of one or more versions of the causal theory of names: Loar 1976; Erwin, Kleinman and Zemach 1976, "The historical theory of reference" ('the historical theory' is the name for the causal theory preferred by Donnellan); McKinsey 1976, "Divided reference in causal theories of names", and 1978, "Names and intentionality", to which Bertolet 1979, "McKinsey, causes and intentions", is a response; Canfield 1977, "Donnellan's theory of names"; Linsky 1977, *Names and Descriptions*, chapter 5; McKay 1984, a critical study of Devitt 1981a.

**4.4*

For a little more on the *qua* -problem for names, see Devitt 1981a: section 2.10.**

5

Theories of reference: other terms

5.1 Description theories of natural kind terms

Our task in this chapter is to consider how far the causal approach to reference can be extended to terms other than names. Insofar as it cannot, other "mechanisms of reference" must be found. Perhaps description theories of reference will have a place with some other terms. In the first five sections we shall consider general terms (2.5) and mass terms. (A mass term refers cumulatively: "any sum of parts which are water is water"; Quine 1960: 91.) In the last two sections we shall consider singular terms other than names.

There are many different sorts of general terms and mass terms. We shall start by considering ones that refer to natural kinds.

Just as there are description theories of names, so also are there description theories of natural kind terms; of general terms like 'tiger', and mass terms like 'gold', referring to observable natural kinds; of general terms like 'atom', and mass terms like 'oxygen', referring to unobservable natural kinds. Speakers of the language associate various descriptions with each term. Using the terminology of Frege, we can capture these description theories as follows: one of these descriptions, or most of a cluster of them, expresses the sense of the term, which determines its reference. Using the terminology of the leading positivist, Rudolf Carnap, we can capture the theories as follows: one of these descriptions, or most of a cluster of them, expresses the *intension* of the term, which determines its *extension*. If only one description counts, the view is analogous to the classical description theory of names (3.1). If a cluster of descriptions counts, the view is analogous to the modern description theory of names (3.2).

There are also description theories of understanding a natural kind term. Understanding a term consists in grasping its sense or intension; it consists in associating the right descriptions. So, according to a description theory, the successful user of a natural kind term has identifying knowledge of the kind.

We shall focus our discussion on general terms referring to observable natural kinds and on simple rather than cluster theories. We draw on Kripke (1980) once again, and also on Putnam (1975).

The descriptions associated with our example, 'tiger', would be along the lines, 'large carnivorous quadrupedal feline, tawny yellow in colour with blackish transverse stripes and white belly'. Another example is 'lemon', for which the descriptions would be along the lines, 'pale yellow, tart, oval, citrus fruit'. 'Tiger' or 'lemon' refers to the members of whatever kind its associated descriptions, or most of them, apply to.

Just like description theories of names, description theories of natural kind terms give a nice solution to the problem of identity statements (2.5, 3.1). There is no appearance of triviality about

Cordates are renates

because though 'cordates' and 'renates' are co-referential, they are associated with different descriptions (with 'having hearts' and 'having kidneys').

But just like description theories of names, these description theories have some immediate problems (3.1–3.2). There is the problem of choosing which of the many descriptions a speaker associates with a term are the ones that express its sense and determine its reference. There is the problem of variations in descriptions from person to person, leading to unwanted ambiguities.

More seriously, there is the problem of unwanted trivialities. It is likely that the descriptions expressing the sense and determining the reference of 'tiger' will include 'striped'. If so,

Tigers are striped

should seem trivial in just the same way that

Bachelors are unmarried

does. Yet it does not seem so.

Many philosophers were prepared to grasp the nettle and say that sentences like the one about tigers were indeed trivial. It was common to think of them as analytic and hence necessarily true and known *a priori*. The triviality problem for natural kind terms does seem easier to live with than the analogous one for names. But it is not very easy.

The descriptions associated with a term like 'tiger' tend to be ones referring to gross observable characteristics – for example, being striped. These characteristics are the result partly of inner nature and partly of environment. Consequently, unusual environments can produce anomolous members of a natural kind: tigers may have only three legs, lack stripes, or be as tame as a domestic cat; lemons may not be yellow, oval, or tart. Yet, according to description theories, it should be impossible for such objects to be tigers and lemons respectively.

A fantasy due largely to Kripke (1980: 119–21) shows that a description associated with a natural kind term might turn out to be not true of *any* member of the natural kind. We can imagine discovering that tigers do not have any of the properties we think them to have. They really have very different properties, including the unusual one of having an uncanny effect on humans: they cause humans to have illusions of large carnivorous quadrupedal felines . . . Perhaps they are extra-terrestrials, pets left behind by von Daniken's extra-solar helpers.

These immediate problems for description theories are serious but not catastrophic. What are catastrophic, once again (3.3), are the problems of ignorance and error. Putnam's example of 'elm' and 'beach' (1975: 226–7) is a vivid one of ignorance. He, like most of us, cannot describe the difference between elms and beeches nor pick one from the other in a crowd of trees. He does not have the identifying knowledge required by description theories. Yet he is perfectly able to use 'elm' to refer to elms and 'beech' to refer to beeches. Whales provide a good example of error. Central to what most people used to associate with 'whale' was the description 'fish'. This description is false of whales. Yet all those people referred to whales by 'whale'.

Reference to a natural kind can occur despite the speaker's ignorance of, or error about, that kind. Identifying knowledge of the kind is not necessary for reference. Neither is it sufficient.

Suppose that in some hitherto unexplored place we discover some animals that fit all the descriptions usually associated with 'unicorn'. Does this likeness to unicorns establish that these animals are the referent of 'unicorn'? It does not. They *may* well be the referent, of course, if our unicorn myths had their origins in sightings of animals of that kind. However, it is much more likely that such animals have nothing to do with our term 'unicorn' and that their resemblance to unicorns is a mere matter of chance. If so, the term does not refer to them.

Reference borrowing helps description theories again, particularly if the borrowing is from scientific experts. But all the problems of the description theory of reference borrowing must surface again. That theory requires identifying knowledge where none may exist; in particular, a person may not know how to identify the experts who are doing the lending (3.4).

Probably the most influential argument against description theories of natural kind terms is Putnam's Twin-Earth fantasy (1975: 223–7). We have given a version of this fantasy before (3.5). Putnam's argument concerns a mass term, 'water' and involves the following version of the fantasy. Suppose that Twin Earth is exactly like Earth except that, where on Earth there is H_2O, on Twin Earth there is a water-like substance, XYZ. This substance is clear, drinkable, odourless, and so forth. The substance is called 'water'. When Oscar, on Earth, uses the term 'water' he refers to water ($=H_2O$) When his Twin-Earth *doppelgänger* uses 'water' he refers to XYZ. Yet Oscar and Twin Oscar are in exactly the same internal states. There can be nothing about their states, no capacity to describe or identify, that would pick out H_2O rather than XYZ, or vice versa. (If this seems a little implausible about a contemporary Earthling, who would probably believe that water is H_2O, place Oscar and his twin in 1750 when nobody knew the chemical composition of water.)

The moral of this is that no association of descriptions or mental images will express a sense that is sufficient to determine reference. "Meanings just ain't in the head". Indeed to suppose that they could be in the head is to adopt a magical theory of reference, as we pointed out (3.5). Description theories for natural kind terms must be rejected.

The Twin-Earth fantasy also brings out an important feature of description theories: their essential incompleteness (3.5). According to description theories, the reference of 'tiger' is determined by the reference of such words as 'carnivorous; and 'striped'. What then determines *their* reference? If there is to be any reference at all, this buck passing must stop. Some terms must get their reference not in virtue of assocation with other terms, but in virtue of the relations language and mind have to things outside themselves. Causal theories require precisely such relations.

5.2 A causal theory of natural kind terms

A causal theory of natural kind terms, like one for names, divides in two (4.1). First, there must be a theory of reference fixing, which explains how a term is linked to its referent in the first place. We shall offer, once again, a theory of the causal groundings of the term in its referent. Second, there must be a theory of reference borrowing, which explains the social transmission of a term to those having no contact with its referent.

As a first approximation, the grounding of a natural kind term includes both an ostensive component and a structural component. In the paradigm cases, these terms are introduced into the language by perceptual contact with samples of the kind. The extension of the term is then all those objects, or all that stuff, having an internal structure of the same sort as the ostensively given samples. So, a term like 'gold' is introduced by causal contact with samples of gold. The term refers then to all and only that stuff which is of the same kind as these samples. The nature of this relation, *being of the same kind*, depending as it does on the internal structure of the samples, is discoverable only by scientific research; we discover the property that makes it the case that something is of the same kind as some given lump of gold by empirical investigation. It follows that users of a natural kind term need not, and most normally do not, know the necessary and sufficient conditions for membership of the relevant kind. Quite often, nobody knows.

The extent of ignorance is even greater than this. In many cases, most of those who use a natural kind term will not be acquainted with the kind: they borrow their reference from others by a procedure just like that for names. Such reference borrowers are unlikely to know not only the necessary and sufficient conditions for membership of a kind but also any effective method of identifying members. Those of us who are as ignorant as Putnam about trees are in this situation with 'elm' and 'beech'.

Putnam brings out the significance of reference borrowing by talking of "the linguistic division of labour" (1975: 227–8), as we have mentioned before (3.5). Language is a social phenomenon. People are equally able (in principle) to use each term of language in their interactions with the world even though they are not equally able to relate that term to the world. How? Because they each gain the benefit of their linguistic involvement with others. Those on whom everyone ultimately depends are, of course, those who have grounded the term. These grounders may be experts, able to give identity conditions, but it is not essential that they be. What matters is that they have, as a matter of fact, linked the term to the world.

Consider the case of an apprentice jeweller learning the term 'platinum'. A sample of platinum is pointed out to him with the words, "That is platinum". He gains an ability to use the term to refer to platinum, an ability grounded in the metal by this introduction. His later uses of the term, exercising that ability, will refer to the metal in virtue of their causal link to it. He will come across further samples of platinum and so his use of the term will be multiply grounded. He will use the term 'platinum' to his friends in banking, building and butchering thus enabling them to borrow the reference from him. In such a way the causal network for a term grounded in a natural kind is established and grows in a linguistic community.

The causal theory of natural kind terms, like that of names, is not only a theory of reference but also a theory of sense and competence (4.1). We identify the sense of a term with the type of causal chain on which its reference depends. Each such chain is grounded (unless there is reference failure). As a result, the internal structure of the natural kind is part of the sense of the term.

Competence with a natural kind term is gained in a grounding or by reference borrowing. It consists in having thoughts that stem in the appropriate way, directly or indirectly, from groundings. It consists in being linked appropriately into the causal network for the term. Our view of this competence will be set out in more detail later (8.8) after we have discussed thoughts (chapter 7).

Multiple grounding is important with natural kind terms, as it was with names (4.3), in handling certain mistakes and the phenomenon of reference change. If reference were fixed solely by the samples involved in the dubbings of a kind, reference would be immutable. However, a natural kind term is grounded just as effectively by subsequent groundings. A few of these may, by mistake, be in samples of a different kind. Intuitively, this should not affect reference. Theoretically, we can set these mistaken groundings aside as insignificant in number relative to those in the original kind. Should they not be relatively insignificant – should the mistakes be systematic, leading to a change in the pattern of groundings – then the reference of the term will change. Such a change can, of course, also be brought about deliberately: people decide to use an old term in a new way and so initiate a new pattern of groundings.

If the pattern of groundings changes by mistake not by decision, then there will be a period whilst the change is taking place when there will be no determinate matter of fact which of the two kinds the term refers to. The situation is analogous to one for names (4.3) and requires the same solution: the introduction of notions of *partial reference* into our theory. However, this is beyond the scope of this book.

Grounding, according to the above account, involves perception of a sample. This is possible when the natural kind term refers to observables but is clearly not if it refers to unobservables; for example, 'atom' and 'oxygen'. This is a difficult problem. What we must look for is some quasi-perceptual contact with unobservables through instruments.

There are other serious problems to be solved before the causal theory of natural kind terms can be regarded as complete. We shall now consider these briefly.

**5.3 The *qua*-problem

Users of a natural kind term need not know necessary and sufficient conditions for membership of the kind referred to. Most users, at least, need not even know an effective method of identifying members of the kind. Is any knowlege of the referent required at all? The rejection of description theories and acceptance of a causal theory may seem to suggest not. Would such a suggestion go too far?

A similar question arose for names (4.4). A consideration of reference borrowing did not then encourage any knowledge requirement, but a consideration of grounding did. We concluded that the grounder must associate a general categorial term with the name being grounded. Perhaps this association amounts to knowledge of the object (should the object satisfy the terms and hence the grounding be successful). The requirement certainly amounts to a move away from a pure-causal theory of grounding to a descriptive-causal theory.

Consideration of groundings again encourages a knowledge requirement and the departure from a pure-causal theory.

Note first that some knowledge seems implicit in our account already: the knowledge that the sample *is* a member of a natural kind. There are many kind terms other than natural kind ones; for example, there are terms like 'bachelor' referring to socio-legal kinds and terms like 'pencil' referring to artefacts. People often use these other terms in ostensive contact with samples of the appropriate kind. We shall consider what relevance this has to the reference of these terms in the next section. Yet, clearly, whatever relevance ostensive contact does have for these other terms, it cannot have the same relevance as it does in the groundings of a natural kind term. There must be something about the grounding situation that makes it the case that it *is* a grounding of a natural kind term and not talk about, say, an artefact. Something must be going on that makes the nature-determining internal structure of the sample relevant to the future reference of the term in a way that the nature-determining internal structure of a bachelor is not relevant to the future reference of 'bachelor'. Something must pick the sample out *qua* member of a natural kind. That something must be the mental state of the grounder. The grounder must, in effect and at some level, "think of" the sample as a member of a natural kind, and intend to apply the term to the sample as such a member.

The *qua*-problem is much more extensive than this. The term is applied to the sample not only *qua* member of a natural kind but also *qua* member of one particular natural kind. Any sample of a natural kind is likely to be a sample of many natural kinds; for example, the sample is not only an echidna, but also a monotreme, a mammal, a vertebrate, and so on. In virtue of what is the grounding it in *qua* member of one natural kind and not another? As a result of groundings, a term refers to all objects having the same underlying nature as the objects in the sample. But *which* underlying nature? The samples share many. What makes the nature responsible for the sample being an echidna the one relevant to reference rather than the nature responsible for it being a mammal (a nature it shares with kangaroos and elephants)?

In discussing names we pointed out that it had to be possible for a grounding to fail: nothing of the appropriate sort is present (4.4). This is true also of natural kind terms. The term 'witch' is empty – there are no witches and never have been – despite many purported groundings of the term in various women. Those groundings all failed. The term 'phlogiston' is empty and yet there was certainly something present in the grounding situation causing the phenomena that led to the introduction of the term; sometimes it was oxygen. In virtue of what did these terms fail to be grounded in hysterical women and oxygen, respectively?

Something about the mental state of the grounder must determine which putative nature of the sample is the one relevant to the grounding, and should it have no such nature the grounding will fail. It is very difficult to say exactly what determines the relevant nature.

People group samples together into natural kinds on the basis of the samples' observed characteristics. They observe what the samples look like, feel like, and so on. They observe how they behave and infer that they have certain causal powers. At some level, then, people "think of" the samples under certain descriptions and as a result apply the natural kind term to them. It is this mental activity that determines which underlying nature of the samples is the relevant one to a grounding. The relevant nature is the one that is, as a matter of fact, responsible for the properties picked out by the descriptions associated with the term in the grounding. If the sample does not have these properties – if, for example, the alleged witch does not have the power to cast spells – then there will be no relevant nature and the groundings will fail.

In sum, the grounder of a natural kind term associates, consciously or unconsciously, with that term, first, some description that in effect classifies the term as a natural kind term; second, some descriptions that determine which nature of the sample is relevant to the reference of the term. These associations raise a number of questions. In particular, we wonder whether they amount to knowledge. They may amount to knowledge, just as similar associations with names may (4.4). We shall consider these matters further in section 5.5 and again later (14.4).

One of us (Sterelny) thinks that a further requirement on the grounding of a natural kind term is required to solve the *qua*-problem: the grounder must be able to discriminate members of the kind with reasonable reliability. For the most part, members should not go unrecognized as members, and non-members should not be classified as members.

We do not pretend that these remarks are close to a complete solution to the *qua*-problem. One difficulty is that there are *individual* differences between members of a natural kind; think of the differences between people for a vivid example. These differences are often the result of nature not nurture. Suppose that a natural individual difference is among the properties picked out by the determining descriptions in a grounding? The underlying nature made relevant to reference by this grounding should then include that individual difference. So, the resulting reference should be not to all other members of the natural kind but only to objects, if any, that share the nature responsible for that difference. Something has gone wrong.

Differences between sub-groups of a kind pose an even greater problem. Consider the term 'swan'. Before Australia made its great contribution to philosophy, all observed swans had been white. It seems certain that among the descriptions playing a determining role in the grounding of 'swan' up to that time, 'white' played a central role. So the reference of the term should have been restricted to objects sharing the nature that made those swans white. Yet the reference was not so restricted. 'Swan' referred then, just as it does now, to swans which lack the nature making some of them white; *viz.* to black swans. Some change in the theory is called for.

A consideration of the *qua*-problem for names led us away from a pure-causal theory to a descriptive-causal theory of groundings (but not of reference borrowing; 4.4). So too has the *qua*-problem for natural kind terms. These moves have a price. First, they raise the possibility of refutation by arguments from ignorance and error (3.3); for example, Kripke's fantasy about tigers (5.1) poses a problem. Second, we have emphasized the essential incompleteness of description theories of reference: they explain the reference of some words in terms of the reference of other words, leaving the latter unexplained (3.5, 4.2, 5.1). To the extent that a descriptive-causal theory is descriptive, it has the same incompleteness. The categorial term that plays a role for a name, the description that classifies a term as a natural kind term, and the descriptions that determine the relevant nature of the samples of a natural kind, all raise further problems of reference. In virtue of what do they refer?

We are torn two ways in explaining reference. The interest in an ultimate explanation pushes us away from description theories toward causal theories. But causal theories confront the *qua*-problem. Attempts to solve that push us back toward description theories, hence postponing the ultimate explanation. We must look for some very basic terms which do not give rise to *qua*-problems and so are amenable to treatment by a pure-causal theory. Likely candidates are the categorial terms referred to in our discussion of names, and simple demonstratives to be discussed later (5.7). On this foundation, other relatively basic terms can be satisfactorily explained by descriptive-causal theories. All the basic terms can then be used to explain the non-basic ones by description theories.

We shall go on to consider some more of these other terms now.**

**5.4 Other kind terms

Putnam, who did so much to launch the causal theory of natural kind terms, saw the theory has having much wider application; it stretched even to kind terms like 'pencil' and 'paediatrician' (1975: 242–5). We are as enthusiastic for conquest as any causal theorist could be, but the wise imperialist knows his limitations. We think that Putnam goes way too far.

Putnam reaches his views of 'pencil' from a consideration of the description theory. If we apply that theory to 'pencil', certain sentences involving both the term and its associated descriptions should be trivial; they should seem necessary, known *a priori*, and analytic (5.1). Putnam supposes that 'artefact' is one of the appropriate associated descriptions for 'pencil'. He again resorts to science fiction to reject the description theory.

> Imagine that we someday discover that *pencils are organisms*. We cut them open and examine them under the electron microscope, and we see the almost invisible tracery of nerves and other organs. We spy upon them, and we see them spawn, and we see the offspring grow into full-grown pencils – there are not and never were any pencils except these organisms. (1975: 242)

This shows that 'Pencils are artefacts' is not trivial; we could discover that pencils are not artefacts at all. So *being an artefact* is not part of the meaning of 'pencil'. Putnam moves straight from this conclusion to his view that 'pencil' is to be treated causally like 'water' or 'gold'; it refers to anything having the same underlying nature as our sample pencils (1975: 243).

What is wrong with this refutation of the description theory, as Stephen Schwartz points out (1978), is that Putnam has picked the wrong description; 'artefact' is not a description that expresses, even partly, the meaning of 'pencil'. We can indeed imagine that pencils are organisms or that they grow on trees. Change the example and we do not have to use our imagination to make the point. A pencil is a tool to serve a human purpose. So too is a paperweight. Some paperweights are not artefacts but perfectly natural objects: stones or pieces of drift-wood. Yet these objects are all part of the extension of 'paperweight'. So-called "artefactual kind" terms need not refer to artefacts! They may refer to objects that are habitually used for some function even though they were not designed and produced for that function. (Through lack of a suitable alternative, we shall also call these terms referring to tools and instruments "artefactual kind", but we will always add scare quotes to distance ourselves from the usage; 2.7)

A plausible description theory of 'pencil' will attend not to the accidental fact that pencils are artefacts, but to the function of pencils and how they must peform that function. A pencil is a *writing instrument*; the writing must be *by graphite* (or something similar? Note that pens are not pencils); and so on. Similarly, the appropriate description for 'chair' will be found by attending to the fact that chairs are things to sit on and to the fact that they have backs and legs (stools are not chairs).

A description theory along these lines – a description of function together with a description of certain physical characteristics – is plausible for basic "artefactual kind" terms. Many "artefactual kind" terms are not basic in that they are defined in terms of other "artefactual kind" terms. For the non-basic ones a straightforward description theory, making no direct reference to functions seems appropriate. Thus the meaning of 'sloop' is given by 'boat having a single mast with a mainsail and jib' (Schwartz 1980: 1983); that of 'dagger' by 'short two-edged weapon with sharp point'. These descriptions contain the basic, or at least more basic, "artefactual kind" terms, 'boat' and 'weapon'.

We think that the description theory of reference fixing for the non-basic terms may be correct. Perhaps the description theory of the basic ones is, too, but we shall briefly explore a causal alternative. The alternative is not a pure-causal theory of the type Putnam seems to be urging, but a descriptive-causal theory. The pure-causal theory faces a massive *qua*-problem, as we shall soon see.

The descriptive-causal theory for the basic "artefactual kind" terms is analogous to that for natural kind terms (5.3). The descriptive element is taken over from the description theory. It is the description of physical characteristics ('graphite' for 'pencil', 'back' for 'chair'). The causal element arises from groundings in samples. Whereas on the description theory, the reference-determining function is fixed by an associated description of the function, on the descriptive-causal theory it is fixed by the objects in the sample used to ground the term. The term refers to any object (with the physical characteristics) that has the same function as the objects in the sample.

A key difference between the description and descriptive-causal theory of reference fixing for basic "artefactual kind" terms is that the former requires, but the latter does not, that those acquainted with samples of the kind should *know* their function. Could such a person use one of these terms successfully even though ignorant of, or wrong about, the function of the objects to which it refers? If so, the description theory is wrong.

It is much harder to find the counter-examples to show that the description theory is wrong about "artefactual kind" terms than it was to show that it was wrong about natural kind terms. The difficulty is that whereas most people do not know the underlying natures of natural kinds, most people do know the functions of tools and instruments. The best place to look for counter-examples to the theory is to cases where religious or social beliefs mystify the function of certain artefacts. We shall not go into the matter any further.

We noted at the beginning of the last section that a person grounding a natural kind term must associate with it something that makes it a term for a natural kind rather than an "artefactual kind"; that something must make the underlying nature of the sample relevant to reference. Our discussion here reinforces that remark. If a description theory of reference fixing for "artefactual kind" terms is correct, then ostensive contact with samples is irrelevant to their reference. So there must be something associated with natural kind terms that distinguishes them from "artefactual kind" terms by making the ostensive contact relevant to reference. On the other hand, if a descriptive-causal theory of "artefactual kind" terms is correct, then the function of the samples is relevant to reference. So there must be something associated with those terms, and something else associated with natural kind terms, that makes the function of the samples relevant to the reference of the former, and the underlying nature of the samples relevant to that of the latter.

This discussion of the initial *qua* -problem brings out the failings of Putnam's pure-causal theory of "artefactual kind" terms. This theory "leaves it to the world to decide" what a term refers to: it refers to whatever kind the samples exemplify. But a sample may exemplify many kinds; for example, the one object can be a cat, a pet, and a paperweight. There must be something going on in the ostensive contact with an "artefact" that makes its function, not its nature or socio-legal status, relevant to reference.

The pure-causal theory for natural kind terms faced a more extensive *qua* - problem than this: a sample exemplifies not just many kinds but many *natural* kinds. Our descriptive-causal theory for "artefactual kind" terms faces a similar problem: a sample may exemplify more than one basic "artefactual kind" – for example, a paperweight and a doorstop.

We have been talking about a descriptive-causal theory of reference for "artefactual kind" terms. That sort of theory can be combined with a pure-causal theory of reference borrowing, as we illustrated in our discussion of names (4.4) and natural kind terms (5.3). We shall consider whether it should be so combined after our discussion of socio-legal terms like 'paediatrician'.

If the description theory applies to 'paediatrician' then the likely associated description is 'doctor specializing in the care of children'. Putnam doubts that the theory does apply because it could turn out that paediatricians are not doctors but Martian spies (1975: 244). In our view, Schwartz has once again responded correctly to Putnam's attack on the description theory (1980: 193-4). Certainly paediatricians could turn out to be Martian spies, but that is irrelevant to the theory: the above associated description does not entail that they are not Martian spies. The description does entail that they are doctors. So it *would* count against the description theory if they could turn out not to be doctors, but Putnam has given no good reason to suppose that they could so turn out.

We think that the description theory of reference fixing may well apply to 'paediatrican'; that it may well apply to non-basic "artefactual kind" terms; and that it may well apply to many other terms; for example, 'bachelor', 'vixen' and 'hunter'. This is no threat to our theory of language, because the reference of all terms appealed to in a description theory must ultimately be explained causally.

What view should we take of reference borrowing for the terms discussed in this section? There seem to be three options.

1   A pure-causal theory, of the sort that we have claimed applies to names and natural kind terms, might be appropriate here too. A non-yachtsman might use 'sloop' to refer to sloops without knowing even that they are boats, so

long as he is at the end of a chain of borrowing from someone who associates the appropriate descriptions with the term.

2   An alternative picture is a descriptive-causal theory: a borrower need not associate descriptions adequate to fix reference but must associate some central ones. Perhaps you cannot refer to sloops, even as a borrower, unless you realize that they are boats; to daggers unless you realize that they are edged weapons.

3   A final possibility, for terms covered by a description theory of reference fixing, is to deny that the terms can be borrowed at all. Perhaps you cannot use 'paediatrician' to refer to paediatricians unless you yourself associate the reference-determining descriptions.

We shall not choose between these options. Likely enough, different options are appropriate for different kinds of terms. (We have not included a description theory of reference borrowing as an option because the earlier arguments against it strike us as decisive; 3.4.)**

**5.5 Associated descriptions and knowledge

We are committed to the association of reference-determining descriptions with terms by speakers: the association of a categorial description with a name in its grounding (4.4); of various descriptions with a natural kind term in its grounding (5.3); and of various descriptions with "artefactual kind" and socio-legal terms (5.4). In traditional theories, this sort of association amounted to the speaker having knowledge. Should we go along with this tradition? There is one important consideration against it. We will see later (8.5) that there are suggestive though not decisive reasons for locating our linguistic competence in a psychological subsystem, a *module*. One characteristic of that module is that information in it is not automatically and fully accessible to the central intellectual processor of the speaker. If the associations are modularized, then they are not knowledge. They are information *in* the speaker, not *of* the speaker.

If we set aside this possibility, there seems no reason to deny that these associations constitute knowledge. But what sort of knowledge? Some description theorists have taken it to be semantic knowledge. We shall argue against this view later (8.7). If the speakers must have knowledge, it is knowledge that, for example, daggers are weapons, not that 'dagger' refers to weapons.

This position leads to a problem: if reference-fixing information is not modularized, but is integrated with the speaker's ordinary stock of information, something must distinguish it from that ordinary stock. There must be something to distinguish the association represented by the following beliefs:

Bachelors are unmarried
Bachelors tend to die younger than married men.

There is a privileged connection between 'bachelor' and 'unmarried' that there is not between 'bachelor' and 'tend to die younger than married men'. The modularity hypothesis would yield one account of this privilege: 'bachelor' is linked to 'unmarried', but not to the other term, in the reference-determining structure for 'bachelor' in the module. But, we are setting aside that hypothesis. We must find something special about the reference-determining knowledge.

Traditionally, the special features of this knowledge has been thought to be that it was *a priori* knowledge (3.1) of *necessary* truths. Often these features were explained in terms of a third: the sentence was *analytic*, "true by virtue of meaning" (2.5). The knowledge was "not derived from experience", hence was *a priori*, in that it was gained in the learning of the language.

Our descriptive-causal and description theories clearly commit us to something like an analyticity thesis: to the extent that the reference of one term depends on another, a sentence linking the two will be true in virtue of the semantic properties of the words involved. Nonetheless, we are cautious about adopting the traditional labels for our view. This is partly because they have kept bad company with theories in semantics and epistemology that we wish to distance ourselves from (chapter 14). It is also partly because the labels may give the illusion that the problem has been solved, rather than merely labelled. The problem is to find a psychologically and semantically salient difference between two descriptions such that one, but not the other, helps to fix the reference of a term. To say that the connection between 'bachelor' and 'unmarried' yields an analytic truth is to announce this special connection, not to say in what it consists. We could say that 'bachelors are unmarried' is analytic, perhaps necessary, and (rejecting modularity) *a priori*, but there is not much theoretical mileage in doing so. (We return to this issue in section 14.4.)

Pure-causal theories of reference apply to "very basic" terms and describe direct links between language and the world, unmediated by any other term. Further direct links are described by descriptive-causal theories which apply to "basic" terms that depend for their reference partly on other terms. Finally, the terms covered by description theories are "non-basic" ones only indirectly linked to reality: they depend for their reference entirely on other terms. We have given examples of the latter two types of theory. For the pure-causal theory, we have gestured toward categorial terms and foreshadowed a discussion of demonstratives (5.7).**

**5.6 Donnellan's distinction

In this section and the next we shall return to the discussion of singular terms. Our focus will be on ones other than names.

We start with definite descriptions, the basic form of which is, 'the *F*'. Our discussion so far suggests that the mechanism of reference for these terms are certainly not open to our causal approach. For, we have followed Russell's theory of descriptions: 'the *F*' denotes *x* if and only if '*F*' applies to *x* and to nothing else (3.1). Reference to *x* does not depend on a causal link to it, but rather on the unique application of a general term to it. We think that a distinction made by Keith Donnellan (1966, 1968) shows that the right story for definite descriptions is more complicated than this. Definite descriptions are ambiguous. Russell's theory does fit one meaning, but the other is to be treated causally.

Donnellan distinguishes two uses of definite descriptions – an "attributive" use and a "referential" use:

> A speaker who uses a definite description attributively in an assertion states something about whoever or whatever is the so-and-so. A speaker who uses a definite description referentially in an assertion, on the other hand, uses the description to enable his audience to pick out whom or what he is talking about and states something about that person or thing. (1986: 285)

Donnellan illustrates the two uses with a number of examples, including the following pair:

> Attributive use. A group of people happen on the savagely mutilated body of the harmless Smith. One says, "The murderer of Smith is insane".

> Referential use. A group of people are present in court where Jones is being tried for the murder of Smith. Throughout the trial, Jones behaves very strangely. One of the group says, "The murderer of Smith is insane".

Donnellan points out how different are these two uses of 'the murderer of Smith'.

In the first case, if Smith was *not* murdered but, say, attacked by wild dogs or hit by a meteor, the description is empty; it refers to nobody. As a result, the utterance containing it fails to predicate insanity of anyone and so cannot be true. This is just what Russell's theory implies.

In the second case, however, things are different. Even if Smith was not murdered, the description is not straightforwardly empty. In using the description, the speaker has Jones in mind and seems to have succeeded in referring to him. Suppose that Jones, despite his innocence, is insane. Then there seems to be a respect in which the speaker has said something true. So, apparently, despite the fact that 'the murderer of Smith' does not uniquely apply to Jones (indeed it does not apply to him at all), the speaker used the definite description to predicate a truth of Jones.

Consider a different situation. Suppose that Jones is both innocent and feigning insanity because he fears a conviction. Further, Smith really was murdered by a madman. Yet the utterance in the second case does not seem to be straightforwardly true. The problem is that the speaker had Jones in mind in using 'the murderer of Smith' and Jones is not insane. The speaker does not seem to be referring to the real killer, who does of course uniquely satisfy 'murderer of Smith'. Russell's theory does not seem to apply to this use.

We think that what examples of confusion and mistake like this indicate is that definite descriptions are ambiguous. The truth conditions of statements containing them vary according as the description is referential or attributive. (Donnellan himself is rather equivocal about the signifiance of his distinction.) We do not think that examples like this alone *establish* this ambiguity; other explanations of the examples are possible. However, when the examples are joined by the considerations to follow, we think that the ambiguity is established.**

**5.7 Designational terms

Suppose that definite descriptions are indeed ambiguous. What then are the mechanisms of reference for each meaning? Those for an attributive description are clear already. They are the Russellian ones set out earlier; reference depends on unique application of a general term. But what are the mechanisms for a referential description? In virtue of what does it refer to its object?

When using a description referentially, the speaker has a particular object in mind. In discussing names we pointed out that the reference of an ambiguous name depends on which object the speaker has in mind. We went on to give a mostly causal account of this (4.2, 4.4): the speaker had a particular object in mind in using a name because a d-chain grounded in that object was causally active in producing the use of the name. This indicates a possible answer to our question. Perhaps we should say that the mechanism of reference for a referential description is (mostly) a causal one like that for names. So the person had Jones in mind, and referred to him, because it was his experience of Jones during the trial that prompted his use of 'the murderer of Smith'. We might extend our usage: the person referred to Jones in virtue of a d-chain.

This possible answer is encouraging for the view that definite descriptions are ambiguous. It shows how there could be a use of descriptions that does not depend on Russellian mechanisms of reference; the use depends instead on causal d-chains. However, we should like more than Donnellan's examples of confusion and mistake to convince us that there actually is this other referential use. More is to be found by considering demonstratives and personal pronouns, and comparing them with "imperfect" definite descriptions.

Demonstratives like 'this' and 'that', and personal pronouns like 'he', 'she' and 'it' are often "deictic": they are used out of blue to the "point to" something present (or recently so), rather than being used "anaphorically" to cross-refer to something previously mentioned. Someone observing Nana might say, "She is hungry". In virtue of what did he designate Nana? He designated her because the causal link from Nana to the speaker, a link established in perceiving Nana, led to the utterance; he designated her in virtue of a d-chain grounded in her.

The *qua* problem for names led to a move from a pure-causal to a descriptive causal theory theory of reference; a descriptive element entered into the characterization of a·d-chain (4.4). The simple demonstratives, 'this' and 'that', and the pronoun, 'it', have near enough no descriptive content and seem amenable to a pure-causal theory (in their deictic use). In contrast, the pronouns, 'he' and 'she', do have some descriptive content: they indicate the gender of the referent. It is plausible to think that the reference of 'she', for example, is partly determined by what 'feminine' applies to: in a successful deictic use, its d-chain is grounded in whatever feminine object is playing the appropriate causal role. So, we explain its reference (in its deictic use) by a descriptive-causal theory.

Complex demonstratives like 'that man' have still more descriptive content. It is plausible to think that the mechanisms of reference for deictic uses of them are also partly causal, partly descriptive. So, if a person at the trial is prompted by Jones's behaviour to say, "That man is insane", he designates Jones partly in virtue of the fact that Jones is a man, and partly in virtue of the fact that Jones played the appropriate causal role. Underlying his use of 'that man' is a d-chain characterized partly descriptively and partly causally.

Consider, now, "imperfect" descriptions. These are definite descriptions like 'the book' and 'the table' which are very often deictic and yet which do not come close to denoting anything. They do not come close because general terms like 'book' and 'table' apply to millions of things not to just one. If these descriptions were treated as they stand in the Russellian way, they would all fail to refer. The way to save the Russellian view of them is to see them as elliptical versions of much longer descriptions that the speaker has in mind. We think that it is much more plausible to see them, in their normal use, as like complex demonstratives. So, 'the book' is like 'that book' in depending for reference on a d-chain from the book in question to the utterance.

Return to the scene of the trial. The person who said, "That man is insane", might have been prompted by the same experience to say, "The man is insane". That sentence would have served his communicative purposes as well as the one he uttered; it would have meant very much the same. So, if it is plausible to claim that reference for the complex demonstrative, 'that man', is determined by d-chains, it is plausible to claim the same for the imperfect description, 'the man'. And it is very plausible to claim this for the complex demonstrative. Denotation has no more to do with the reference of 'the man' than it has to do with that of 'that man'.

The moral of this is that there are deictic uses of demonstratives, pronouns, and definite descriptions, which share a mode of reference depending on d-chains. These singular terms differ in the amount of their descriptive content: at one extreme, 'this', has no such content; 'she' has a little content; 'that book' and 'the book' have quite a lot. There is no reason to stop at this point. Even definite descriptions that are very rich in content have a use depending on d-chains. These are the descriptions like 'the murderer of Smith' which featured in Donnellan's examples.

We conclude that definite descriptions really are ambiguous: aside from the attributive use explained by Russell, there is a use to be explained partly causally. Donnellan called this use "referential". However, we use 'refer' as a generic term for all modes of reference and so this name is not appropriate for us. Since this use of a description depends on d-chains for reference, it is appropriate to call it "designational".

A description used designationally yields a designational token. So also does a deictic use of a demonstrative or personal pronoun. All of these tokens are designational terms.

Just as a person can borrow the reference of a name from another, so also can he borrow the reference of a designational description. The person at the trial can tell a friend all about Jones using, say, 'the man on trial'. On the strength of this, the friend is in a position to use that description designationally. When he does so use it he will have Jones in mind in virtue of a d-chain stretching back from his use through the reference leader to Jones himself.

We have offered a pure-causal theory for only some designational terms: the deictic uses of 'this', 'that' and 'it'. The others are treated by a descriptive-causal view. These others have a descriptive content and we think it plausible to suppose that this content is important to their reference. If we are right about this, when the person says, with Jones in mind, "The murderer of Smith is insane", he will not have succeeded in designating Jones if Jones is innocent. His description token is designational and so it will not matter to reference that Jones is not the *unique* murderer of Smith, but it will matter that he is not a murderer of Smith at all. In this we seem to depart from Donnellan (though he is rather equivocal, as we have remarked; 5.6): the description is not *straight-forwardly* empty, because of the causal link to Jones, but it is empty nonetheless.

In the previous chapter, we wrote about names as if they were all introduced in a face-to-face dubbing (4.1). This is certainly the common form of introduction, but it is not universal. Names for an object can be introduced in its absence using a definite description. If that description is designational, then there will still be a d-chain underlying the name. However, the description may be attributive. Thus, it seems that the name 'Jack the Ripper' was once introduced in London by an attributive description along the lines of, 'the murderer of those prostitutes'. The description, and hence the name that depends on it, refer to whoever committed those murders; people had nobody particular in mind; the terms were not grounded in anyone. A name of this sort is attributive. Names of the normal sort, discussed in the previous chapter, are designational names. (This amounts to accepting a description theory of reference fixing for attributive names. Description theories of names seem so false in general because, first, so few names are like 'Jack the Ripper' in being attributive; second, because the description theory of reference borrowing is false for all names.)

Finally, it has been argued by Charles Chastain that *in*definite descriptions – those of the form 'an *F*' – have a use analogous to designational definite descriptions (1975).

The standard interpretation of the sentence, 'A mosquito is in this room', takes it as equivalent to the existentially quantified sentence, 'There is something that is both a mosquito and in this room'. So the sentence is true if somewhere or other in the room there is a mosquito, whether noticed or not. Interpreted in this way an indefinite description is analogous to an attributive definite description without the uniqueness requirement.

However, there seems to be another use of an indefinite description where the speaker has a particular object in mind. Suppose that the above sentence was uttered by Fiona after hearing a particular mosquito, x. She gets some insecticide, sprays the room, and withdraws saying, "That will kill it". The spraying does kill a mosquito in the room, y, previously unnoticed, but x survives. Now 'it' in Fiona's second sentence is clearly anaphoric, referring to whatever 'a mosquito' in the first sentence refers to. On the standard quantificational interpretation, 'a mosqito' refers not to any particular mosquito but to any mosquito at all; to x or y or any one of the billions of mosquitoes in the world. So, on that interpretation, Fiona's second sentence is true: y is indeed a mosquito killed by the spraying. However, the sentence seems false because Fiona had x in mind and x is still alive. It seems that 'it' in the second sentence refers to x. So 'a mosquito' on which 'it' depends for reference must also refer to x. There is a designational use of indefinite descriptions.

This completes our discussion of word meaning. We shall now move on to consider syntactic structure.**

Suggested reading

5.1

Classical versions of the description theory for general terms in general, and natural kind terms in particular, are to be found in Mill 1961, *A System of Logic*: book I, chapter 2, section 5; and in Carnap 1956, *Meaning and Necessity*: section 4.

** A prominent recent manifestation of the theory is the "componential analysis" movement in transformational grammar. The founding document in the movement is Katz and Fodor 1963, "The structure of semantic theory", reprinted in Fodor and Katz 1964, *The Structure of Language*, and in Rosenberg and Travis 1971. This theory was further developed by Katz 1972, *Semantic Theory*. Fodor has since abandoned it, but Katz gives a lengthy defence of it in, "Logic and language" (1975), in Gunderson 1975, *Language, Mind and Knowledge*.**

In effect, positivist philosophers of science developed and defended a description theory of theoretical terms. Clear introductions to their views are to be found in Hempel 1966 *Philosophy of Natural Science*: chapter 7; and in 1954, "A logical appraisal of operationism". Lewis's paper, "How to define theoretical terms", reprinted in Lewis 1983, is a sophisticated version of such theories, minus the positivist prejudice in favour of observational descriptions.

For Kripke's refutation of the description theories of natural kind terms, see *Naming and Necessity* (1980: 116–35, 156–7). For Putnam's, see "Is semantics possible?" in *Mind, Language and Reality* (1975), and "Meaning and reference" (1973), both reprinted in Schwartz 1977. An expanded version of the latter forms an early part of "The meaning of 'meaning'" also in Putnam 1975 (and in Gunderson 1975).

The difficulty of giving description theories for most terms arises from the difficulty of finding definitions for them. This is brought about nicely by Fodor in "The present status of the innateness controversy", particularly pp. 283–92, in his *Representations* (1981a).

5.2

Kripke's causal theory of natural kind terms is set out briefly in *Naming and Necessity* (1980: 153–9). Putnam's theory is set out in some detail in the above papers together with "Explanation and reference" and "Language and reality" in Putnam 1975.

5.3

David Papineau points to the *qua*-problem in *Theory and Meaning* (1979): chapter 5, section 7. For some other criticisms of the views of Putnam and Kripke, see Fine 1975, "How to compare theories"; Zemach 1976, "Putnam's theory on the reference of substance terms"; Mellor 1977, "Natural kinds"; Dupre 1981, "Natural kinds and biological taxa"; Unger 1983, "The causal theory of reference"; Donnellan 1983, "Kripke and Putnam on natural kind terms"; Kroon 1985, "Theoretical terms and the causal view of reference".

Our own earlier discussions of these problems are : Devitt 1981a, chapter 7; Sterelny 1983a, "Natural kind terms".**

5.4

Putnam's discussion of other words is in "The meaning of 'meaning'", Putnam 1975, pp. 242–5. Schwartz responds in "Putnam on artifacts" (1978) and "Natural kinds and nominal kinds" (1980). Kornblith 1980, "Referring to artifacts", is a defence of Putnam.**

5.5

Quine is the most famous sceptic about analyticity and *a priority*. This goes with his scepticism about meaning in general; see the suggested readings to 1.3. See also the readings on analyticity in part 1 of Rosenberg and Travis 1971.**

5.6

Donnellan's classic paper, "Reference and definite descriptions" (1966), is very readable. It has been reprinted in many places including Steinberg and Jacobovits 1971, Rosenberg and Travis 1971, and Schwartz 1977. Donnellan's response to a critic, "Putting Humpty Dumpty together again" (1968), is also helpful. Donnellan is critical not only of Russell's theory but also of Strawson's criticism of Russell in "On referring" (1950). That paper has also been reprinted many times including in Caton 1963 and Rosenberg and Travis 1971. Bertolet 1980, "The semantic significance of Donnellan's distinction", brings out nicely the problems of interpreting exactly what Donnellan is claiming.**

5.7

For more details on this approach to demonstratives, pronouns and definite descriptions, see Devitt 1981a: sections 2.5–2.7. Kripke casts doubt on the view that descriptions are ambiguous in "Speaker's reference and semantic reference"

(1979). For a response, see Devitt 1981b, "Donnellan's distinction". A similar view is urged in Wettstein 1981, "Demonstrative reference and definite descriptions". Bertolet 1986, "Donnellan's distinctions", reflects upon these two papers and offers a different perspective of what Donnellan has done. (In Devitt 1981a and 1981b, there is less commitment to a descriptive-causal approach than there is in the present text. Related to this, the uses of 'designation' and its cognates in those works differ in excluding almost all descriptive elements.)

Chastain 1975, "Reference and context", in Gunderson 1975, is an extensive and interesting discussion of singular terms along lines similar to those urged here; see pp. 201–15 particularly for the source of our views on indefinite descriptions.**

6

Syntactic structure

6.1 Introduction

Our aim is to explain meaning in terms of truth conditions (2.1). Truth conditions are to be explained in terms of reference and syntactic structure (2.2). We have devoted several chapters to explaining reference. We have said little about syntactic structure beyond bringing out its obvious relevance to truth conditions (2.2) and mentioning the problems of explaining it (2.4).

The bearing of syntactic structure on the truth conditions of simple sentences like 'Reagan is wrinkled' was easy enough to explain. However, most sentences are much more difficult to deal with. The problems can be roughly divided into two sorts, one which has particularly occupied logicians, and the other, grammarians. The logicians have concentrated on what are intuitively the basic underlying structures of a natural language. The logicians represent each structure in the symbols of formal logic and seek a theory explaining that structure's role in determining truth conditions. Some of these underlying structures – for example, those involving quantifiers – have proved very difficult to explain. The grammarians, on the other hand, have been concerned with the structure of the actual sentences of a natural language, seeking a mapping of each sentence into a "semantic representation" or meaning. An appealing idea is that these semantic representations have the sorts of structures studied by the logicians. This idea makes the work of logician and grammarian nicely complementary. Unfortunately, the idea is not one that is shared by many grammarians (though there is one contemporary group pursuing this line of thought: the "Montague grammarians"). We shall see later that many have a rather different conception of meaning, and of the place of syntax in it, from the one we are urging (6.4–6.5).

We are setting aside the findings of the logicians as too difficult for this book (2.4). In the present chapter, we shall discuss the findings of the grammarians, in particular, the revolutionary findings of Noam Chomsky and his followers.

There are reasons for an interest in structure independent of an interest in truth conditions. Many strings of English words would sound queer if ever uttered. Why? In many cases the strings do not form proper sentences. Consider, for example, 'the Opera House likes was' and 'who did John believe the rumour that came'. These strings are simply *ungrammatical*. What makes a string of words ungrammatical and hence not a sentence? We need a theory that tells us which structures are to be found in English (and other natural languages). Any string that is not of an acceptable structure will sound queer.

A cautionary word is appropriate here. Seeming queer is neither necessary nor sufficient for being ungrammatical. It is not sufficient because strings of words may seem queer for other reasons: they may be too long and complicated to be quickly understood; they may be irrelevant; they may be too boring to be worth stating; they may be absurdly false. Ungrammaticality is just one possible explanation for queerness. It is the most plausible one in some cases – for example, those in the last paragraph – but not at all plausible in others; for example, 'It was whilst kicking heads on Mars that Thatcher first ran into Reagan'. In some cases it is not immediately obvious what is a plausible explanation for the queerness; consider, 'Mount Everest plays good ping pong' and 'Colourless green ideas sleep furiously' (a favourite example of the linguists). In fact, initial judgements of plausibility simply reflect our folk theory (1.3). What we need before making a final decision on which strings are or are not grammatical is a theory of grammaticality.

Seeming queer is not necessary for being ungrammatical because some grammatical failures are so common as to pass almost unnoticed. This is particularly true of failures in speech. Our ordinary speech is liberally sprinkled with false starts, 'um's and 'ah's, slips of the tongue, and so on. Such speech is strictly ungrammatical but does not strike us as queer.

Our two interests in structure converge. When we seek to explain meaning and truth conditions, which items are we concerned with? We are concerned only with the possible sentences of the language; ungrammatical strings of words have no truth conditions (but see the qualifications in 7.4). All (indicative) sentences have truth conditions; further, those conditions depend in part on the syntactic structure that makes a string grammatical and hence a sentence.

We should emphasize that the notion of grammaticality that concerns us is a *descriptive* one, not a *normative* one. We are not concerned with how a person ought to speak, according to the approved standards of her society. We are concerned with a notion that applies to the language she does, as a matter of fact, speak; a notion that applies to her idiolect, however much that may depart from the approved standards.

Chomsky's approach to explaining grammaticality is called *transformational generative grammar* or, more simply, *transformational grammar*. It aims to specify the possible sentences of a given language and to give a syntactic description of those sentences. It thus meets both our interests. Nevertheless, we cannot take over its findings *en bloc*. Chomsky and his followers have formulated the question they seek to answer in a different way. Whereas we see a grammar as explaining some of the properties of linguistic symbols, these grammarians see it *primarily* as explaining linguistic competence, a property of people (on which we have already made some preliminary remarks: 1.2, 2.6, 3.1, 3.2, 4.1, 5.1, 5.2).

At the beginning we remarked on the bewildering nature of the study of language (1.1). It is often hard to see what question a theory is trying to answer and whether different theories are concerned with the same question. This problem is acute in studying the transformational grammarians. One would think that explaining structure is one thing, explaining competence, a different though related thing. Yet the grammarians run them together, as we shall demonstrate later (8.2). And there are other puzzles. Why suppose that a grammar explains competence at all? The grammarians think that the grammar does so because competence consists in *tacit knowledge* of the grammar. Further, some of this knowledge is said by some to be innate. Why suppose that speakers know any more about grammar than the little they learn at school?

These puzzles are appropriately dealt with in part III. They are the main concern of chapter 8. However, our discussion has already indicated where we think the main trouble lies: in the failure to distinguish sharply between the linguistic competence of speakers and the syntactic structure of linguistic symbols. Competence, together with various other aspects of the speaker's psychology and the external environment, produce linguistic symbols, but a theory of the one is not a theory of the other.

The distinction we are insisting on should not be confused with the grammarians' one between competence and performance. A theory of performance is concerned with those factors which, together with competence, bear on the production (and understanding) of linguistic symbols; such factors as memory, attention and interest. So a theory of performance is like a theory of competence in being psychological. It is a theory of the production (and understanding) of linguistic symbols, not a theory of the products, the symbols themselves. It is the latter theory that we are anxious to distinguish from the theory of competence.

A major motivation for the grammarians' distinction between competence and performance is their observation that much of a person's linguistic performance is a poor reflection of her competence: it is full of the grammatical failures (relative to her idiolect) that we have already mentioned. The competence which concerns the grammarians is an *idealization*: it is those aspects of the speaker's psychology that, were it not for the other factors, would lead the speaker to produce only grammatical sentences. Similarly, we are concerned not with the actual linguistic symbols produced by speakers but with an idealization of them (except when considering speaker meaning; 7.4).

Without more ado, we shall return to the task of examining the properties of linguistic symbols.

6.2 Sentence structure

It is obvious that a sentence has *some* structure; it matters which order the words are in. Our first aim is to show that there is much more to the internal structure of a sentence than this. It will turn out that sentence structure is surprisingly complex: there are persuasive arguments for the view that sentences have two distinct but related structures.

1   We have already alluded to one reason for thinking that sentences have structures. Some strings of words sound queer because they are ungrammatical (6.1). What is it for something to be grammatical? In the case of some simple languages – for example, the sign language divers use for underwater communication – there is nothing more to being grammatical than being on a list of conventional signals. But no such explanation is possible for any natural language, for the list would have to be indefinitely long. There are, for example, indefinitely many good English sentences. Clearly, a natural language is a *system*. Only thus could it be *productive* (1.2, 2.2). It must consist of a finite number of rules specifying the ways in which words can be combined. How could this work? Only if words are collected into syntactic categories: nouns, verbs, prepositions, adverbs, and so on. The rules will then specify how these categories fit together; they will describe the general pattern of grammatical sentences. So, to take an oversimple example, one such pattern in English might be: Name – Transitive Verb – Name. Plugging in words of the appropriate category yields a sentence. Thus the rules specify the ways in which words of a finite number of syntactic categories can be legitimately combined to form an infinite number of sentences. These rules reveal the structure of sentences. A sentence is grammatical in the language in virtue of having one of those structures (and being made up of words in the language: "the slithy toves did gyre and gimble in the wabe" is not English).

2   Many sentences in a language are *structurally ambiguous*. They have ambiguities that are additional to any lexical ambiguities that they may contain. For example:

Tex likes exciting sheep
Spanish money lenders are more avaricious than cautious.

These sentences are ambiguous in ways that cannot be traced to the ambiguity of any words they contain. Their truth conditions vary even though reference is held constant. Thus, is it being said that Tex enjoys causing sheep to become excited? Or is it that he enjoys the company of interesting and stimulating sheep? Either way Tex has a problem, of course, but they are very different problems.

How can this ambiguity be explained? As a first approximation, we can say that 'Tex likes exciting sheep' has two distinct structures. One will group 'likes' and 'exciting' together as a *constituent* of the sentence; the other will group 'exciting' and 'sheep' together as a constituent. This shows that sometimes there is more than one way of assembling words into subsentential constituents of a sentence. There is more to the structure of a sentence than simply the order of the words out of which the sentence is built. There are *intermediate layers* of sentence organization between the level of words and the level of the sentence itself. The sentence with 'Spanish money lenders' illustrates the same phenomenon. It may be about lenders of Spanish money, in which case 'Spanish money' is a constituent. Alternatively, the sentence may be about Spanish lenders of money, in which case 'Spanish money lenders' is a constituent but 'Spanish money' is not.

It is common to represent the internal structure of sentences as *trees* which display the *hierarchical organization* of sentences. If the sentence is structurally ambiguous, it gets more than one tree. These trees are called *phrase-structure* trees, because they organize the sentence elements into successively larger constituents, or phrases, of the sentence.

Take as an example the two trees for 'Tex likes exciting sheep':

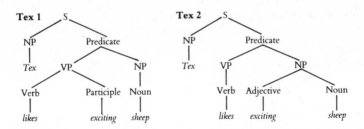

Both Tex 1 and Tex 2 are oversimplified: the details should not be taken too literally. But they are right in dividing S (the sentence) into two basic units, NP (noun phrase) and Predicate. Tex 1 differs from Tex 2 only in the structure of its predicate. In Tex 1 the predicate is composed of a complex VP (verb phrase) and simple NP; in Tex 2 the reverse is the case. As a result of these different underlying structures, the sentence has two sets of truth conditions and two meanings.

In our other example, the source of the ambiguity is in the first major constituent of the sentence (its *subject*). Thus, when the sentence concerns the lenders of Spanish money, it is represented as follows (ignoring the structure of the predicate):

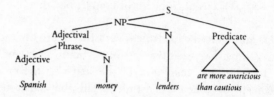

Note that 'Spanish money' is a constituent of this tree: there is a single node – Adjectival Phrase – that dominates the elements 'Spanish' and 'money' *and no other elements*. That is not true of the alternative interpretation, where the sentence concerns Spanish nationals:

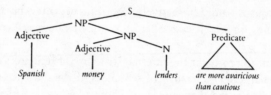

In this tree, NP dominates 'Spanish' and 'money', but it is also dominates 'lenders'. So 'Spanish money lenders' is a constituent but 'Spanish money' is not.

3   Consider the following pairs of sentences:

Alex can lift Natasha
Can Alex lift Natasha?

Chess is generally played by obsessives
Is chess generally played by obsessives?

They will want to buy two children
Will they want to buy two children?

The first sentence of each pair is a statement; the second, the correlative question. Clearly the form of the one is related to the form of the other. How can we capture that in our theory of English sentencehood? Were we to restrict ourselves to examples like these, nothing could be easier: the question has the same form as the statement except the first two words occur in reverse order. But it is easy to see that this will not work in general:

Chess generally is played by obsessives
Generally chess is played by obsessives
Is chess generally played by obsessives?

The third sentence, not the second, is the question that corresponds to the first.

Perhaps we should amend our generalization: the question has the same form as the statement except that *the first verb* of the statement appears at the front of the question. This generalization covers our examples to date. And it commits us to more internal structure than word order because it requires us to classify words into groups, in particular, to classify some as verbs. But it won't do. The regularity that links questions to statements is dependent on a more complex structure.

Consider the following:

Chess players who get to be grandmasters are generally obsessive
*Get chess players who to be grandmasters are generally obsessive?

Our revised generalization predicts that the string marked "*" is the correlative question. But that string is no sentence at all. The correlative question is:

Are chess players who get to be grandmasters generally obsessive?

The verb that needs to be moved in this case is the second one.

Examples of this kind can be made indefintely complex. Thus:

Chess players who get to be grandmasters who can hold their own in tournaments in Zambia in which candidates for the world championship play are generally obsessive
Are chess players who get to be grandmaster who can hold their own in tournaments in Zambia in which candidates for the world championship play generally obsessive?

The relationship between this statement and question is essentially the same as in our other examples, but in this case it is the fourth verb that needs to be moved. Clearly, no simple numerical story will capture the relationship. Instead, we need to appeal to a structural fact about sentences: they are organized into two major constituents. Conventionally, these are called the subject (which is an NP) and the predicate. So, taking one of the simpler examples, we can illustrate the basic organization of the indicative sentence:

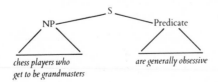

In terms of this fact of sentence structure, we can now say (roughly) how a question is related to its correlative statement: the question has the same form as the statement except that the first verb *of the statement's predicate* appears at the front of the question.

So far, we have argued that sentences have a structure consisting not just of words in sequence, but of words organized into successively larger constituents or phrases. That structure can be conveniently represented as a tree. All this was orthodox before Chomsky. His great insight was to see that many facts about sentences could be explained if we took them to have a richer structure still.

6.3 Motivating transformational grammar

Chomsky claims that we need to see a sentence as having *two* structures, both represented as trees. The two structures are linked together. One of them he calls the *deep* (or *base*) structure. The other, which we have been discussing, he calls the *surface* structure. Chomsky and others have assembled an enormous amount of evidence in support of the view that we need two kinds of structure to explain grammaticality. What follows is a tiny sample.

4   Consider ambiguity again.

    Riveting rhinos can be infuriating

is structurally ambiguous. It might mean either that it can be infuriating to rivet rhinos or that rhinos who rivet can be infuriating. However, this ambiguity is quite different from those considered in 2 above (6.2). There the ambiguity arose from different ways of grouping words into constituents of the sentence. Here it arises *within* the constituent 'riveting rhinos'. It is as though that phrase can go proxy for two distinct phrases: 'the process of riveting of rhinos' and 'rhinos who rivet'. How can a phrase act as though it is the reduced remnant of some more complex expression? Perhaps underlying the ambiguous sentence are distinct deep structures, but some process collapses or erases the distinction in the surface structure. Oversimplifying mightily, the alternative deep structure could be something like this:

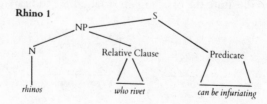

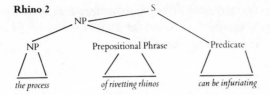

Rhino 2

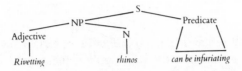

Transformational rules link both deep structures to a *single surface structure* by deleting and moving elements in the subject. We can represent the common surface structure as follows:

The sentence has two sets of truth conditions and two meanings not because it has two surface structures (as does 'Tex likes exciting sheep') but because it has two deep structures.

5   Some sentences come in pairs. Consider, for example, these two groups:

Jane beat Tarzan { carefully / with a dead snake / yesterday

Carefully / With a dead snake / Yesterday }, Jane beat Tarzan.

The sentences in these two groups are related. The structural relations within the pair 'Jane beat Tarzan with a dead snake' and 'With a dead snake, Jane beat Tarzan' are the same. Despite their different word order; they have the same truth conditions and hence meaning. The phenomenon is very common in English and other languages. Here is another pair:

It is hard to eat soup with chopsticks
To eat soup with chopsticks is hard.

If we make a distinction between deep and surface structure, these phenomena fall into place. Though the members of each pair have different surface structures, reflected in their different word orders, they share a deep structure. Thus, the deep structure for 'Jane beat Tarzan with a dead snake' and its correlate might be something like this:

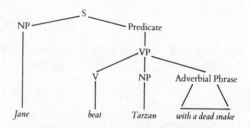

These examples illustrate the option in English of *Adverb Preposing*. There are many other options that have the same result: sentences with different surface structures have the one deep structure. Traditional grammar has already identified *Passivization*: each transitive sentence in the active has a corresponding sentence in the passive. Here are some examples illustrating other options:

> Igor threw up his lunch
> Igor threw his lunch up.

> The man who trumped my ace is an idiot
> The man is an idiot who trumped my ace.

The first is an example of *Particle Movement*: the particle attached to a verb may appear at the end of the sentence. The second is an example of *Extraposition from NP*: the clause modifying a subject NP may appear at the end of the sentence. In all such cases, the distinction between surface and deep structure enables us to capture the idea that two distinct sentences are really variants of each other.

6   Just as there are some sentences that look different but are fundamentally the same, there are some sentences that look the same but are fundamentally different. Chomsky has made one sort of example famous:

> Noam is easy to please
> Noam is eager to please.

These two sentences seem to have exactly the same structure, apparently differing only in a single word. Appearances are deceptive. The sentences are members of very different families as the following pairs show:

> It is easy to please Noam
> *It is eager to please Noam.

*Noam is easy to please Lyndon
Noam is eager to please Lyndon.

The strings marked '*' are not acceptable sentences. The first pair exemplifies a construction, apparently related to those of the original sentences, which permits 'easy' but not 'eager'. The second pair exemplifies one which permits 'eager' but not 'easy'. Despite the surface similarity of the original sentences, this contrast shows that the sentences have very different deep structures.

In the last section we saw that sentences are not merely strings of words: they have rich structures that can be represented by phrase-structure trees. These structures determine which strings of words are grammatical and hence sentences. In this section we have given some of the evidence that sentences have a richer structure still: that they have deep structures as well as surface ones. Deep structures explain structural ambiguities; the structural identity of sentence variants; the structural differences between apparently similar sentences. We must now summarize the theory of transformational grammar that Chomsky constructed to account for these facts. It is known as *the Standard Theory*.

6.4 The Standard Theory of transformational grammar

Chomsky calls a theory of a language its *grammar*. As we have seen, his insight was to distinguish between two levels of structure. The deep structure of a sentence determines the so-called *thematic* relations within a sentence. These are the basic grammatical relations between the major constituents of the sentence. This structure defines the subject, object, and indirect object of the verb. It defines the structure of the predicate (whether it has adverbial or prepositional elements). It defines the overall hierarchy of the clauses in complex sentences. Initially, it was also thought to determine the meaning of the sentence. And that has been a guiding assumption of the above discussion. But we shall soon see (6.5) that some came to abandon this view.

The surface structure determines the phonological interpretation of the sentence: it determines the way it sounds. In doing so, it settles matters of stress, intonation, emphasis, and so on. Thus, while two surface structure variants of the one deep structure will not differ in basic grammatical make-up, they may contrast pragmatically or stylistically in important ways. For example, collo-quial English permits *Topicalization*:

Max bit Sam
Sam, Max bit him

share a deep structure but contrast in emphasis.

Chomsky thinks of a grammar as a system of rules organized into four subsystems. One of these, the pronunciation subsystem or *Phonological Component*, we shall say nothing about. Another consists of the tree-building rules plus a lexicon; this is the *Base Component* of a grammar. It determines the deep structures permitted in the language.

A third subsystem mediates the relations between deep and surface structure. That subsystem is the *Transformational Component* containing the transformational rules. (It is because of this component, of course, that the whole approach has become known as transformational grammar.) These rules connect deep and surface structures by mapping one tree onto another: a chain of intermediate trees link deep and surface structure. For example, the surface structure of the topicalized sentence 'Sam, Max bit him' might be produced in two steps. First a copying transformation might turn

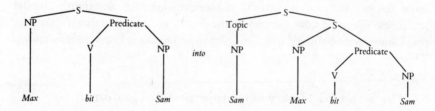

and then a pronominalization rule produces:

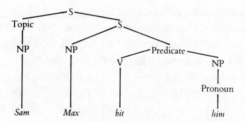

A transformational rule thus contains two elements. One specifies the type of tree on which it operates. This is called the rule's *structural description*. The other specifies the *structural change* the rule effects.

In sum, the first systematic expositions of transformational grammar developed in the mid-1960s yielded the following picture:

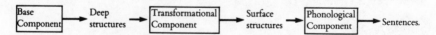

How does this story fit with the account of meaning we have been urging? So far, it seems to fit well. We claim that the core of a sentence's meaning is its truth conditions (chapter 2). Truth conditions, in turn, are a function of the referential role of the words in the sentence together with its syntactic structure. The deep structure of a sentence seems to provide just the structure we want. For, what is the "deep structure"? It is a set of words assigned a syntactic structure; it is like a sentence under structural analysis. If we abstract from the words in the deep structure, we are left with a pure structure. And that seems to be the underlying structure we need to combine with the reference of the words to get the truth conditions of the original sentence.

Consider the pairs of sentences in 5 (6.3) which we said shared a deep structure; for example, 'Jane beat Tarzan carefully' and 'Carefully, Jane beat Tarzan'. The members of each pair differ from one another in their structure and yet they are fundamentally similar: they have the same meaning and truth conditions. According to the above story, that similarity is captured by their sharing a deep structure. Truth conditions are determined by referential roles and the structure revealed before the transformation rules operate.

Of course, the task remains of showing precisely how the truth conditions depend on that underlying structure. That is a task on which logicians have begun to shed light, but which we are setting aside (2.4, 6.1). What the deep structure seems to provide is the right structure for that final task.

This is how we take transformational grammar, but it is important to note that it is not the way the grammarians themselves take it. Rather, they think that meaning is explained by a *fourth* subsystem of the grammar, the *Semantic Component*.

The Semantic Component is a system of rules relating deep structures to further structures, *semantic representations*, which are "possible interpretations" of sentences.

(The Base, Transformational, and Phonological Components have been omitted for simplifiction.) Semantic representations are structures of basic *concepts*, usually thought to be common to our species. Thus, a simplified version of the semantic representation for 'chase' (cf. Katz 1966: 167), mapped to it by the Semantic Component, might be:

(ACTIVITY: (PHYSICAL) (MOVEMENT) (SPEED): (FAST) (FOLLOWING (x)))), (PURPOSE: (TO CATCH (x)))).

The capitalized words name semantic primitives: basic, unanalysable, human concepts. So, the meaning of a single word, 'chase', is explained by a complex structure of concepts. This sort of decomposition is characteristic of the approach.

To understand this approach it is important to note that the grammarians have a very different view of the problem of meaning from ours (cf. 1.1). We see language–world relationships as posing *the* central problem of meaning. Thus truth and reference are the central notions in our theory of meaning. In contrast, the grammarians give no place in semantics to language–world relationships. For example, Jerrold Katz, in a standard exposition of their approach, does not mention truth and reference at all in specifying the basic problems of semantics (1972: 5–6). Instead, the grammarians are concerned with such problems as synonymy, similarity of meaning (e.g. between 'cat', 'elephant' and 'snake'), redundancy (e.g. 'A naked nude posed for the vicar'), ambiguity and entailment.

The Semantic Component provides an attractive solution to the grammarians' semantic problems. Synonymy is explained by sameness of semantic representation; similarity of meaning, by a common concept in representations; redundancy, by a repeated representation; ambiguity, by having more than one representation; entailment, by the inclusion of one representation in another.

The major objection to the grammarians' theory of meaning is that it does ignore the central problem: language–world relations. As a result, the theory is seriously incomplete. *At best*, it explains the semantic properties of words in terms of primitive concepts. But, what determines the particular nature of each such concept? In virtue of what does the concept TO CATCH concern catching rather than, say, Maggie's fist or the price of eggs? *At bottom, the grammarians do not explain meaning but take it for granted. For, their primitive concepts are nothing but unexplained meanings.*

It is not surprising that Chomsky and his followers are least convincing when handling aspects of meaning that go beyond syntax, because they are part of the *structuralist* tradition (of which more in chapter 13). As John Searle points out, that tradition saw language as a "self-contained formal system" (1972: 30) – a favourite analogy was chess. But language differs crucially from such systems as chess in having representational powers; it represents situations in the world. It is because it does this that it has its central place in our lives.

Beyond this major objection, we *need* have nothing but a verbal disagreement with the grammarians. Where we use the theory of reference to flesh out syntactic structures with word meanings, they use the Semantic Component of the grammar. What they do with the Semantic Component, talking of concepts, we could do with the theory of reference, talking of words. For example, we could take over the above explanation of 'chase' as follows: the reference of 'chase' is to be explained in terms of the references of 'activity', 'physical', 'movement', 'speed', 'fast', 'following', 'purpose' and 'to catch'. This would be to adopt a description theory of reference for 'chase' along the lines suggested earlier for handling non-basic terms (5.4). We could similarly take over their explanations of synonymy, similarity, and so on. Finally, where the grammarians rest content with primitive concepts, thus provoking the major objection, we could offer causal theories of reference of basic terms.

Though this ecumenicalism is possible in principle, it is unlikely in practice. The grammarians tend to overdo the business of decomposing into a structure of primitive concepts. So, taking over their explanations would probably commit us to description theories of reference where we would think that causal theories – pure or descriptive – were appropriate.

In sum, the Standard Theory's handling of word meaning is seriously incomplete in leaving primitive concepts unexplained. Further, it seems to overdo decomposition. In other respects the Theory fits nicely into the account of meaning we have been urging. Deep structure seems to provide the structure of natural language sentences that we seek. Subject it to logical analysis, add a theory of reference, and we might hope to have the core of a theory of meaning.

We shall now consider some problems that have arisen for the Standard Theory and the responses to them. But before that we should note that some matters relevant to the discussion of syntactic structure that we are setting aside for later chapters. First, we have been attempting to describe the sorts of syntactic structures that natural language have. There is a further question to be considered. In virtue of what does a particular sentence have whatever structure it has? We shall suggest that structure is explained ultimately in psychological terms: it is a matter of "conceptual role". This will be discussed briefly in section 7.5. Second, we have been concerned with transformational grammar as a theory of the syntactic structure of linguistic symbols. Yet Chomsky and his followers offer it primarily as a theory of the competence of native speakers (6.1). We shall consider it as a theory of competence, and the conflation of these two explanatory aims, in chapter 8.

**6.5 Problems for the Standard Theory

In the light of the Standard Theory, we might put our views as follows: sentence meaning is determined by deep-level structure and what goes into explaining reference. The grammarians themselves thought, in effect, that sentence meaning was determined by deep-level structure and structures of primitive concepts. Either way, the meaning of a sentence is determined solely by word meaning and deep structure; surface structure is linked to meaning only via deep structure. This was sometimes expressed: "transformations preserve meaning". That was an assumption of transformationalists until the late 1960s; it was part of the Standard Theory. Since then that theory has run into problems which have led to much more complex accounts of the relations between surface structure, deep structure, and semantic representations.

The problems arise from the interaction of quantifiers, negation, and *movement rules*.

Many transformation rules are movement rules: they change the order of the elements of a sentence. We mentioned several in 5 (6.3). One of these was Passivization. The sentences

> Maggie kicks heads
> Heads are kicked by Maggie

have the same deep structure. It is plausible to think of this deep structure as approximating the active form. So Passivization turns

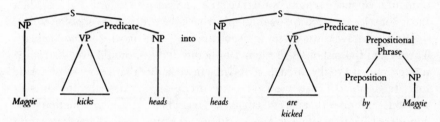

Consider now the following sentences involving quantifiers and negation:

> Many arrows didn't hit the target
> The target wasn't hit by many arrows.

Against a background of examples of Passivization like our one above, it is natural to think of the second sentence as the passive of the first. And that was what the Standard Theory led many to conclude. The problem is that there is a subtle, but important, difference in the truth conditions of these two sentences. 'Many arrows didn't hit the target, but many did' is consistent: many missing is compatible with many hitting. However, its counterpart, 'The target wasn't hit by many arrows, but it was hit by many', is inconsistent. So Passivization seems to go against the assumption that transformations preserve meanings; the change in the order of 'many' and 'not' changes meaning.

This turns out to be a general phenomenon. The order in which quantifiers like 'many', 'some', 'few', and 'most', occur either with each other, or with negation, is semantically important. Here is another example:

> Most women love no men

is not equivalent to

No men are loved by most women.

Some examples do not involve negation:

Few elephants bite many tigers
Many tigers are bitten by few elephants

The first sentence means that few elephants are habitual tiger biters; the second, that many tigers are rarely elephant-bitten.

These examples challenge our assumption:

(a) surface structure is linked to meaning only by deep structure (transformations preserve meaning).

The first thing we should do is identify the *other* assumptions that lead to this challenge. After all, if our simple rule for Passivization goes against (a), why is that not sufficient ground for rejecting the rule and looking for another? Why not look for a rule that makes

The target wasn't hit by many arrows

the passive of

Not many arrows hit the target

which is equivalent? The answer is that the Standard Theory operated with the following implicit assumptions as well:

(b) Transformational rules are simple: they do only one thing at a time. Further, they are formal: they apply in virtue of the structure of the input tree, not its meaning.
(c) Deep structures are similar to surface structures: transformations change deep structures, but not radically.
(d) Transformation rules are the only rules we need to link surface and deep structures.

It was the commitment to these other assumptions that led to the clash with (a). Our problem with Passivization shows that these four assumptions cannot be held jointly.**

**6.6 Contemporary transformational grammar

What is to be done? There are three major responses. Each of them maintains the Standard Theory's two levels of structure, but relates them together differently.

The first response, historically, was *Generative Semantics*. This response developed a grammar that retained (a) at the expense of (c) and (d), and, perhaps, (b).

The defense of (a) required solving two problems. The first was to find plausible and distinct deep structures for the sentences in each of the troublesome pairs. This task was not too difficult. However, the resulting deep structures, modelled on the "logical forms" of predicate calculus, were much more abstract and less like surface structures than their predecessors. They divided sentences into two basic caegories, V and NP, but these categories have little connection with the traditional notions of verb and noun phrase. So assumption (c) went. Consider the simplest of our examples. The proposed deep structures were along the following lines:

Few elephants bite many tigers

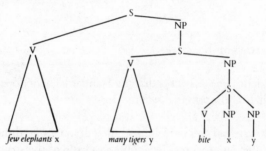

Many tigers are bitten by few elephants

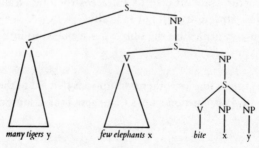

The most important new transformation needed to derive the sentences from these deep structures is *Quantifier Lowering*. The quantifiers involved are restricted: variable '*x*' ranges not over all objects, but only over elephants; '*y*' ranges only over tigers. Thus, Quantifier Lowering inserts the quantifier 'few elephants *x*' into the space occupied by the variable '*x*' (2.4); similarly, 'many tigers *y*' for '*y*'. So, for the first sentence, we get (after "tree-pruning"):

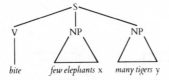

Subject Formation, and various rules that mark the verbs for tense and nouns for number, then yield the surface structure. The same process applies for the second sentence except that Passivization changes the order of '*x*' and '*y*' first (and "marks" the verb for the later auxiliary verb 'to be').

This leads to the second problem. For this story to work, Passivization has to be *obligatory* in the second case, and *impossible* in the first. Otherwise, both sentences could arise from both deep structures; the sentences would be a synonymous ambiguous pair. To solve this problem, the generative semanticists introduced a new type of rule, *global derivational constraints*. This abandoned assumption (d).

So saving assumption (a) has costs: new transformations; new and more powerful sorts of rules; less sentence-like deep structures. Most transformational grammarians thought these costs were too great. This reaction was exacerbated by other aspects of Generative Semantics. We have mentioned that the Standard Theory tended to overdo the decomposition of word meaning into primitive concepts (6.4). Generative Semantics took decomposition to extremes: hardly any words corresponded to primitive concepts. Since Generative Semantics made the deep structure do double duty as the semantic representation, these decompositional excesses had to be captured in deep structure. This led to even more abstract deep structures and more elaborate transformations.

If Generative Semantics is stripped of its more extravagant claims about decomposition, it is not obvious that it should be abandoned. However, as a matter of fact, it largely has been abandoned in favour of one of the two other alternatives.

Since Generative Semantics preserves assumption (a), it is as congenial to our programme for explaining meaning as the Standard Theory. Deep structure reveals the meaning relevant structure of sentences.

The next alternative we shall consider is known as the *Extended Standard Theory*. In effect, it was an attempt to maintain assumptions (b)–(d) by making the dropping of (a) seem more congenial. It did this by reassigning some (but not all) semantic jobs that had been done by deep structure. Crucially, some of these jobs were assigned to surface structure. Whereas on the Standard Theory the Semantic Component operates only on the deep structure to yield semantic representations, on the Extended Theory it operates on *both* the deep and surface structures. So, meaning is determined by both structures (and primitive concepts).

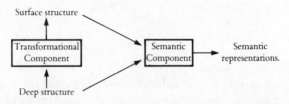

One aspect of meaning transferred to the surface structure is *scope* (2.4). That is how the Extended Theory deals with the problem of passives. The difference in meaning between, for example, 'Few elephants bite many tigers' and 'Many tigers are bitten by few elephants' lies in the scope of the quantifiers 'many' and 'few': in the first sentence, 'many' lies within the scope of 'few'; in the second, the reverse is the case. By assigning scope to surface structure, the Extended Theory can continue to treat the second as the passive of the first, both sentences being obtained by simple transformations from the one deep structure.

The Extended Standard Theory does not suit our programme as well as Generative Semantics does: we have to look to both deep and surface structure to find the structure relevant to truth conditions and hence meaning. However, this complication results in little more than a loss of elegance; the relevant structure is still there to be found.

More recently, an alternative has been urged called *Trace Theory*, which also seeks to maintain (b)–(d). It takes over from the Extended Theory the idea of handling scope in the surface structure. Its innovation is to claim that all the information in the deep structure is also to be found in the surface structure: the surface bears "traces" of the deep. This being so, the surface structure can be the only input to the Semantic Component. We have the following picture:

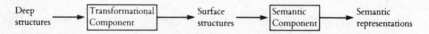

The great advantage of this over the Extended Theory is that meaning is determined by only one structure. Trace Theory is thus simpler. (Generative Semantics, of course, shares this advantage, but differs from Trace Theory in making deep structure not surface structure the determining one.)

Trace Theory recasts the explanations that motivated transformational grammar in the first place. Consider, for example, the ambiguity of 'Riveting rhinos can be infuriating'. The Standard Theory explained this as follows: the sentence has a single surface structure derived from two deep structures. Trace Theory varies the explanation: the sentence has two surface structures which differ because they are derived from different deep structures.

The problem for Trace Theory is to develop a plausible theory of transformations that supplies a trace for each feature of the deep structure. Some of the transformations rules of the Standard Theory supply this already and so can simply be taken over. Topicalization is an example. The surface structure of the topicalized 'Sam, Max bit him' contains 'him' as the trace of 'Sam'. So we can recover the deep structure, 'Max bit Sam', from the surface. Passivization also seems to be an example: the 'by' marks the original, deep structure subject of the verb. However, many Standard transformations do not have this property. For example, the surface structure we gave for the ambiguous 'Riveting rhinos can be infuriating' (6.3) bears no trace that identifies which of its two possible deep structures applies. Trace Theory must find new transformation rules, yielding new surface structures, to remedy this lack.

There is one rather striking bit of evidence for Trace Theory and against the other theories. The evidence comes from phonetics. According to all the theories, surface structure determines the way a sentence sounds; it is the only input into the Phonological Component (6.4). So there should be no phonetic differences between sentences without surface structure differences. Yet on the Standard Theory, Extended Standard Theory, and Generative Semantics, there do seem to be such phonetic differences. For example, if a person means by the rhino sentence that it can be infuriating to rivet rhinos, he will emphasize 'rhinos'; whereas if he means that rhinos who rivet can be infuriating, he will emphasize 'riveting'. Such differences in the deep structure are reflected in the sounds and so should be indicated by the surface structure. Provided Trace Theory can fulfil its programme, it will accommodate such phenomena: the surface structure that determines the sound will bear a trace of the relevant deep structure.

Though phonetic differences of this sort are nice evidence for the existence of traces, the Theory does not require that all traces be sounded. It can allow that some traces are silent. There can be surface structure differences without phonetic differences.

According to Trace Theory, the truth-relevant structure that we seek for our programme is to be found in the surface structure. So this final alternative to the Standard Theory is also congenial.

In sum, difficulties for the Standard Theory have led to three major alternatives. From our perspective the differences between them are largely technical. Each can provide the truth-relevant structure that our programme requires to explain meaning. And each preserves the distinction between deep and surface structure which we take to be the central insight of Chomsky's revolution. Exactly how these structures are related, and exactly how they provide the truth-relevant structure, is up for grabs.**

Suggested reading

6.1

Montague's papers are collected together in *Formal Philosophy* (1974). See Dowty, Wall and Peters 1981, *Introduction to Montague Semantics*, for further information on the approach of Montague grammarians.

6.2–6.4

Chomsky's two early classics are *Syntactic Structures* (1957) and **Aspects of the Theory of Syntax* (1965)**. A more readable work is *Topics in the Theory of Generative Grammar* (1966), parts of which are reprinted under the same title in Searle 1971, *The Philosophy of Language*.

Katz 1966, *The Philosophy of Language*, chapter 4, gives a good account of the Standard Theory. **This can be found in a less readable form also in Katz and Fodor 1963, "The structure of a semantic theory", reprinted in Fodor and Katz 1964, *The Structure of Language*, and in Rosenberg and Travis 1971.**

Searle 1972, "Chomsky's revolution in linguistics", reprinted in Harman 1974, *On Noam Chomsky*, gives a good overview of transformational grammar emphasizing its difference from its predecessors.

There are many introductory texts in transformational grammar. Two good ones are Akmajian and Heny 1975, *An Introduction to the Principles of Transformational Sytax*, and Baker 1977, *Introduction to Generative-Transformational Syntax*. A more philosophical and critical introduction is given in Sampson 1975, *The Form of Language*.

**6.5–6.6*

For Generative Semantics, see McCawley 1972, "A program for logic", in Davidson and Harman 1972, *Semantics of Natural Language*; Lakoff 1971, "On generative semantics", in Steinberg and Jacobovits 1971; and McCawley 1971, "Prelexical syntax", and Seuren 1972, "Autonomous *versus* semantic syntax", both reprinted in Seuren 1974, *Semantic Syntax*.

For the Extended Standard Theory, see Jackendoff 1972, *Semantic Interpretation In Generative Grammar*. For an early discussion, see Chomsky 1971, "Deep structure, surface structure, and semantic interpretation", in Steinberg and Jacobovits 1971.

For Trace Theory, see Chomsky 1980, *Rules and Representations*, chapter 4.

See Janet Fodor 1977, *Semantics*, for a good account of all theories (except Trace Theory) presented in a way suitable for those without a technical background. Kempson 1977, *Semantic Theory*, chapter 10, gives an overview of the debate between defenders of the theories (again, except Trace Theory) and, in chapter 6, discusses decompositional approaches to word meaning.**

PART III

LANGUAGE AND MIND

7

Thought and meaning

7.1 Thoughts as inner representations

Our focus so far has been on meaning, a property of linguistic items. This focus has frequently led to remarks about the mental states of language users, the people who produce the linguistic items. For meaning clearly depends in various ways on those states. In particular, it has proved impossible to discuss meaning without discussing linguistic competence or understanding. In this part of the book, the focus will be on those areas of the mind that are relevant to language. We start with thoughts.

Thoughts – or, as they are sometimes called, "propositional attitudes" – are inner states: beliefs, desires, hopes, fears, etc. Why suppose that are such inner states? Because we need to in order to explain our behaviour. Why does Oscar vote for Reagan? We answer in terms of beliefs and desires: he believes that Reagan is dangerous; he believes that a dangerous president is more likely to stop the Russians; he desires that the Russians be stopped and so on. Thoughts are behaviour-controlling states.

We think that thoughts are also *representational*. They are inner representations (and misrepresentations) of the external world; they have *content*. The desire to meet Jane Fonda is different from the desire to meet the prettiest CIA agent simply because these two thoughts have different representational contents. (Note that this would be so even if Jane Fonda were the prettiest CIA agent: the problem of opacity again; 2.5.) Further, the content of a thought is causally relevant. It is because a person desired *to meet Jane Fonda* that he lined up at a certain stage door. If he had desired *to meet the prettiest CIA agent*, he would have done something else. Similarly, if Oscar had believed that *a dangerous president was the last thing he wanted*, he would have voted for somebody else.

Thoughts differ not only in their representational content: the same content can be involved in a belief, a desire and so on. Thus, we can believe that Mum will come, hope that Mum will come, or fear that Mum will come. What then is it to have a thought? It is to have a certain attitude – for example, that of believing – to a certain content.

In sum, thoughts are inner states of people (and possible other things) that have their causal powers partly in virtue of their representational content and partly in virtue of the attitude people have to them.

There is an ambiguity in the ordinary term 'thought'. It can be used, as we have above, to refer to a mental state: the having of an attitude to a content. It can also be used to refer simply to the content. In this use it is rather like 'proposition'. We shall use it both ways.

7.2 The linguistic character of thought

What kind of inner representation are thoughts? At the very least, they must be language-like in character.

First, thoughts seem to have the same semantic properties as sentences of human languages. (a) Thoughts have referential relations with the world, just as sentences do. Oscar's belief that Reagan is dangerous refers to Reagan in just the same way as the utterance 'Reagan is dangerous' does. (b) Beliefs, like assertions, are true or false. Desires and hopes are not, but they are like requests in having compliance or satisfaction conditions (2.4). (c) Thoughts, like sentences, can stand in inferential relations. Oscar might have arrived at his belief by inferring it from his beliefs that all Christians are dangerous and that Reagan is a Christian.

Second, thoughts have the syntax of sentences. One reason for thinking this comes from the explanation of (c). How could Oscar infer his belief from the other two mentioned? Oscar is exemplifying the fact that he has caught on to the validity of all inferences of the form:

All Fs are G
a is F
So, a is G.

Oscar's inference is an instance of this form. So in explaining Oscar's inference, we attribute certain forms to his beliefs. These forms are syntactic structures that the beliefs can share with sentences.

Another reason for attributing a syntax to belief is that thought, like language, is productive. People do not learn to produce and understand sentences one by one: they learn the elements of sentences and recipes for putting those elements together (1.2). This requires, as we pointed out (2.2), that sentences have syntactic structure. Similar remarks are true of thoughts. People have the capacity to think indefinitely many thoughts that they never have, and never will, think. For, they have gained the concepts contained in those thoughts and have acquired the recipe for putting those concepts together. This capacity requires that thoughts have syntactic structure.

Finally, thoughts are like sentences in being abstract. The sentence 'Orson weighs 130 kg' tells you nothing about Orson other than his mass (1.2). Similarly, the thought that Orson weighs 130 kg. Images, maps and diagrams may be *associated with* thoughts, particularly with perceptually based ones, but they are not themselves thoughts. Depictive representation is too rich and ambiguous to capture the content of thought; a picture of Reagan is no more a representation of the belief that Reagan is wrinkled, than it is of the belief that he is Caucasian, or of the belief that he is surprisingly hairy for an old man. Moreover, no pictures could come close to capturing the beliefs that Reagan is dangerous, that turtles make poor lovers, and that high interest rates could cause a banking collapse. In sum, many thoughts are unpicturable; any picture could be associated with many thoughts. Thought and talk are abstract, and abstract in the same way.

It seems clear that our system of inner representation and our system of linguistic representation are importantly similar. In the light of this, it is tempting to suppose that our inner system *is* our public language; that our "language of thought" is our language of talk. This idea has more than simplicity to recommend it, for our cognitive capacities seem closely correlated with our linguistic capacities. The general development of the two capacities goes hand in hand. Further, it is very plausible to suppose that our ability to think certain thoughts depends on language. Could we have had beliefs about aircraft, or desires about nuclear bombs before we had words for aircraft and bombs? (We return to this matter of the dependency of thought on language in chapter 10.)

The idea also has some introspective support. Speech often *seems* to be thinking out loud; thought often *seems* to be talking to oneself. Moreover, consider a familiar barrier a person must break through in learning a foreign language: learning to "think in the language". Until she crashes through this barrier, she uses the foreign language by translating back and forth to the familiar home language. Or, so it seems to introspection.

The deliverance of the inner eye should be treated with caution, especially in this case. For, an equivocation lurks here. We have used 'thought' as an umbrella term for beliefs, desires, wants, hopes, and the like. We have conceived of these as long-term informational states: as relatively persistent representational states that contribute to the control of our behaviour. Thoughts as revealed by introspection are, at best, their activated counterparts. When Bruce observes Peacock on the hustings and thinks, "Lovely gear, but it takes more than Gucci shoes to run a country", his thought is a fleeting mental episode that is, at best, some reflection of an underlying behaviour-controlling state. Even if introspection is right and these conscious mental episodes do employ our public language, it does not follow that our long-term representations are in our public language.

Nonetheless, we think it is plausible to suppose that learning a public language is learning a language to think in. So, acquiring our first public language involves a vast expansion in our ways of thinking. This is not to suppose that all thinking is in the public language. The higher animals and pre-linguistic children think, but obviously not in a public language. And some mature human thought is not in such a language either: consider our thought about music or chess, for example. So the thesis is that *most* mature human thought consists in having attitudes of believing, desiring, hoping, etc., to mental sentences in a public language. And the content of those thoughts is the meaning of those sentences. We shall now consider some objections to this thesis.

7.3 Do we think in a public language?

One objection can be dismissed quickly. When a living brain is examined, we find no cerebral blackboard on which sentences are written. Nothing inside the head *looks like* a sentence. This objection is confused. What *does* a sentence look like? Sentences, unlike pictures, are medium-independent (1.2). Whereas the relation between picture and pictured is, in some vague sense, natural or intrinsic, that between name and named is arbitrary. Practical problems aside, anything could be used to refer to anything. Indeed we are familiar with a range of very different physical types being used for the one semantic type (4.2); a sentence may appear as a sequence of acoustic vibrations, as marks on paper, as a sequence of flags, as electric pulses of various kinds, and so on. So there is nothing incoherent in the idea that sentences could come in a neural medium as well. Tokens in the medium of thought, just like tokens of speech or braille, can be natural language sentences.

Noam Chomsky is responsible for a more serious objection. He has argued for a highly cognitivist account of linguistic competence. He thinks that human language use is rule-governed in a very strong way. Linguistic behaviour is controlled by rules represented in the mind of the speaker, rules of which the speaker is cognizant. Knowledge of these rules tells the speaker which strings of words are sentences and what sentences mean. Finally, many of the rules governing linguistic behaviour are *innate*. We are born pre-programmed with information about the kinds of rules we will need to learn in learning a language. We have innate knowledge of "universal grammar".

Chomsky's picture is not one we can accept. If a speaker understands English in virtue of knowing rules for its employment, these rules cannot be in English.

If you do not already understand Japanese, a Japanese-Japanese dictionary is no help to you. Similarly, if you do not already understand English, a system of rules in English telling you how to construct sentences, and what they mean, is no help. It follows that the speaker must represent those rules in a language of thought that is not English; and, of course, it cannot be any other public language either. It is "Mentalese". How rich must Mentalese be? Jerry Fodor has appealed to learning theory in arguing that Mentalese has to be at least as rich as any public language it governs (1975). He goes further, in his inimitable way: Mentalese, in its rich entirety, is innate.

We have, in effect, conceded some place for Mentalese in allowing that not all thinking is in a public language. However, the place we give it is very different from the above. We think of Mentalese as the impoverished system of representation of the higher animals and pre-linguistic children; and as supplement to the public language representations of the adult human. The above rich view of Mentalese arises from the assumption that linguistic competence consists in *knowlege*, an assumption we shall argue against in the next chapter (8.3-8.4). Further, though it is obviously the case that innate structures make thinking possible, we doubt that any of the language of thought is, in any interesting sense, innate (8.9-8.10).

The final objection stems from the work of Paul Grice. Grice, and following him many others, have given psychological theories of meaning: they have explained the semantic by appeal to the psychological. More specifically, Grice offered explanations of the meaning of utterances in terms of the intentions of utterers. We are in general sympathy with Grice's approach, as will become more apparent in the next section. This poses a *prima facie* problem for our view. The intentions of utterers, like their beliefs and desires, are attitudes to sentences in the language of thought. The content of an intention is given by the meaning of the sentence involved. How can we both identify such mental sentences with public ones and explain the meaning of the public ones in terms of the mental ones? There is a threat of circularity in our explanation. We shall remove the threat in section 7.5. But first we must consider Grice's view of meaning.

7.4 Grice's theory of meaning

At the beginning of chapter 2, we mentioned the vagueness and ambiguity of the term 'meaning'. Grice starts from an awareness of this. This leads him to distinguish a number of species of meaning. He first pares off what he calls "natural meaning". In 'foetid breath means tooth decay', 'means' is roughly synonymous with 'is a reliable sign of'; it identifies a species of meaning that is not restricted to language and other symbolic systems. Grice goes on to identify two important species of "non-natural meaning" or "meaning$_{NN}$": on the one hand, there is the *standard*, *literal*, or *conventional* meaning of a sign; on the other, there is *what a speaker means by* the sign on some given occasion.

Mostly conventional meaning and speaker meaning coincide, but sometimes they do not. Thus, in *The Old Dick* the protagonist describes a thug as 'so primitive that he could regenerate missing limbs'. The literal or conventional meaning of this utterance is of course a falsehood; even the dimmest tough cannot sprout new arms and legs. But what speaker means by the utterance is true, for what he means is that the thug is exceptionally stupid.

Metaphors like this one about the thug provide support for the distinction between speaker meaning and conventional meaning. In any such non-literal use of language, a speaker means something that is suggested by, but is not the same as, the conventional meaning.

Further support for this distinction can be found from situations where there seems to be speaker meaning without conventional meaning. Consider the original development of language. Presumably this development was replete with examples of noises and gestures being used with communicative intent – with speaker meaning – before there existed a settled system of conventions for so using them. Communicative effort that was at least partly successful must have been a precondition for the development of linguistic conventions. The conventions came from regularities in speaker meanings. Even now, there is speaker meaning without conventional meaning when people without a common language are thrown together: they attempt to communicate by gestures, mime and the like.

In a metaphor, a speaker deliberately brings about a divergence of speaker meaning from conventional meaning. Divergence can also be accidental. When we say to someone, "You didn't say what you meant", we are usually indicating just such a divergence. Accidental divergences, like metaphors, are very common. In any case of divergence, there are two distinct meanings of a sign to assess. So, for example, we can talk of both the speaker reference and the conventional reference of a term. And, a slip of the tongue may be conventionally ungrammatical, and hence lack conventional truth conditions, and yet have a speaker syntax and truth conditions. (This bears on the qualifications mentioned in 6.1)

** A distinction of this kind also applies to pragmatic features of sentences, and in particular to illocutionary force (2.3). Consider, for example:

I promise that if you butt your cigarette on my rook again, I'll call the tournament director

Is it within your capacities to pass that jug of water? My wooden leg has caught fire.

The first of these is likely to be intended as a threat, perhaps a warning. The second is unlikely to be a question about the hearer's qualifications as a waiter. Yet these sentences have the conventional forms, respectively, of a promise and a question. Adapting Grice's terminology to these cases (known in the literature as *indirect* speech acts), we might say that their conventional force is different from their speaker force. These differences are, at least, analogous to those between conventional and speaker meaning. To the extent that illocutionary force is part of meaning – and we think that it is to some extent (2.3) – the differences are further examples of those between conventional and speaker meaning.**

We shall suppose then that the distinction is real. Which sort of meaning is more basic or prior? Grice thinks that speaker meaning is prior to conventional meaning. The discussion above suggests that he is right. It reveals cases of speaker meaning without, or independent of, conventional meaning. Yet conventional meaning cannot be similarly detached from speaker meaning.

At first sight it may seem that a sentence can have conventional meaning without a speaker meaning anything by it: a monkey might randomly type out – or, to be more modern, a computer might randomly print out – the works of Shakespeare; the wind may carve out the words 'Reagan is dangerous' in the Mojave desert. But does a chance occurrence really have meaning? Notice that there is no fact of the matter *which* Reagan the desert sentence refers to and, therefore, no fact of the matter *which* conventional meaning has. Wherever a token is of a type that is ambiguous within a language, or between languages, it is impossible to assign it a conventional meaning in the absence of a speaker meaning; for its conventional meaning depends on which convention the speaker had in mind (4.2). Even if the token is of an unambiguous type, it is doubtful if there is any point to assigning it a conventional meaning. And even if there is a point, these examples do not cast any doubt on the fundamental Gricean view: a sentence could not have conventional meaning which is not derived from *past* regularities in speaker meanings.

We conclude that speaker meaning is indeed prior to conventional meaning.

What account can we give of speaker meaning? A communicative intention, Grice thinks, is in some way reflexive. You intend to communicate by means of your audience's recognition of *that very intention*. He is led to this view by a certain contrast. Suppose Tom wishes to induce in Dick the belief that Dick's lover is having an affair with Harry. He might use one of the following two procedures:

(a) Tom arranges for Dick to see a photograph of his lover and Harry in compromising circumstances
(b) Tom draws a picture of Dick's lover and Harry in such circumstances and shows it to Dick.

Grice makes the following claims in this connection. First, he suggests that the photograph has natural meaning but no meaning$_{NN}$; only the drawing has speaker meaning. Second, there is a crucial difference in the role intentions play in the two cases. Dick may come to the target belief from the photograph without any view of Tom's intentions. He might, for example, think that his discovery of the photograph is an accident. Contrast this with the case of the drawing. Unless Dick takes Tom to be drawing a picture of his lover and Harry, and drawing it with the point of inducing the target belief, Dick will not come to that belief. If he takes Tom to have a different purpose, say of producing an interesting drawing, Tom will not achieve his aim. Dick must recognize Tom's intentions and Tom knows this.

Grice's remarks on this case are plausible enough. They lead him to the following account of speaker meaning:

> '*A* meant something by *x*' is (roughly) equivalent to '*A* intended the utterance of *x* to produce some effect in an audience by means of the recognition of this intention'; and we may add that to ask what *A* meant is to ask for a specification of the intended effect.... (Grice 1957: 442)

Later work by Grice and others led to many revisions and complications. The results were elaborate and baroque structures of nested intentions. We shall not concern ourselves with these complications. Nevertheless, to give their flavour, we reproduce one of Grice's later tries:

> '*U* meant something by *x*' is true iff *U* uttered *x* intending thereby: (1) that *A* should produce response *r*, (2) that *A* should, at least partly on the basis of *x*, think that *U* intended (1), (3) that *A* should think that *U* intended (2), (4) that *A*'s production of *r* should be based (at least in part) on *A*'s thought that *U* intended (1) [that is, on *A*'s fulfilment of (2)], (5) that *A* should think *U* intended (4). (Grice 1969: 156)

Even this definition proves insufficiently complex to rule out all the suggested counter-examples. What should we think of such an account of speaker meaning? Is it supposed to be psychologically real? If so, it is not very plausible; we do not seem to have this complex of nested intentions when we speak. Grice's early response to this worry was rather vague. He disclaimed "any intention of peopling all our talking life with armies of complicated psychological occurrences" (1957: 443). What then are we to make of his talk of intentions? His answer is not clear but seems behaviouristic: to have these intentions is simply to behave in a certain sort of way.

> Explicitly formulated linguistic ... intentions are no doubt rare. In their absence we would seem to rely on very much the same kinds of criteria as

we do in the case of nonlinguistic intentions where there is a general usage. An utterer is held to convey what is normally conveyed ... we require a good reason for accepting that a particular usage diverges from general usage ... (1957: 443)

This line of thought will not do. Behaviourist accounts of most mental states are hopeless (8.6). If the Griceans are right about speaker meaning, then the complex structure of intentions that they talk about must be part of the unconscious mental life of speakers.

Why are Grice's definitions so exceptionally complex? The answer, we suggest, is to be found in his view of his task. He sees himself as doing "conceptual analysis" or the "analysis of ordinary language": his definitions are attempts to analyse an ordinary concept of meaning. We shall discuss conceptual analysis in some detail later (14.4). Meanwhile, we note two features of it that help with our current question. First, an analysis must be constructed out of elements familiar to all: common-sense concepts. As a result the weight of Grice's analysis of meaning is born by only two notions: intention and belief. Second, an analysis must be both necessarily true and knowable *a priori*. So, Grice's analysis has to be inviolable to our intuitions about *any situation that can be imagined* in a "thought experiment". The complexity of Grice's definitions reflects the difficulty, perhaps even the impossibility, of covering such an enormous range of possible counter-examples using such a thin stock of basic elements.

We have a different view of the task in the philosophy of language (1.3, 14.1; see also 2.7). From our naturalistic perspective, the most that an analysis could reveal is our implicit folk theory of language. The discovery of that theory is only the beginning of the task. It is an open empirical question just how good that theory is. How well does it explain the phenomena? It may be wrong. It will almost certainly be incomplete.

In the light of this, if conceptual analysis reveals a distinction between speaker meaning and conventional meaning, then it reveals that folk make that distinction. What matters to us, primarily, is not whether folk do make it but whether it is theoretically profitable to make it. We have indicated that we think it is. Next, if analysis shows that it is difficult to explain speaker meanings in terms of familiar notions, this may indicate that folk intuitions about some alleged counter-examples are mistaken: folk theory is wrong here. Or it may indicate that folk have no explanation of speaker meaning; folk theory is incomplete here. We may have to seek an explanation that involves unfamiliar notions. This explanation may appeal to aspects of our psychological organization that differ from intentions and beliefs in being undreamt of in folk psychology.

We have a deeper objection to Grice's approach to speaker meaning. At best it will help to distinguish communicative acts from other human behaviour **(and, perhaps, distinguish the different illocutionary forces of communicative acts).** It tells us nothing about the *content* of such acts; *nothing about what distinguishes one speaker meaning from another* **(beyond, perhaps, their illocutionary force).** In virtue of what does a speaker mean by 'Armadillos are dangerous' that armadillos are dangerous and not, say, that turkeys gobble? Grice answers that the speaker intended to convey the former belief not the latter. But in virtue of what was it *that* belief that he intended to convey? What makes it the case that the content of the belief he intended to convey was *armadillos are dangerous* not *turkeys gobble*? The Griceans provided no answer.

The failure to answer this question is a serious weakness of the Gricean programme. How is the question to be answered? Our earlier discussion of the language of thought (7.2) suggests that the content of thought, and hence speaker meaning, is to be explained by appeal to the conventions of a public language. But how can we combine such an explanation with our present acceptance of the Gricean view that speaker meaning is prior to conventional meaning? We do seem to be caught in the circle that threatened earlier (7.3).

7.5 Avoiding the circle

The apparent circle is generated as follows. Consider some utterance. What the speaker means by the token he utters is determined by the content of the thought that causally underlies it (7.4). That content is identified with the meaning of the sentence involved in the thought. Our discussion suggests that this meaning will be determined by the conventions of a public language, for the language of thought is largely the natural language of the speaker (7.2). Yet, according to the Gricean view we accept, the conventional meaning of a sentence in a public language is to be explained in terms of regularities in speaker meanings. That conventional meaning must depend in some way on what people have commonly meant by words of the physical type exemplified in the sentence; and on what they have commonly meant by sentences of that structure (7.4). We have illustrated this dependence, in effect, in our theory of the introduction of names (4.1, 4.3) and natural kind terms (5.2).

In sum, we seem caught in the following circle: (a) speaker meaning is explained by thought content; (b) that content is explained by the meaning of the thought sentence; (c) that meaning is explained by conventional meaning; and (d) conventional meaning is explained by speaker meaning.

To break out of this circle, we need to examine (c) closely. The suggestion that the meaning of a thought sentence is to be explained by conventional meaning makes the thought content dependent on convention. This is completely at odds with the Gricean insistence on the priority of speaker meaning.

It is only in one respect that a thought seems to have its content in virtue of conventions. This respect arises from our account of the social and collective nature of referential mechanisms for the "basic" terms covered by causal theories of reference: ones like names and natural kind terms that depend for their reference on groundings. With such terms, people borrow their reference from others; there is a division of linguistic labour (3.5, 4.1, 5.2). Someone of our century can use 'Socrates' to think about a certain ancient philosopher only by being plugged into a causal network grounded in Socrates. This network was established and maintained by the convention of using a certain sound type and a certain inscription type to refer to the philosopher. Such uses participate in the convention. The meaning of any thought token of 'Socrates' that arises out of that network is thus partly explained in terms of the convention. Similarly, most of us have thoughts about protons in virtue of being linked to them by the network for 'proton', a network established by the conventional linguistic practices of physicists.

The solution to our problem with these basic terms is indicated by the qualifications that must accompany such accounts of the dependence of thought content on convention. *Some* people *once* used 'Socrates' to think about the philosopher without depending on the convention: the people who named him. Similarly, 'proton'. Furthermore, all those involved in *subsequent* groundings of a term have thoughts that are, to that extent, dependent for their content not on convention but on direct confrontation with the appropriate object(s) (4.3, 5.2). Indeed, it is the regularities of speaker meaning arising out of these convention-independent thoughts that establish the convention; it is in this way that speaker meaning is prior to conventional meaning.

Whenever the speaker meaning of a basic term arises from a thought that regrounds a term in its referent, that meaning is not entirely dependent on convention. Generally, insofar as a speaker borrows a reference, her meaning is to be largely explained by the convention; insofar as she is grounding a term, her meaning is not to be so explained.

That is how we break out of the circle with the basic terms. There is no circle at all with all other aspects of the content of thought. For the other aspects are dependent not on convention but on the conceptual role of thoughts: on their function or role in the cognitive processes of the thinker.

Consider, first, the syntactic structure of a thought. In virtue of what does it have the structure of a predication, a quantification, or whatever? Entirely in virtue of its conceptual role. Briefly, this role is explained in terms of the thought's possible inferential interactions with other thoughts and ultimately with sensory input and behavioural output. Thus, the thoughts 'Reagan is wrinkled' and 'Thatcher is tough' share a syntactic structure in virtue of a similarity in their roles in our cognitive lives. Similarly, 'All politicians are rich' and 'All police are corrupt', which share a different structure and role.

It is difficult to say more about what determines the syntax of thought and we shall not attempt to. The main point is that it is not determined by the conventions of language. Indeed it is the regular use of a certain spoken form to express thoughts with a certain syntactic structure that leads to that form being the conventional one for that structure.

These remarks on structure supply our answer to a question raised at the end of section 6.4: "In virtue of what does a particular sentence have whatever structure it has?" The conventional structure depends on regularities in speaker structure; speaker structure depends on conceptual role.

Consider, second, non-basic terms like 'paediatrician', 'bachelor', and 'hunter'. Description theories seem appropriate for them (5.4). Their meaning in thought is determined jointly by their reference-determining association in thought with other terms, and by basic terms on which they ultimately depend. Their meaning in thought in turn determines what speakers mean by the terms in utterances. Regularities in those speaker meanings then yield conventional meanings. Since the association with other terms in thought is a matter of conceptual role not convention, the only conventional aspect to the meaning of non-basic terms in thought is what they inherit from the basic terms.

Third, conceptual role contributes even to the meaning of a basic term in thought. A term has to function as a name to have the meaning of a name, whatever its causal origins in groundings and reference borrowings. Similarly, a natural kind term has to play the role of a general or mass term. More strikingly, our retreat from pure-causal to descriptive-causal theories of these terms requires that they be associated with descriptions in groundings (4.4, 5.3). These associations are again matters of conceptual role.

** Fourth, such aspects of illocutionary force as enter into the meaning of a thought are explained, in the first instance at least, by conceptual role. What gives a thought the force of a question, statement, threat, or promise, we suppose, is its interactions with various beliefs, desires, intentions, and the like (2.3). The regular use of a certain spoken form to express a certain illocutionary force may lead to that form being the conventional one for that force.**

In our rejection of description theories and adoption of causal theories of reference, we have enthusiastically adopted Putnam's slogan, "Meanings just ain't in the head" (3.5, 5.1). Like all slogans, this one can mislead. It is aimed at the view, derived from description theories, that meanings are determined *entirely* by what is in the head. The point of the slogan is to emphasize that extra-cranial links to reality are also important. However, the slogan should not mislead one into supposing that no aspect of meaning is determined by what is in the head. We have just seen some that are.

We shall now fill out this solution to the apparent circle with some speculations about the origins of language. These speculations will bring out the way conventions *facilitate* thought. This is a very different matter from the one we have been examining: conventions *explaining the content* of thought.

7.6 The origins of language

We had thoughts before we were able to say anything, and before we learned any linguistic conventions. This is true of us as a species, and of us all individually. The higher animals can think but probably not talk. We suppose that these preconventional thoughts – primeval, babyish, or non-human – are very primitive, so primitive as to be unlike the thoughts of language-using adults. These early thoughts preceded the learning of conventions, but we need not suppose that they are innate. Presumably we have innate dispositions to respond in different ways to different stimuli. These predispositions, together with the stimuli we receive, lead us and our biological kin to represent the world in thought. It is because of the causal relations amongst these representations, and between the representations and the world, that the representations refer as they do. Though these early thoughts are primitive, we need not suppose that they are structureless; presumably they have crude structures.

Mental representations of the world come with theorizing about it. We feel a pressing need to understand our environment in order to manipulate and control it. This drive led to our early ancestors, in time, to express a primitive thought or two. They grunted or gestured, *meaning something by* such actions. There was speaker meaning without conventional meaning. Over time the grunts and gestures caught on: linguistic conventions were born. As a result of this trail blazing it is much easier for others to have those primitive thoughts, for they can learn to have them from the conventional ways of expressing them. Further, they have available an easy way of representing the world, a way based on those conventional gestures and grunts. They borrow their capacity to think about things from those who created the conventions. With primitive thought made easy, the drive to understand leads to more complicated thoughts, hence more complicated speaker meanings, hence more complicated conventions. If this sketch is right we have, as individuals and as a species, engaged in a prodigious feat of lifting ourselves up by our own semantic bootstraps.

The picture is of a language of thought expanding with the introduction into it of a public language. The language is public in having a conventional form, the regular association of sounds with speaker meanings. Feedback goes both ways. No conventions can be established without the existence of the appropriate speaker meanings. But the existence of conventions facilitates speaker meaning. And conventions introduce into the language of thought mental representations that are causally based on, and have the same meaning as, the sounds that figure in the conventions. The language of thought incorporates more and more of the public language, but remains a little ahead of it. We still have the capacity to think beyond the conventional established public language, as is shown by our ability to express new thoughts in new words. We can now think thoughts which a century ago were unthinkable.

We suppose that the development in humanoid society of complex and rich public language was very slow. In contrast its development in a contemporary child is very quick. This is to be expected, for the child gets the benefits of past struggles. The stimuli he receives include many linguistic ones: sentences conventionally related to thoughts that are complex in both structure and content. These stimuli make it much easier to have these complicated thoughts.

We could state the primacy of speaker meaning as follows. Speaker meanings create the conventional written and spoken forms of the language. But it is because we have learned those conventions that we are able to have the rich variety of thoughts, and hence produce the rich variety of speaker meanings, that we do. The *creation* of a convention requires some people to have thoughts the contents of which are not fully dependent on conventions. Once created each convention encourages other people to have new thoughts. Often the contents of many of those thoughts are to be explained partly in terms of that convention. Thought contents explain the conventions that explain *other* thought contents. There is no circle in the explanation.

Suggested reading

7.1

For an overview of the relations between thought meaning, meaning in language, and pragmatics – an overview we partly agree with – see Harman 1968, "Three levels of meaning", reprinted in Steinberg and Jacobovits 1971.

7.2

See Harman 1973, *Thought*, particularly pp. 54–9, 84–92, Harman 1975, "Language, thought, and communication", and Fodor 1975, *The Language of Thought*, particularly pp. 27–33, for arguments that thoughts are linguistic in character. Note that Harman thinks as do we, that the language of thought is mostly the public language of the thinker. Fodor argues against this view. Fodor's arguments are discussed sympathetically in Sterelny 1983b, "Mental representation: what language is brainese".

Block 1981, *Readings in Philosophy of Psychology, Volume 2*, Part One, "Mental representation", is a useful collection of readings on the topic. It has a helpful introduction.

** For powerful critiques of the view that thoughts could be images, see Pylyshyn 1973, "What the mind's eye tells the mind's brain", and Fodor 1975, chapter 4. See also Block 1981, Part Two, "Imagery".**

7.4

Grice first put forward his theory in "Meaning" (1957), reprinted in Steinberg and Jacobovits 1971, and in Rosenberg and Travis 1971. **His later works are much more difficult: "Utterer's meaning, sentence meaning, and word meaning" (1968), reprinted in Searle 1971; "Utterer's meaning and intentions" (1969).** For a short, readable, development of Grice's ideas, see Armstrong 1971, "Meaning and communication". For longer developments, see Bennett 1976, *Linguistic Behaviour*, **and Schiffer 1972, *Meaning*.**

For an argument that speaker meaning is not prior to conventional meaning, see Millikan 1984, *Language, Thought and other Biological Categories*, chapter 3.

Any attempt to explain conventional meaning must consider David Lewis' famous work, *Convention: A Philosophical Study* (1969). See also his follow-up essay, "Languages and language" (1975) in Gunderson 1975, reprinted in Lewis 1983. ("Languages, language, and grammar" in Harman 1974 is made up of short excerpts from both.)

7.5–7.6

The view of meaning sketched in the text is a version of the "two-factor" theory: meaning is determined partly by the links between mind and world, and partly by the structure and functioning of the mind. A theory of this sort is developed and defended in Field 1978, "Mental representation", reprinted in Block 1981; Lycan 1981b, "Toward a homuncular theory of believing"; McGinn 1982, "The structure of content" in Woodfield 1982, *Thought and Object*. Such theories are defended in Sterelny 1984, review of Woodfield 1982. They are criticized in Burge 1979, "Individualism and the mental", and in Pettit and McDowell 1986, *Subject, Thought and Content*. Block (in press), "Advertisement for a semantics for psychology", is a nice overview and defence of two-factor theories.

** Causal theories of thought about an object, like that in the text, are rejected in a difficult book, Evans 1982, *The Varieties of Reference*. He defends "Russell's Principle", according to which thought about an object requires discriminating knowledge of the object. This view is criticized in Devitt 1985, a critical notice of the book.**

8

Linguistic competence

8.1 Introduction

In the previous chapter we have related language to beliefs, desires and other thoughts. Another mental state that is relevant to language is *linguistic competence*. This is the state that enables a native speaker to use her language successfully. We have already said something about competence (1.2, 2.6, 3.1, 3.2, 4.1, 5.1, 5.2). This chapter will say a lot more, particularly about Noam Chomsky's view of competence.

Chomsky began the movement in linguistics known as transformational generative grammar. Our discussion of syntactic structure was largely devoted to this movement (chapter 6). However, we pointed out that transformational grammar was not offered primarily as a theory of the syntactic properties of linguistic symbols, but as a theory of linguistic competence, a property of people (6.1). In fact, the transformational grammarians run the two sorts of theory together, as we shall argue in the next section.

This conflation of syntax and competence is just one of the puzzles about transformational grammar. Here are some others which we shall also discuss.

1   Why suppose that a grammar explains competence at all? The transformational grammarians think that the grammar is "internalized" by the native speaker and is thus "psychologically real". But why suppose that (8.6)?
2   The grammarian's most common expression of their views suggest that a grammar is psychologically real in a special way. They identify competence with knowledge of the rules of grammar: each truth about English, hard won by the grammarian, is said to be "tacitly" known by English speakers already (8.3-8.5).
3   Further, some rules - those of "universal grammar", allegedly common to all natural languages - are said to be innately known (8.9). Why suppose that speakers know any more about grammar than the little they learn at school?

4 Finally, the grammarians attach great importance to, and have surprising confidence in, the grammatical intuitions of native speakers (8.5).

As a result of such puzzles as these, controversy has raged at the very foundations of transformational grammar on the issues, *What does a Grammar Explain?* and *What is a Grammar About?* This controversy has led to a considerable literature but little of this has centred on what we see as the major puzzle: the failure to distinguish sharply between the linguistic competence of speakers and the syntactic structure of linguistic symbols. We shall now consider this puzzle.

8.2 The conflation of syntax and linguistic competence

In chapter 6 we presented a theory of sentence structure that derives from Chomsky. We saw a transformational grammar as giving a syntactic description of all the possible sentences of a language. Chomsky agrees. Thus, in the opening pages of *Syntactic Structures*, the work which began transformational grammar, we find:

> The fundamental aim in the linguistic analysis of a language L is to separate the *grammatical* sequences which are sentences of L from the *ungrammatical* sequences which are not sentences of L and to study the structure of the grammatical sequences. (1957: 13)

The concern is with sentences, *a human product*.

However, often in the same breath, Chomsky says something very different: the concern is with linguistic competence, *a characteristic of the human mind*. Thus, in another classical work, *Aspects of the Theory of Syntax*, after some remarks like the above, Chomsky says:

> The problem for the linguist . . . is to determine . . . the underlying system of rules that has been mastered by the speaker–hearer . . . Hence, in a technical sense, linguistic theory is mentalistic, since it is concerned with discovering a mental reality underlying actual behaviour. (1965: 4).

There are very many such claims in the works of the transformational grammarians. For them, a grammar is not just a description of the structure of sentences; even more it is an account of the speaker's linguistic competence: the system of rules that he has "internalized". A grammar is part of psychology.

The conflation of a theory of syntax with a theory of competence did not start with Chomsky. Indeed, it seems to have a long history (see, for example, Saussure 1966: 77, 90). Nevertheless, the conflation is bewildering. To bring this out, let us start with some further explanation of the distinction between these two sorts of theory.

To help to make this distinction sharp we shall set aside private symbols, the ones that occur in the language of thought (7.2–7.3). We shall attend only to the public symbols, ones written, spoken and so on. However, the distinction between syntax and competence applies equally in the private realm.

Linguistic competence is a mental state of a person, posited to explain his linguistic behaviour; it plays a key role in *the production of* that behaviour. Linguistic symbols are the result of that behaviour; they are *the products of* that behaviour. They are datable placeable parts of the physical world: sounds in the air, marks on the page, and so on. They are not mental entities at all. A theory of a part of the production of linguistic symbols is not a theory of the products, the symbols themselves. Of course, given the causal relation between competence and symbol, we can expect a theory of the one to bear on a theory of the other. But that does not make the two theories identical.

In part II, we were interested in the properties of symbols that make them good for certain purposes. What is it about them that leads people to produce and respond to them as they do? In brief, we were interested in meaning (1.2). Syntactic structure is an important part of meaning. We discovered that properties like being a name, being a verb phrase and being passive are part of the explanation of grammaticality. Analogously, we might be interested in what makes a certain movement of a ball a good tennis shot. The answer would be in terms of such properties as speed, direction and height. Or we might be interested in what makes a certain chess move good. The answer would be in terms of the myriad possible game continuations; perhaps, in each of these the move gives white an advantage and no other move guarantees this. In all of thse cases we are concerned with objects or events in the physical world "outside the head".

However, in each case we might have another concern which is very much with something "inside the head" (or, at least, "inside the body"). What is the explanation of the behaviour – certain movements of hand and arm, perhaps – producing good sentences, tennis shots or chess moves? To answer this, we need a psychological (perhaps, physiological) theory, a theory of competence; we need a theory that explains, for example, how white knew that a particular chess move was good. Such a theory is different from a theory of the objects produced by the behavioural output of a competence: different from a theory of linguistic symbols, tennis shots or chess moves.

In sum, linguistic competence, together with various other aspects of the speaker's psychology, produces linguistic behaviour. That behaviour, together with the external environment, produces linguistic symbols. A theory of symbols is not a theory of competence.

To distinguish the theory of symbols from psychology is not to make it mysterious. We do think that linguistics, as the theory of symbols, has a certain autonomy from other theories, including psychology. However, given our physicalism (1.3), we must see this autonomy as only relative: in some sense, linguistics must ultimately be explained in physical terms. But this requirement does not remove the autonomy of linguistics any more than it removes that of, say, biology or economics.

Ideally, we would show how linguistics was dependent on physics, thus removing all mystery. That is too much to expect at this time. Meanwhile there is no reason to be particularly suspicious of the relative autonomy of linguistics.

Linguistics is a social science. Like all social sciences, it seems to be immediately dependent on psychological facts and facts about the natural environment. The nature of this sort of dependency is complex and hard to describe. Yet each social science proceeds largely undisturbed by the lack of a complete description. And so it should.

Consider some examples. What makes a physical object a pawn or a dollar? What makes a physical event a vote or unlawful? Nothing intrinsic to the objects and events in question; rather, it is the psychological states, within certain environments, of people involved with those objects and events. Exactly what states, what involvement, and what environment, is hard to say. Yet people quite properly feel free to theorize about chess, money, elections and the law. Similarly, we should feel free to theorize about linguistic objects and events.

Our theorizing about linguistic objects has, in fact, been very much concerned to explain their properties in terms of psychological states and relations to the environment. The zenith of this concern was in the last chapter. Whilst respecting the relative autonomy of linguistics, we have sought to explain it in other terms.

Distinguish the theory of symbols from the theory of competence. Which is linguistics? This might be interpreted as a boring verbal question about what we should call 'linguistics'. We have applied that name to the theory of symbols. The transformational grammarians apply it to both theories – the conflation – but *primarily* to the theory of competence. However, there is an interesting and important way of interpreting the question. Is the work offered under the name 'linguistics' true, or approximtely so, of symbols or of competence? We have already assessed the work of the transformational grammarians as a contribution to the theory of symbols (chapter 6). In this chapter, we shall be assessing it as a contribution to the theory of competence. From this perspective, a transformational theory can be true only if the grammar it describes has been internalized by speakers.

We think that linguistic theories are *not* mostly about competence. By taking their theories to be about competence instead of symbols, the grammarians turn possibly true theories into almost certainly false ones.

In emphasizing the distinction between competence and symbol, we have made another one which is also important: that between behaviour and symbol. In the next chapter we shall tackle doubts about the explanatory role of truth, doubts which reflect upon our whole semantic programme. We think that these doubts stem largely from confusing linguistic symbols with the behaviour that produces them.

8.3 Following a rule

We have pointed out that the transformational grammarians usually write as if they had a surprising view of *how* the grammar is built into speakers: the speakers are alleged to *know* "tacitly" the rules of the grammar (8.1). We think that this view is quite mistaken. To show this we need to consider what is involved in following a rule.

Suppose that R is a rule for addition. So R is a mechanical procedure guaranteeing the right answer to problems of addition; it is an algorithm. Consider, now, some object that is an effective adder. We might describe it in any of the following ways:

(a)   It behaves as if it follows R
(b)   It (actually) follows R
(c)   It knows that R is an algorithm for addition and applies it.

The nub of our criticism of the transformational grammarians is this. *At most*, there is evidence that speakers follow the rules of a grammar in sense (b), while the grammarians' theory of competence – in its most common expression – requires that we follow those rules in sense (c). This criticism will take a good deal of expansion.

Many problems have no algorithm for their solution. Thus, there are no mechanical procedures for discovering the laws of nature or for winning at chess. But where we do have one algorithm, we normally have several. For example, there are many different ways of adding, any one of which could be R. We (roughly) illustrate three radically different ones, each dealing with the problem of adding 27 and 8.

(i) Take an empty box. Count 27 marbles, putting each one in the box. Count 8 marbles, putting each one in the box. Count all the marbles in the box yielding an answer of 35.

(ii) Using the decimal notation, represesent 27 by '27' and 8 by '8'. Apply the simple addition rules (one for each pair of single-digit numerals) to the units '7' and '8' to yield '15'. Store '5' in the units and insert '1' in the tens. Apply the simple rules to '1' and '2' to yield '3' in the tens. Combine the '3' with the stored '5' yielding an answer of '35'.

(iii) We can use the binary notation, which has only two basic symbols, '0' and '1', to represent all numbers. The right-hand column is the units; the next to the left is the twos; the next the fours; the next the eights; and so on. A '0' in, say, the eights column means include no 8 to get the number; a '1' means include one 8. We thus represent 27 by '11011' and 8 by '1000'. Apply the simple addition rules to the units '1' and '0' to yield '1'. Store this in the units. Apply the simple rules to the twos to yield '1'. Store this in the twos. And so on through the fours, eights, sixteens and thirty-twos, yielding an answer of '100011'.

Children typically learn to add by an algorithm like (i). Adults typically add by one like (ii). Computers and calculators typically add by one like (iii).

If we were to build a machine, we could make it add by any one of many algorithms. The result of each addition will be the same whichever we choose, but the route to the result will differ from algorithm to algorithm. Now, if R is built into the machine then obviously description (b) will be correct. Even if R is not built in, description (a) may be correct: there may be little or no difference at the level of behaviour between machines using a range of algorithms. But our main point is that description (b) can be correct and yet description (c) be incorrect: a machine can follow R without *knowing that* R is an algorithm for addition. Indeed, if the machine is a pocket calculator, it will certainly *not* know this because it does not *know that* anything. It follows R simply in virtue of its construction.

This denial of knowledge needs clarification, for 'know' is ordinarily used so loosely and widely. Consider the following:

Ralph knows Don Bradman
Ralph knows who Little Caesar is
Ralph knows how to add up by R
Ralph knows rule R for addition
Ralph knows that R is an algorithm for addition.

These sentences illustrate quite different uses of the verb 'know'. We are particularly concerned with the difference between the last three: *knowing-how*, *knowing-a-rule* and *knowing-that*. Knowing-how is in the same family as skills, abilities and capacities. It need hardly be cognitive at all. In contrast, knowing-that is essentially cognitive: it requires belief and mental representation (7.1–7.2); it is "propositional" knowledge. We know how to swim or ride a bicycle but that knowledge does not primarily consist of mental representations; it does not require that we represent to ourselves the complicated behaviour that these abilities involve (even the dimmest fish can swim). When we ride a bicycle, we *just do it*, we don't even think about it. The required processes are built into us by learning, but they are not represented. This is even true of some "intellectual" tasks. Though Ralph *may* know how to add up by R because he knows that R is an algorithm for addition and can apply it – description (c), he is more likely to have the knowledge-how simply on the strength of description (b) being true of him. It is more likely that he follows R in adding without representing it to himself. And if he does have propositional knowledge of R, that is additional to what is required for him to add by R.

What is required for Ralph to know-the-rule R for addition? We are inclined to think that Ralph must know *that* R is a rule for addition. However, the answer to the question is not obvious. Perhaps it is sufficient for his knowing the rule that he knows *how* to add by R. What does seem obvious is that knowing-a-rule is either a matter of knowing-that *or* of knowing-how.

Consider again the pocket calculator. Suppose it is built to follow R. Then its situation is analogous to the more likely situation with Ralph. In that situation, Ralph knows how to add by R. Does the calculator know this too? We sense a strain in ascribing any sort of knowledge to a calculator. But what we are insisting on is that it does not have propositional knowledge of R. In the usual situation, not even Ralph has that knowledge, though he at least has the conceptual capacity to have it. We can be certain that the calculator does not have it because the calculator entirely lacks the capacity.

Finally, consider the cartoon, figure 8.1. The kingfisher catches fish by diving into water. It does not dive vertically, nor does it pursue fish underwater. So, in diving, it must make suitable allowance for the refraction of light: the light refracts as it leaves water for the less dense medium of air. The point of the cartoon is that it would be absurd to suggest that the kingfisher does this as follows: it knows that μ for water-to-air refraction is such and such; it knows the angle ϕ is so and so; it knows that $\mu = \sin\phi/\sin\theta$; it uses this information to calculate the angle θ. The kingfisher has none of this propositional knowledge. There seems less strain in ascribing knowledge-how to the bird than to the calculator; perhaps it does know how to calculate the position of the fish. Whether or not it does, it is clear that its capacity to calculate the position is simply built into it, just as R can be built into a calculator.

In sum, a description of type (b) can be true of a machine, an animal or a human without entailing that the object has the knowledge-that required by a description of type (c). Even if it seems appropriate to ascribe knowledge to the object, this should not lead readily to the view that the object has knowledge-

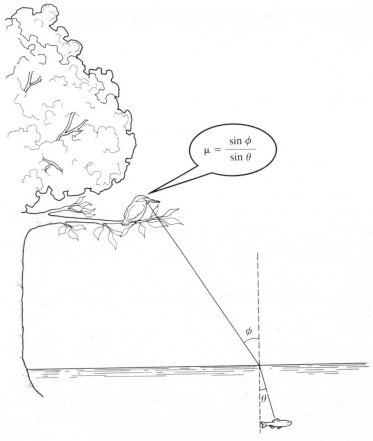

Figure 8.1 (Boden 1984: 153)

that. For the knowledge might be mere knowledge-how, the ascription of which can be licensed by a description of type (b) alone (at least to things not too remote from humans).

We shall now apply this discussion to the transformational linguists' claim that a grammar is a theory of competence.

8.4 The propositional assumption about linguistic competence

A grammar is a set of rules. The set for any natural language is still largely undiscovered. Let us suppose, optimistically, that linguists have discovered some members of the set for English and that future linguists will complete the job. The result will be G, the grammar for English. Our discussion suggests three ways we might describe a competent English speaker's relation to G:

(a)   She behaves as if she follows G
(b)   She (actually) follows G
(c)   She knows that G is the grammar for English and applies it.

For (b) or (c) to be true, the speaker has to have internalized G: it has to have become psychologically real. Our discussion has shown that, though (b) might be true because (c) is, (b) can be true without (c) being so: G may be built into the speaker in the way R may be built into the calculator. In the next section, we shall cast doubt on the view that even (b) is true. However, for the sake of argument, let us suppose in this section that it is true: G is internalized. Our first point is that (c) is false: the internalization is not a case of the speaker's having propositional knowledge. The view that it is we shall call *the propositional assumption* about competence.

The literature provides no good reason for supposing that (c) is true. The supposition is as implausible as the similar ones about Ralph, the calculator, and the kingfisher.

Stephen Stich (1971, 1978b) brings out this implausibility nicely by contrasting the speaker's relation to G with unproblematic cases of propositional knowledge. If a person knows that *p*, we expect him to be aware of *p*, or at least to be able to become aware of it when given a suitable prompt; and we expect him to understand expressions of *p*. The ordinary speaker quite clearly lacks this awareness and understanding for most of G. If a person knows that *p*, his knowledge should join up with other beliefs to generate more beliefs. If a speaker has knowledge of G, it is clearly not inferentially integrated in this way. Consider an example. Without tuition, a speaker is unlikely to have the conceptual resources to understand even the relatively simple claim that '*NP* → *Det* + *Adj* + *N*' is a rule of English. If she knows that this is a rule, her knowledge is largely inferentially isolated from her other beliefs.

The plausible thing to say is that English speakers have only a little propositional knowledge of G, linguists *may* have quite a lot, but that *nobody* now has full propositional knowledge of it.

Do the transformational grammarians believe the propositional assumption? The question has been aired at great length and yet, amazingly enough, no clear answer has emerged. They do not explicitly assert anything like (c). However, they certainly believe that the speaker's relation to G is appropriately called knowledge (or something close).

Chomsky's favourite way of describing this knowlege is not helpful: he says that the speaker *tacitly knows the rules or principles* of her language. Unfortunately, the import of "knows the rules or principles" is not crystal clear. We are inclined to think it requires knowledge-that, but there is room for doubt about this (8.3). The addition of the word 'tacitly' may seem to settle the question. It is absurd to say that a swimmer or bicycle rider has tacit knowledge of the rules or principles of their activities. It is natural to think of a person's tacit knowledge as propositions that he has not entertained but which he would acknowledge in suitable circumstances; for example, Ron tacitly knows that rabbits don't lay eggs, even though the thought has never crossed his mind, because he would deny that they laid eggs if the question were ever to arise. However, we cannot interpret Chomsky as believing the propositional assumption on the strength of this because he knows better than anyone that no matter how the question of G arose, the speaker would not acknowledge the rules. Further, on occasions Chomsky explicitly denies that the speaker's knowledge is knowledge-that (1969a: 86–7; 1969b: 153–4).

The mystery deepens because the grammarians so often write as if the speaker did have propositional knowledge of G and its consequences. Thus Chomsky describes the knowledge as a "system of beliefs" (1969a: 60–1; see also 1980: 225); as "a mental representation of a grammar" (1975: 304). Learning a language is seen as learning a theory:

> It seems plain that language acquisition is based on the child's discovery of what from a formal point of view is a deep and abstract theory – a generative grammar of his language. (Chomsky 1965: 58).

Fodor describes Chomsky's view as propositional (Fodor 1983: 4–10); it is the view that "your linguistic capacities . . . are . . . explained by reference to the *content of your beliefs*" (p. 7). Finally, if the knowledge is not propositional, it must surely be knowledge-how. And it is plausible to think, on the strength of description (b), that it *is* a particularly complicated example of knowledge-how. However, Chomsky denies that it is knowledge-how (1969a: 87) or, at least, that it is knowledge-how without an "intellectual component" (1975: 314–8).

We are left quite uncertain of the nature of the claim that the speaker has knowledge of G. It sometimes seems to be suggested that this knowledge is a third sort, neither knowledge-that nor knowledge-how (e.g. Chomsky 1969a: 87). If this were so, knowledge of G would be *sui generis* and badly in need of an explanation that is never given.

On any interpretation, the grammarians' view includes the implausible thesis that a speaker has a mental representation of G; she *thinks about* G. Gilbert Harman has raised a problem for this thesis (1967). The representation it requires must itself be in a language. What is it to understand that more basic language? If we suppose the more basic language is the same as the original language then we are caught in a vicious circle. If we suppose that it is some other language ("Mentalese" perhaps; 7.3), then its grammar also has to be represented. This requires a still more basic language. And so on. The only way to avoid a vicious circle or an infinite regress is to allow that at least one language is understood directly, without representing its grammar. Why not then allow this of the original language, the one spoken?

The grammarians, particularly Fodor (1975; see also Chomsky 1969a: 87–9; 1969b: 155–6), have some sort of answer to this question. They think that there are good reasons for supposing that in order to *learn* a language you have to understand another one already. However, we can understand that one directly, without representing its grammar, because it is not learned; it is *innate*. We have mentioned this thesis of an innate Mentalese before (7.3) and will consider it in more detail later (8.9–8.10). Meanwhile, we shall see its bearing on the propositional assumption.

8.5 Innate Mentalese and the propositional assumption

The thesis that there is an innate Mentalese finds a plausible setting within a very interesting recent development. This development sees the area of the mind that employs G, the sentence-parsing area, as *modular*. Jerry Fodor is the main exponent of this view (1983), but Chomsky also has a good word for it (1980: 40–7).

Fodor believes that the sentence-parser is one of many modular "input systems" in the mind. His belief in these systems gives him a tripartite division of the cognitive mechanisms. At the skin there are "transducers" the familiar sense organs – which record the stimuli the world provides and send on messages in neural code. Next come the modular input systems. The raw data from the transducers are passed on to these systems for analysis. Finally, there is the central processor. The input systems pass on the results of their analysis to the central processor. What goes on in that processor is what we would ordinarily think of as thinking. Input systems are highly specialized: for example, there is not just one for vision, but one for colour, one for shape, one for face-recognition, and so on. And, of course, there is one for sentence-parsing. The view that there are these modular input systems between peripheral transducers and central processing is controversial. The more popular view is bipartite: there are no sharp boundaries to be drawn once we get inside the transducers; rather, perception and thinking merge into each other.

What is it for a system to be "modular"? Some of the important properties of a modular system are as follows. It is "*domain specific*", specializing in a particular sort of stimulus; for example, sentences or faces. It is "*innately specified*"; its structure is not for the most part "formed by some sort of learning process". It is "*hardwired*", "associated with specific, localized, and elaborately structured neural systems". It is "*autonomous*": it does not share resources of memory, attention, etc., with other cognitive systems (pp. 36–7). It is "*mandatory*": there is no decision to operate; it is automatic, rather like a reflex (pp. 52–3).

So, according to this recent development, G is represented in the innate Mentalese of a modular system with the specific function of parsing sentences. If so, then G is represented *in* the speaker. But far from vindicating the propositional assumption, this development undermines it. Though G is represented in the speaker, the representation is in the wrong place. Knowledge is a species of thought or propositional attitude. Our folk psychology places these attitudes firmly in what Fodor calls "the central processor". It is in virtue of what is going on *there* that a person stands in the required relation to the specified content (but see 8.7 on reference). So the grammarians' insistence on talking of *the speaker's* knowledge of G places G in the central processor. Yet it seemed obvious to many critics that it was not there. The modularity thesis entails that it is indeed not there. If that thesis is correct, it is the sentence-parsing system itself, if anything, which has "knowledge" of G. Mentalese, in which G is represented, is the language of that system not the language of *thought*.

Fodor emphasizes that "there is only *limited central access* to the mental representations that input systems compute" (p. 57). Central processing has access to the output of the systems, but little access to lower levels of analysis. Further, "input systems are *informationally encapsulated*" (p. 64); they have no access to information held elsewhere, in particular to that held by the central processor. In certain respects input systems are "insensitive to what the perceiver presumes or desires" (p. 68). If G is indeed represented in a system that is thus autonomous of the central system – of the system which, as Fodor says, performs such "processes as thought and problem-solving" (p. 103) – we have the best reason in the world for denying that the speaker thereby has any thoughts about G.

In sum, when the thesis that we have an innate Mentalese is combined with the modularity thesis, it does not support the propositional assumption about linguistic competence; rather, it undermines it.

The modularity thesis is highly speculative and controversial. Suppose that it is false. The case against the propositional assumption is not then as clear, but it still exists. For, even if there are not sets of modular input systems analysing the output of each sense organ, the sentence-parser has many of the properties of such systems. At least, it has if Chomsky is anywhere near right about it. For, he thinks of it as a relatively encapsulated "mental organ" inaccessible to our general cognitive capacities. The innate Mentalese is in a relatively autonomous system. So the argument will still go through.

Finally, the propositional assumption about competence is not only a mistake in itself, it encourages other mistakes. First, it facilitates the conflation of a theory of competence with a theory of symbols. For, according to that assumption, a theory of competence is a theory of the syntactical rules known by the speaker. And if the speaker *knows* that a certain rule applies to a linguistic symbol then, of course, it does apply; knowledge implies truth. So, once the speaker's knowledge had been described, there would be nothing further to say about linguistic symbols. Second, the assumption encourages an inflated view of the importance of the intuitions that speakers have about the properties of linguistic symbols. For, if speakers really do know the grammar, it is plausible to see these intuitions as products of that knowledge and hence certainly true. If, on the other hand, speakers do not have this knowledge, then the reliability of such intuitions becomes a much more open question.

8.6 The psychological reality of grammars

In the last two sections we assumed, for the sake of argument, that description (b) was true of the speaker; that she had internalized G, the grammar for English that linguists are on their way to discovering. We shall now examine this assumption. Are the grammatical rules that linguists are discovering psychologically real in each speaker? The transformational grammarians claim that they are. We have our doubts.

First, let us consider G's alleged role. G is thought to play the central role in linguistic *performance*. Along with such other factors as memory, attention and interest, it explains the production and understanding of linguistic symbols. Abstracting from these other factors, the explanation must, it seems, be along the following lines (but see Chomsky 1965, pp. 9, 139–40, where this seems to be denied). Our thoughts are semantic representations. We have a thought we wanted to encode. The Semantic Component maps the thought onto a deep structure. The Transformational Component maps the deep structure onto a surface structure. The Phonological Component enables you to sound it. You have expressed your thought. Decoding runs through the rules in the opposite direction.

Our first doubt is that it is hard to see how recently developed transformation theories *could* be psychologically real. Thus, in Trace Theory the deep structure plays no role in determining semantic representation. Hence, we presume, it plays no role in a theory of understanding. Nor is there any obvious place for it in a theory of production.

Set that doubt aside. Why should we suppose that we are entitled to claim anything stronger than description (a)? After all, grammars are like other algorithms. If there is one set of rules that generates the set of English sentences and assigns appropriate meaning-relevant structures to them, there will be many. Some of these grammars may be less simple and elegant than G but they are all methods for constructing sentences from words nonetheless. Similarly, marble counting is less simple and elegant than using the decimal notation, but it can still be an effective method of adding (8.3). Suppose G' is one of those alternative grammars. Given that G' has the same output as G, why suppose that it is G rather than G' that is psychologically real?

The evidence that transformational grammarians adduce provides little reason for thinking that it *is* G rather than G'. In the beginning, this evidence – for example, 1–6 in sections 6.2–6.3 – was almost entirely about linguistic symbols: about which strings of words are grammatical; about the ambiguity of certain sentences; about the statement forms and question forms; about the synonymy of sentences that are superficially different; about the difference between sentences that are superficially similar; and so on. This evidence is not the behavioural sort needed to throw light on what is going on in the head; on the processes by which the speaker understands and produces sentences. There seems no basis in this evidence for thinking that the speaker has internalized G rather than G'.

Of course, grammarians operate under constraints other than this evidence: they seek the simplest and most elegant grammar. So we can assume that G is preferable to G' on those grounds. But why is that a reason for thinking that G is psychologically real? Suppose that R is the simplest and most elegant algorithm for addition. On that basis alone we are not justified in ascribing R to any calculator that is an efficient adder. What is needed before ascribing R or G to an object is some evidence about its *design*, about how it achieves its effect of producing additions or sentences.

In principle, psycholinguists could provide the evidence we need: evidence about reaction times, the types of errors we make, the relative ease of understanding sentences, the order in which sentences are learned, and so on. Thus, suppose that according to G the active (e.g. 'Maggie kicks heads') is the basic form and the passive (e.g. 'Heads are kicked by Maggie') is the derived form, but that according to G' the reverse is the case. Now suppose that we discovered that actives are learned before passives; that they are easier to understand and remember; that fewer errors are made with them. Evidence of this kind would favour G over G' as an account of psychological reality. In practice, however, psycholinguistics has so far provided very little convincing evidence for the psychological reality of the details of the grammars linguists have produced.

Chomsky and his followers have a standard response to objections along these lines. The background to their response is the rejection of behaviourism.

We have seen how Chomsky improved on his predecessors in the handling of syntax. Where they were content to classify surface elements, he sought the underlying deep structure (6.3). He also improved on his predecessors in the handling of competence, for they were largely behaviourists. Behaviourists deny anything to the mind beyond dispositions to respond in certain ways to certain stimuli. For them the mind, linguistic competence included, is just a set of input/output functions. This reflects the crude empiricist dislike of things unseen; an unwillingness to posit theoretical entities that explain the observed phenomena. Chomsky, in contrast, is enthusiastically theoretical. He thinks that the only way to explain human behaviour is to ascribe complicated inner states *interacting with each other*, as well as with various stimuli, to produce our responses. In other words, he rejects behaviourism in favour of functionalism.

Consider beliefs and desires, for example. No particular desire is tied to a particular kind of input and output. Even if a person wants to get rich and sees a bag of money before her, she may not seize it. Her behaviour is conditional on her other beliefs and desires: she may believe that the money is counterfeit, or want to be honest as well as rich.

Chomsky is right to reject behaviourism. Indeed, its failure to explain linguistic behaviour is particularly vivid because of the *stimulus independence* of that behaviour, remarked on earlier (1.2). It is appropriate to posit theoretical entities underlying our linguistic behaviour even though such posits go beyond the evidence. For, the epistemic life is always risky. However, it does not follow that we should accept Chomsky's account of competence. His account is not the only alternative to behaviourism.

Against this background, the grammarians' standard response to the objections is not surprising. They point out that their claims about grammatical rules are typical scientific hypotheses based on *inference to the best explanation*, a form of inference that has no place in the methodology of behaviourism. We need some account of how we produce and understand English sentences. The best explanation of this is that we have built into us the very same rules that define English sentencehood. So we are entitled to infer that we do have those rules built in. The grammarians go on to draw attention to two aspects of this inference which it shares with *any* inference to the best explanation.

First, it is irrelevant to argue that the conclusion of an inference may be wrong. *Of course* the evidence does not prove the hypothesis conclusively: it is *underdetermined* by the evidence like any other scientific hypothesis. Perhaps other hypotheses would provide better explanations. But again that is true of any hypothesis and is therefore beside the point. Until other hypotheses are produced we are entitled to accept this one.

Second, when we accept a theoretical hypothesis we should interpret it *realistically*: it purports to describe an area of reality underlying our observations. The alternative view is instrumentalism: the view that an hypothesis is simply an instrument for predicting observations on the basis of past observations; it does not describe an underlying reality. Instrumentalism as a general doctrine is discredited, and it would be unjustified discrimination to apply it to linguistics in particular.

In sum, the grammarians conclude that they are entitled to believe that their grammatical rules really do describe the reality underling linguistic behaviour. That reality is psychological, the speaker's competence.

Chomsky offers a nice analogy (1980: 189–92). Suppose that physicists are unable to get any direct evidence about the inside of the sun. The best they can do is construct a theory of the inside that, if it were true, would explain the observed behaviour of the sun. Any such theory may be wrong of course, but they are entitled to believe the best one they can come up with.

We agree with these general observations. It is pointless to object that the conclusion of an inference to the best explanation might be wrong. And, certainly the conclusion should be construed realistically. However, we do not think that those general views yield the desired result in this particular case: they are insufficient to justify the view that G is psychologically real.

The key question is whether the inference to the psychological reality of G is *appropriate*. Nobody knows how to codify inference to the best explanation, but two conditions on appropriate inferences are obvious enough. The proposed explanation must be both good and better than its rivals. It is no canon of science to accept a bad explanation because others are worse, nor to draw explanations out of a hat when we have a range of good ones.

Is G – say a Trace Theoretic version of transformational grammar – a good explanation of competence? Surely we must be agnostic here. So little is known of the computational mechanisms of the mind that we have no idea whether G is a candidate for psychological explanation. Is G better than G´? Again, suspension of judgement is appropriate. What is the reason for preferring G to the many possible alternatives?

Indeed, we can strengthen these remarks for those parts of G allegedly discovered so far. Chomsky asks us to imagine that physicists had constructed a theory correctly predicting the sun's behaviour. If there was general agreement that this was a good theory and the best available, then its tentative endorsement would be appropriate. But transformational grammar is not yet in anything like that position: there has never been a stable consensus about even the rough details of the form and structure of a grammar. We certainly wouldn't attribute solar reality to a theory that was supported only by indirect evidence *and* changed every five years.

Let us exercise our imagination and contemplate a time when the linguistic community has reached a stable consensus on G. Given that psycholinguistic evidence has played so little role in the construction of G *to the present time*, let us suppose for a moment that it has played no role to that future time. So G is adequate only to all the *linguistic* evidence (like that in 6.2–6.3); and, of course, it will be manifestly more simple and elegant than its rivals. We would be impressed by G, but still dubious of its psychological reality. First, we would want evidence that G was a *candidate* for psychological implementation; that the transformational processes it implicated were within the computational ambit of the mind. Second, the very elegance and simplicity of G is rather more evidence *against*, than evidence for, it being the grammar our brain is built to use. If innateness claims are right, our brains are specifically adapted to a certain class of grammars. Stephen Jay Gould has used examples like the panda's thumb to show that adaptations are typically *not* maximally efficient engineering solutions to the problems they solve (1983: 19–31). For, adaptations are of preexisting structures and this constrains the solutions possible. Finally, as David Lewis has pointed out to us, the fact that G is maximally efficient and elegant from the grammarians' point of view does not entitle us to suppose it is optimal from the brain's point of view.

In sum, setting aside psycholinguistic evidence, we do not think that inference to the best explanation does warrant the conclusion that G is psychologically real.

Why do grammarians misapply inference to the best explanation and realism here? We think that their mistake arises from their conflation of the competence of speakers with the syntax of symbols. For, we think that inference to the best explanation does warrant acceptance of linguistic theory realistically construed (within certain limits). But only if it is taken as descriptive of the truth-conditionally relevant syntactic properties of linguistic symbols and not of the competence of speakers. That is how we took it in chapter 6. The grammar is real, but not necessarily *psychologically* real.

We are sceptical of the psychological reality of the grammar linguists are discovering. However, we are not suggesting that this grammar throws no light on that reality. People have the capacity to produce and understand any of an indefinite number of sentences; their capacity is "productive'" (1.2, 2.2). It is plausible to think that this is to be explained by their internalizing *something like* the grammar linguists are discovering. So some of the general features of G are likely to be psychologically real. Furthermore, psycholinguistic evidence is playing *some* role in the construction of G. In the long run, such evidence could be decisive. The problem is that, so far, its role in the choice of grammars has been relatively minor.

So, to some small extent, linguistics is about competence – an internally represented grammar – and is part of the explanation of behaviour. However, linguistics is not *primarily* about competence. For, given the way it actually proceeds, there is little reason to suppose that it casts much light on competence. Yet, it does cast light on the nature of symbols.

8.7 Philosophers on linguistic competence

We have been examining the transformational grammarians' view of linguistic competence. It is time to consider the view of philosophers. We shall lead into this with one further, and quite general, criticism of the grammarians' view.

We pointed out earlier that Chomsky and his followers overlook reference in their theory of meaning (6.4). They overlook it also in the theory of competence. The result is an impoverished view of competence. Even if the grammarians were right and English speakers had internalized G, the most that this could explain is the speakers' *syntactic* competence: their ability to produce grammatical sentences, and to understand such sentences so far as their syntax is concerned. But there is more to full linguistic competence than this: there are semantic aspects this misses. Take a banal example. It is part of the competence of English speakers to use 'lion' to refer to lions and 'tiger' to refer to tigers. A deviant speaker who calls tigers 'lions' is not, in that respect, a competent speaker of English. Nonetheless, he would have full syntactic competence: his deviant English and standard English are syntactically identical.

Chomsky is part of the structuralist tradition that treats a language as a "self-contained formal system" like chess (6.4). But a language is not like that: it represents situations in the world. And understanding it must involve getting its representational powers right. (We shall discuss structuralism in chapter 13.)

The point we are making here is related to the earlier one that we captured with Putnam's slogan: "meanings just ain't in the head" (3.5, 5.1, 7.5). Because meanings are not (fully) determined by what is in the head, having a grammar, or anything else, built into the head cannot be sufficient for understanding meanings.

Philosophers have had a lot to say about linguistic competence. Implicitly, at least, they have been concerned with competence in the full semantic sense, for they have attended to truth and reference. Yet, interestingly enough, they have typically made two mistakes that are parallel to the two major mistakes of the linguists. First, they conflate the theory of competence with the theory of symbols. Second, they write as if that competence consisted in propositional knowledge of the language.

The first mistake is certainly made by Michael Dummett. It is reflected in his slogan, "a theory of meaning is a theory of understanding" (1975: 99). In our discussion of Chomsky, we have distinguished sharply between explaining the syntactic properties of linguistic symbols and explaining the psychological properties of those that produce and understand those symbols (8.2). Just the same point applies when we are concerned not simply with the syntactic properties of symbols but with their full semantic properties (which include syntactic ones, of course).

Where the linguists seem to assume that competence in a language is tacit knowledge that a certain set of grammatical rules apply to the language, philosophers seem to assume that the competence is tacit knowledge of the truth conditions of each sentence: the speaker knows that the sentence is true if and only if certain circumstances hold. This is the second mistake. It seems also to be made by Dummett (e.g. 1976: 69–71), and is important in his argument against realism to be considered later (11.3–11.4). Despite the popularity of this semantic propositional assumption among philosophers, little attempt has been made to argue for it. We think it is as false as the linguists' assumption (8.4).

Harman has raised one objection to the philosophers' assumption (1975: 286), mate to his earlier objection to the linguists' assumption (8.4). The knowledge it attributes to the speaker requires that he have some way of representing to himself the conditions that would make sentences true. But what does competence in the representing language consist in? Either the same problem has reappeared or we are faced with an equal one.

There is a related objection (Devitt 1981a: 97–100). A person can have the required semantic propositional knowledge only if he has the semantic vocabulary of some language. But that portion of the vocabulary is isolatable from the rest of the language, just as is its biological or football vocabulary. A person could be competent in the remainder of a language – in its non-semantic part – without being competent in its semantic part or in the semantic part of any other language. So competence in the non-semantic part does not involve semantic propositional knowledge. So competence in the language as a whole does not either.

The linguists had an answer to Harman's objection that posited an innate Mentalese (8.4). We found the answer unsatisfactory (8.5). The philosophers have no such answer because full semantic competence in a language cannot all be in the head, as we have just pointed out, and so cannot be innate.

We shall now give our own view of linguistic competence.

8.8 Linguistic competence

We think that competence in a language does not consist in the speaker's semantic propositional knowledge. It is a set of skills or abilities, some of them grounded in the external world. It consists in the speaker being able to do things with a language, not in his having thoughts about it. Understanding a language no more involves having propositional knowledge of a semantic sort about the language than being able to ride a bicycle involves propositional knowledge of a mechanical sort about riding.

What then is competence? Our answer does not go very far. It brings together our part-II discussions of word competence, the discussion of conceptual role (7.5), and our recent remarks about syntactic competence (8.6).

Consider first an English speaker's abilities with basic terms, names and natural kind terms (4.1, 5.2). Take as an example her competence with 'cat'. It consists in her being appropriately linked to the network of causal chains for 'cat', a network involving other people's abilities as well as groundings and reference borrowings. To have this ability the speaker must be able to combine 'cat' appropriately with other words to form sentences, a matter of conceptual role. She must be able to have thoughts about cats which those sentences express. Furthermore, these thoughts must be grounded in cats. A Twin Earthian will not have the speaker's understanding, even if she is in other ways similar, if her ability with 'cat' is grounded in different animals. However, the speaker's ability does not require knowledge that 'cat' has any particular semantic or syntactic property.

The *qua*-problem forced us to move from a pure-causal to a descriptive-causal theory of terms like 'cat', thus requiring the association of descriptions for a grounding (5.3). This association of descriptions is another matter of conceptual role. This association may be in a modular input system (8.5). If it is not, then we accept that it amounts to knowledge (5.5). However, even if it does amount to knowledge, the knowledge is not essential for competence; as a result of reference borrowing many who have not grounded a term can be competent with it. Further, the knowledge is not semantic; it is knowledge of the grounding object, not knowledge of the semantic properties of the term being grounded.

Similar points are to be made about competence with non-basic terms, ones to which a description theory applies (5.4). If we can borrow their reference, then competence with them need involve no knowledge. If these terms cannot be borrowed, then knowledge may be involved (5.5). Competence with a term like 'bachelor' would consist in the conceptual role association of the appropriate reference-determining descriptions, as well as competence with each of those descriptions, of course. Thus competence with 'bachelor' presumably requires competence with 'adult', 'unmarried', 'male'. If this association is non-modular, then it is knowledge, but it is knowledge of bachelors not knowledge of the semantic properties of 'bachelor'.

Syntactic competence is the skill of matching sentences of the language with thoughts having appropriate structures. This is also a conceptual role matter. Though we do not accept the view that this competence consists in the speaker having internalized the grammar that linguists are discovering, we do think that something like that grammar must have been internalized. But this internalization is not a speaker's propositional knowledge of the grammar.

** Finally, competence in such pragmatic aspects of language as enter into meaning is similar to syntactic combination: the skill of matching sentences with thoughts having appropriate illocutionary forces.**

Putting all this together, full competence in the language requires causal links to the external world together with appropriate conceptual roles, including the internalization of something like a grammar.

** It is worth noting that competence in using a language can be mediated by skills that are not specifically linguistic. We have, in effect, alluded to this earlier in indicating the way that the context of a remark helps the audience to remove ambiguity (4.2). Consider now, for example, our success at detecting conversational implicatures (2.3). Effortlessly and accurately we determine that something is implied by an utterance in addition to what is said. To do this we must identify the speaker's intentions. That sort of task comes up also in umpteen non-linguistic contexts. There is no reason to suppose that the identification of intentions in the linguistic context involves any specifically linguistic skills. There is no reason to suppose that the mechanisms by which, say, a wife can recognise *threat* from the way her husband washes his hands differ from those that allow her to pick up what he conversationally implies. Part of the evidence on which her inferential machinery operates differs, that is all.**

8.9 Chomsky on innateness

Questions of innateness have arisen on several occasions. We have mentioned Chomsky's claim that there are grammatical rules common to all languages – "universal grammar" – which are innately known by speakers. This requires, of course, an innate language in which to represent those rules: innate Mentalese (7.3). Next, considering Harman's objection to the propositional assumption about competence, we mentioned the claim, made by Fodor at least, that the innate language can represent *all* the rules of any public language (8.4–8.5). Fodor goes even further: the innate language is rich enough to represent not merely grammatical rules but *anything* that a public language can represent (8.3). (Fodor describes himself rightly, and with characteristic seriousness, as a "mad-dog nativist".)

We shall focus our attention on Chomsky's very famous claims about innateness, claims that are thought by him and others to force a reassessment of the traditional debate between empiricist and rationalist over "innate ideas". Rationalists thought that many concepts were innate. Empiricists rejected this. (For more on the nature of this dispute, see section 8.10.) It is thought that Chomsky's claims about innateness strongly support the rationalist side. In considering these claims, it is helpful to distinguish three theses.

First, there is a *boring* thesis. This is the thesis that human beings are innately predisposed to learn languages; it is because of innate structures in our mind that, given linguistic data, almost every human learns a language. The thesis is boring because every informed person, even the crudest empiricist, should believe it and, so far as we know, does believe it. How else could one explain the fact that dogs, for example, cannot learn languages? One needs to go further to make an innateness claim interesting. Chomsky goes further.

Second, there is an *interesting* thesis. This is the thesis – strictly, two theses – that humans have an innate, richly structured, *language-specific*, learning device.

And this device determines that the grammar of any language that a human can learn conforms to the universal grammar. The thesis is interesting because it conflicts with the initially plausible view that the innate structures that make language learning possible are ones that make *all* learning possible; our *general* learning device selects a grammar from the linguistic data. The relation of this conflict to the traditional debate over innate ideas is controversial. We shall not venture an opinion. However, any contemporary empiricist, except possibly one of the crudest sort, can surely afford to remain neutral on the interesting thesis. Chomsky subscribes to that thesis, at least. This section will be mostly devoted to it.

Third, there is a *very exciting* thesis. This is the thesis, already mentioned, that the innate language-acquisition device consists in propositional knowledge of universal grammar. The thesis is very exciting because it goes against any empiricism, traditional or contemporary. It requires a commitment to innate ideas that no empiricist could allow. A great deal of the attention given to Chomsky's claims about innateness comes from construing them in this very exciting way.

We have already argued against the view that competence involves the speaker's syntactic propositional knowledge (8.3–8.5). There is even less to be said for the view that the speaker's innate capacity to acquire this competence – whether in a language-specific device or not – involves such knowledge.

Humans have an innate capacity to learn to swim. Most humans do learn. It is absurd, and quite gratuitous, to say that what they learn is propositional knowledge about swimming. It is even more absurd and gratuitous to say that the innate capacity is such knowledge. Why should we take a different view in considering language?

If there are good arguments for the view that the universal grammar is not simply built in but *represented*, then they are arguments for it being represented in a modular input system, or something similar. In which case, it is that system, if anything, that has the innate knowledge (8.5). And even then it would have to be knowledge without reference (8.7).

Does Chomsky hold the very exciting thesis? It is hard to be confident of an answer here as it was earlier to the analogous question about the propositional assumption (8.4). He frequently writes as if he held the thesis (e.g. 1965: 27, 58). And according to Fodor,

What Chomsky thinks is innate is primarily a certain *body of information*: the child is, so to speak, "born knowing" certain facts about universal constraints on possible human languages. (1983:4)

However, it seems that Chomsky is not concerned to distinguish the very exciting from the merely interesting thesis (1969b: 155–6; 1975: 319).

The interesting thesis has two parts. First, it requires that there be a specific "language-acquisition device". Second, it requires that this device constrains possible human languages to ones having certain characteristics; there are set of "linguistic universals" comprising a universal grammar. We shall consider these in turn.

Three considerations can be advanced in favour of there being a language-acquisition device. First, any evidence for the modularity of mind is evidence for the device. For, if the mind is partly constituted by a set of "domain specific", "innately specified" input systems between transducers and the central processors, then it is very plausible that the language-acquisition device is one of those systems, or the core of one of them – the sentence-parser. However, a problem for this consideration is that evidence for the modularity of the sentence-parser is Fodor's favourite (though not sole) evidence for the modularity of mind. Apart from that, the modularity thesis is highly controversial, as we pointed out (8.5).

Second, a consideration that Chomsky and Fodor return to repeatedly is the *poverty of stimulus* received by the language learner. It is claimed that the grammatical rules picked up by the child are abstract, subtle and unobvious. They would be extremely difficult for her to derive by simple induction from the limited data available to her. She must have a head start: the kinds of hypotheses about the language that she considers must be tightly constrained.

This thought can be made to look very plausible. For instance, a child must learn that the subject can be moved out of structures like

Egbert believed that who was a parricide?

to

Egbert believed whom to be a parricide?
Whom did Egbert believe to be a parricide?

Yet it cannot be moved out of apparently similar structures like

Egbert believed the slander that who was a parricide?
Egbert believed that Esme and who were parricides?

For, none of the following are grammatical:

*Egbert believed whom the slander to be a parricide?
*Egbert believed whom Esme and to be parricides?
*Who did Egbert believe the slander to be a parricide?
*Who did Egbert believe Esme and to be parricides?

The pattern here certainly looks abstract, subtle and unobvious. And so too are many others in G, which we have conceded must be something like what English speakers have internalized (8.6).

Though plausible, this argument for a language-acquisition device should be taken with caution. Why suppose that a general learning device could not explain the child's learning such abstract patterns? Chomsky and his followers tend to restrict their opponents to crude empiricist methods of learning (see particularly Katz 1964: 247). Those who are sceptical of an innate language-acquisition device are allowed only simple induction and association of ideas. But these methods are hopelessly inadequate to explain learning *in general*. So one possible response to Chomsky is to posit a richer and more sophisticated innate *general* learning device. In effect, this is the response made by Putnam (1967: 297–8). Its difficulty, as Chomsky points out (1969a: 79–80), is its vagueness. Nobody nows how to construct an adequate general learning device.

Thirdly, the final consideration in favour of an innate language-acquisition device is one we think fairly unproblematic. It is that language learning is *sui generis*: it is quite unlike the acquisition of other cognitive skills. (a) It is done very young. (b) The data the child receives is degraded, often not consisting of good sentences. (c) There is little explicit instruction. (d) The level of achievement is quite uniform by comparison to other intellectual skills. (e) All children, whatever their language, acquire elements of linguistic capacity in the same order. Acquisition is developmentally uniform across individuals and cultures.

What we are talking about here is, of course, the acquisition of the *spoken* language: speaking and understanding. Indeed, the significance of these five points is demonstrated by the contrast between this acquisition and that of the *written* language: writing and reading. The latter acquisition has no specific evolution and most of the five points do not apply to it. Yet one would expect that the two acquisitions would be equally difficult for a general learning device.

All things considered, we think that it is plausible to suppose that humans do have an innate language-acqusition device. Does this device constrain possible human languages to those having certain characteristics? Is there really a universal grammar made up of a set of linguistic universals, as Chomsky claims?

Stephen Stich has raised some doubts (1978a), on which we shall draw heavily. First, he has pointed out that there is a "logical space" beween the supposition that we have just found plausible and this claim about universal grammar, a space that Chomsky seems to overlook.

To establish that there is a universal grammar we would need to start with an exhaustive study of existing languages to see if they do have (non-trivial) features in common. Chomsky and his followers have made progress on this. They claim, for example, that it is always the case that transformation rules move only constituents – the elements out of which sentences are built (6.2). The rules cannot add or delete anything; they cannot move anything but a constituent. Thus, 'boy loves' in 'Every boy loves his mother' is not a constituent and so cannot be moved.

The next step is an inference to the best explanation. We explain the presence of a feature in all actual languages by supposing that the language-acquisition device prevents us learning any language without it; it is a linguistic universal.

We have two worries about this inference. The first, due to Putnam (1967), is that the common features may be better explained by supposing that all languages are "descended from a single common ur-language whose details have been lost in pre-history" (Stich 1978a: 283). The second is that the common features may be artefacts of the method theorists use to construct grammars, rather than indications of what is common to the grammars actually internalized by speakers (8.6).

In sum, we think that it is plausible to think that there is an innate language-acquisition device, but are not convinced that this device embodies a universal grammar. We reject the view that speakers have innate knowledge of universal grammar or of anything else about their language.

**8.10 Fodor on innateness

We move on from Chomsky's innateness thesis to Fodor's (1975, 1981a). Fodor believes that there is an innate Mentalese with the conceptual resources of any public language:

> at least one of the languages which one knows without learning is as powerful as any language that one can ever learn. (1975: 82)

Fodor's view rests on current learning theory. He emphasizes that this theory is implicitly or explicitly intellectualist; learning consists literally in the formulation and testing of hypotheses. These hypotheses must be framed in a system of representation. This view has important consequences both for the acquisition of language (1975) and the acquisition of concepts (1981a).

Consider concepts. If the intellectualist picture is correct, concepts can only be learnt by the construction of internal representations that define that concept. Thus the concept *radio telescope* can be learnt only if the learning mind already has the resources to define that concept. It follows that undefinable concepts cannot be learnt at all. Fodor thinks that they can be *acquired* but, nevertheless, they are in an important sense innate.

Consider language. How could the word 'tiger' be learnt? The learner must internally represent an hypothesis along the following lines: 'tiger' applies to *x* if and only if *x* is a tiger. Thus to learn the word for tigers, one must already have a way of representing tigers; one must have the concept *tiger* or an equivalent complex of concepts.

Furthermore, Fodor thinks (1981a: 264–76) that every theory of language acquisition (and conceptual growth), *even empiricist theories*, is committed to this strong innateness thesis! The much discussed dispute between rationalist and empiricist on innate ideas (8.9) comes down, in his view, only to a dispute on the numbers and kind of primitive, or basic, concepts. Empiricists think that only a fairly restricted class of "sensory" concepts are primitive, whereas rationalists think that almost all concepts that are not "patently phrasal" (p. 273) – concepts like *largest barnacle on a whale's fluke* – are primitive.

The innateness thesis stretches credulity – even, we suspect, Fodor's – way past its limits. It implies that there is no growth in the expressive power of the conceptual system of the individual or of the race: in some sense, human beings are born with the *gene*, *neutrino*, *videocamera*, and *bachelor*, and always have been. By what conceivable evolutionary process could we be so endowed?

Fodor's discussion is very ingenious. Where has he gone wrong? Our discussion will be brief. We shall start by highlighting the ambiguities in Fodor's thesis. We shall then suggest that in any strong or interesting form it is very implausible.

First, concepts cannot innately refer. Reference of all concepts depends on the grounding of the basic ones. Groundings involve an experiential interaction between the person and the world and so could not be innate. To this extent at least, anything innate could be a concept only in an impoverished sense. Fodor does not think that reference is innate. He thinks that the innate concepts require "triggering" by the environment (pp. 273–4). His triggering is like our grounding; it supplies the reference. However, where we see groundings as important to the nature of concepts, Fodor treats triggerings as if they merely activated a nature already present. This is an important difference, as we shall see below.

Furthermore, Fodor's argument from concept learning only requires that primitive, or basic, concepts are fully innate (triggering aside). Complex concepts like *left-hand drive* and, perhaps, *bachelor* and *videocamera*, which are made up of basic ones, may be innate only in that the ones that go to make them up – that define them – are innate. What are innate are the building blocks for any concept we might have. It is not claimed that all possible concepts are innately built.

The basic concepts are "brute-causal" (1981a; 273): they are made available by the triggering of an appropriate stimulus. Complex concepts, in contrast, are "rational-causal" (p. 273): they are not made available by mere triggering, but by an inductive process involving hypothesis formation and confirmation. Fodor differs from the empiricist in thinking that almost all concepts that are not patently phrasal are "brute-causal".

We wonder whether Fodor's innateness thesis is really as radical as it appears. Perhaps it is a sheep in wolf's clothing. Everyone should agree that it is in virtue of innate structures that we are capable of learning any concept that we do learn. What more is the thesis claiming? Fodor accepts that we learn to construct many concepts out of basic ones. He accepts that the reference of the basic concepts is not innate. What then is innate? It must be something else about the basic concepts.

Here the difference between triggering and grounding is important. Triggerings activate a nature already present. But in what could such a nature consist? This pre-triggered structure must be neutral between the concept of, say, an echidna and the concept of a Twin echidna. But if Fodor's thesis is not to decay into triviality, there must be a pre-triggered structure that is the concept-to-be of an echidna, not, say, the concept-to-be of a kangaroo.

An empiricist can give some sort of answer to this challenge by appealing to the innate "structure of the sensorium" (p. 275). An innate structure for, say, redness, would be *for redness* because it would consist in, or include, a disposition to respond to red stimuli but not to blue ones or to high-pitched ones. That structure would be predisposed to redness. Similarly, the fledgeling duck has an innate concept of mother; it has a disposition with the operative rule, "if it moves it's mother" (p. 280).

Second, Fodor seems to take over this answer, extending it to his much greater set of basic concepts (pp. 274-5). This yields a non-trivial interpretation of his views at the cost of plausibility. The problem is that a particular triggering of an innate structure is necessary and sufficient for the availability of hardly any concept. Our discussion of the *qua*-problem (4.4, 5.3-5.4) shows that mere triggering is insufficient to make available almost any concept in the grounding. The only exceptions would be concepts amenable to a pure-causal theory of reference. Any concept, such as a natural kind one, that is covered by a descriptive-causal theory cannot be gained in a "brute-causal" way.

More strikingly still, a particular triggering is not necessary for any concept that can be made available by reference borrowing (4.1, 5.2-5.4). For, the triggering in such a case is by *a word* and words are arbitrary (1.2): any word can be used for anything. Almost all the most plausible candidates for basic concepts can be made available by reference borrowing, for they are the ones covered by a descriptive-causal theory; natural kind concepts are examples, once again.

What is innate about a basic concept cannot then be a disposition to respond to a certain trigger. Is there anything else about it that could be innate?

Fodor does allow that a basic concept might have an internal structure (p. 279; though not one that plays a role in explaining its acquisition). The conceptual role of a concept, or a non-trivial part of it, might be thought to be innate. But not only does Fodor himself argue that "most concepts are internally unstructured" (p. 283); as well, the facts of reference borrowing once again counts against the proposal. Reference borrowing shows that a person can have most of the plausible candidates for basic concepts without making the associations with other concepts required by the proposal. You can have a concept though ignorant of, or wrong about, its referent (3.3, 5.1).

Perhaps we have a stock of structures, the roles of which *qua* natural kind concept or *qua* artefact concepts are innate. But these would be "blank files" until triggering, with nothing that could be identified as the concept of *an echidna* rather than that of a kangaroo, an elephant, or whatever.

The issues that Fodor has raised are difficult. This is not the place to attempt to resolve all the difficulties. A full response to Fodor requires an alternative account of concept acquisition and its role in language learning. We have offered only a brief sketch (7.5–7.6). Furthermore, there are many complexities in the relation between triggering and learning we have not explored. Nevertheless, we doubt that there is a construal of Fodor's thesis that is both non-trivial and plausible.**

Suggested reading

8.1

Block 1981, Part Three, "The subject matter of grammar", contains a number of papers which give a good idea of the current state of the controversy over grammar. It starts with a helpful (and witty) survey by Fodor, "Introduction: some notes on what linguistics is talking about" (1981b). We have joined the controversy in "Linguistics: What's wrong with 'the right view'", Devitt and Sterelny in preparation a.

Soames 1984, "Linguistics and philosophy", is one work that attends to our main puzzle: the failure to distinguish between competence and syntactic structure.

8.2

The conflation is to be found in almost any transformationalist acount of the aim of a grammar and in much of the practice. The early pages of the following works by Chomsky are examples: "On the notion 'Rule of Grammar'" (1961), *Aspects of the Theory of Syntax* (1965), *Topics in the Theory of Generative Grammar* (1966); see also Katz 1971, *The Underlying Reality of Language and Its Philosophical Import*, chapter 4.

We have attempted a diagnosis of the conflation in Devitt and Sterelny (in preparation a). Soames 1984, "Linguistics and psychology", also criticizes the conflation and, like us, sees grammar as primarily a theory of symbols.

8.4

Harman 1967, "Psychological aspects of the theory of syntax" (reprinted in Rosenberg and Travis 1971, and in Stich 1975, *Innate Ideas*), part I, criticized Chomsky's doctrine of tacit knowledge. This led to a revealing interchange in Hook 1969, *Language and Philosophy*: Chomsky 1969a: 86–9; Harman 1969: 143–8; Chomsky 1969b: 152–6. See also Nagel 1969 (reprinted in Harman 1974) and Schwartz 1969 in the same volume. For later statements of Chomsky's views, see "Knowledge of language" (1975) and *Rules and Representations* (1980), chapter 3. (In the latter work, Chomsky talks of the speaker "cognizing" the grammar rather than tacity knowing it. This is to meet the objection that the speaker could not have the justification for her beliefs that knowledge requires. The terminological change is beside the point of our objection.)

Stich 1971, "What every speaker knows" argues clearly and persuasively for the view that the speaker need know nothing. Graves *et al.* 1973, "Tacit knowledge", is a reply. Stich 1978b, "Beliefs and subdoxastic states", objects to the way the distinction between beliefs and other states that causally underpin beliefs has been ignored.

Harman 1975, "Language, thought, and communication", helpfully relates views on speaker's knowledge to general views about language.

8.5

An early statement of Fodor's view can be found in his 1968 paper, "The appeal to tacit knowledge in psychological explanations", reprinted in Fodor 1981a. **Fodor 1983, *The Modularity of Mind*, is a detailed argument for modularity.** Fodor 1985, "Precis of *The Modularity of Mind*", is a summary of the argument, following by criticisms and Fodor's response.

We have explored the significance of linguistic intuitions in more detail in Devitt and Sterelny in preparation a.

8.6

For Chomsky's opposition to behaviourism, see his famous 1959 review, reprinted in Fodor and Katz 1964, of Skinner's classic *Verbal Behaviour* (1957). Fodor 1981a, *Representations*, pp. 1–16, gives a good account of behaviourism and of its relation to its successor, functionalism. **Quine's scepticism about meaning (see suggested reading for 1.3) seems based on a behaviourism like Skinner's.**

For doubts about the psychological reality of grammars, see Stich 1972, "Grammar, psychology, and indeterminacy", and Katz 1977, "The real status of semantic representations", in Block 1981; also Soames 1984.

Chomsky 1980, pp. 189–201, provides a clear statement of the standard response to doubts about the psychological reality of the grammar.

8.7–8.8

For more on this approach to competence, see Devitt 1981a, sections 4.3–4.5; 1984a, *Realism and Truth*, sections 12.5–12.6.

For Dummett's views see "What is a theory of meaning?" (1975), pp. 105–9, 121–5; "What is a theory of meaning? (II)" (1976), pp. 68–71. **Davidson is another influential philosopher who seems to conflate competence with meaning and to have a propositional view of the former, but his views are difficult to pin down: see several of his papers in *Inquiries into Truth and Interpretation* (1984), particularly, his classic 1967 paper "Truth and meaning", and the 1973 paper "Radical interpretation".**

McGinn 1982, "The structure of content", criticizes Dummett and Davidson for conflating the theory of competence with truth-conditional semantics.

8.9

For Chomsky's views of innateness, see 1965: 47–59; 1980: chapters 4 and 6. See also his contributions to the following collections: Searle 1971; Hook 1969; Stich 1975; Piatelli-Palmarini, *Language and Learning* (1980); Block 1981.

Many papers by others in these collections are also helpful on innateness. See particularly: those by Putnam and Goodman in Searle; those by Quine, Goodman, and Harman in Hook; those in part III of Stich; all papers in Piatelli-Palmarini; those in part IV of Block. Lenneberg 1964, "The capacity for language acquisition", in Fodor and Katz 1964, is an early statement of the "interesting" thesis. Ryle's paper, "Mowgli in Babel", in *On Thinking* (1979), challenges the poverty-of-stimulus argument.

See Stich 1978a, "Empiricism, innateness, and linguistic universals", for a sceptical view of the thesis that all human languages must conform to a universal grammar.

**8.10

Fodor's views are set out at length in *The Language of Thought* (1975) and more succinctly in his contribution to Piatelli-Palmarini 1980. He tries to show that their consequences are not *quite* as implausible as they seem at first sight in "The present status of the innateness controversy" (1981a). Churchland 1980, "Language, thought and information", is a critique of Fodor. Sterelny 1983b, "Mental representation", is a somewhat more sympathetic treatment. Neither of these works takes account of the rescue operation in Fodor 1981a. We attempt to deepen our understanding of these mysteries in Devitt and Sterelny in preparation b, "Detoxifying Fodor's paradox".**

**9

Truth and explanation

9.1 Introduction

In the preceding chapters we have developed a theory of meaning. The core of meaning, we have claimed, is truth conditions (2.1, 2.3); meaning is essentially representational (7.2). We have then set about explaining the notion of truth that this theory requires in terms of reference and syntactic structure. In this way we hope to construct a naturalistic and physicalistic theory of meaning. Only if we can explain truth satisfactorily are we entitled to it (1.3). Most of our discussion has focussed on *entitlement*. However, in recent times, several philosophers have been concerned with *need*. Do we really need truth to explain meaning? We did say something in answer to this question, but not much (2.1). This chapter will be wholly concerned with it. Nevertheless, our discussion can only be a brief introduction to what has proved to be a very difficult problem to grasp, let alone solve.

We have used 'meaning' as a blanket term to cover the special properties of linguistic symbols that enable them to play their striking role in our lives (1.2). So the question of need comes down to this. Is there something about linguistic phenomena that requires truth in its explanation?

Should the answer to this question be negative, a large part of the discussion in this book may be rendered pointless. If we don't need truth to explain anything, then we don't need reference and syntactic structure to explain truth. Entitlement loses its point. Unless there is some other need for reference and syntactic structure, we should not concern ourselves with explaining them. Typically, those who favour the negative answer see it as threatening reference in particular.

Doubt about the need for truth stems first of all from the way the question is posed. We have identified the content of most thoughts with sentences in the public language of the thinker. Even those that cannot be so identified, are linguistic in character (7.2). So meaning, and anything that goes into explaining it, is as much a property of thoughts as of items in a public language. Indeed,

Gricean considerations show thought meaning to be prior to the conventional meaning of public symbols (7.4–7.6). The doubt arises because it is hard to see why we need to explain thought meaning, hence any other sort of meaning, in terms of truth conditions and hence reference. We posit thoughts to explain behaviour, the line runs, but there is nothing about behaviour, even linguistic behaviour, that requires truth for its explanation. We shall consider this line in section 9.3.

Our discussion of the distinction between syntax and competence (8.2) gives some indication of where we think this line goes wrong. Put simply, it goes wrong in seeing linguistics as part of psychology. The task is not the psychological one of explaining linguistic *behaviour* but the linguistic one of explaining linguistic *symbols*. The symbols (at least, the public ones) are not the behaviour itself but the *products* of the behaviour. Truth is needed to explain the symbols. We shall argue this in section 9.4.

It is easy to be complacent about the notion truth because it seems so useful and so ubiquitous. The word 'truth' and its cognates are on everyone's lips. This gives rise to the conviction that there *must* be a need for it somewhere. Explaining language seems the obvious place for that need. So, many people find it difficult to take the question of need seriously.

The complacency should not survive the discovery that much of the utility of truth can be accounted for by seeing it not as an explanatory notion but simply as a logical one like disjunction or quantification. This notion (or notions) is that of *disquotational* or *redundancy* truth. Since such a notion does not explain anything about the world, it does not itself need explanation in terms of reference, or anything else. Awareness of disquotational truth is the second cause of doubt about the need for truth to explain language. We shall consider disquotational truth in the next section.

9.2 Disquotational truth

Those who think that truth is a purely logical notion place a central emphasis on the *disquotation principle*. This principle notes that the following two sentences are equivalent:

'The Rolling Stones are the world's greatest rock and roll band' is true
The Rolling Stones are the world's greatest rock and roll band.

The two sentences have the same epistemic load; if we can justifiably assert one, we can justifiably assert the other. Intuitively, they say the same thing. The first exhibits what Quine calls *semantic ascent*: when we are in a position to assert a sentence, we can instead put quotation marks round it and add 'is true'. Disquotation is just coming down again.

Some argue that this style shift is essentially all there is to truth, and certainly some examples seem to support that view. For instance, instead of saying

> Max said that Hitler was mad, but if that's true, then he was cunningly mad

we could say

> Max said that Hitler was mad, but if Hitler was mad, then he was cunningly mad.

Or, in conversation, instead of

> Max: Hitler was mad.
> Justine: That's true.

we could have

> Max: Hitler was mad.
> Justine: Hitler was mad.

In other words, 'true' seems *redundant*. Hence, this approach is sometimes called the *redundancy* theory of truth.

Admittedly, even in these examples, the 'true'-free translations we have offered are not pragmatically the same as the sentences using 'true': they have a repetitious air. But that disappears if we add 'indeed' or emphasize 'was' in the translations. There is nothing odd about

> Max: Hitler was mad.
> Justine: Hitler was indeed mad.

However, semantic ascent is much more useful than these examples suggest. It, or some other device playing the same role, may well be indispensible in natural language. For, the real point of it is abbreviation. It enables us to assert briefly something that may otherwise be very tedious, if not impossible, to assert.

Suppose that Imogen wishes to express her agreement with the claims made in a certain article. She can say simply,

> What that article says is true.

Without 'true', she would have to assert all the claims made in the article. If she can remember all the claims she could, of course, manage this. However, it would be tiresome to try.

Frequently, people cannot identify all the sentences that they want to assent to. In such cases, their beliefs are beyond assertion altogether without 'true'. (a) Someone may have heard Goldbach's Conjecture ("Every even number is the sum of two primes") and believe it true even though he has forgotten exactly what it is. With the help of 'true', he can say,

Goldbach's Conjecture is true.

Without it, he must remain silent. (b) The political beliefs of a once numerous, though fast dwindling, group could be expressed thus:

Everything Chairman Mao said was true.

Anyone who has not kept track of all the Great Helmsman's utterances – which, surely, is everyone – is faced with an impossible task in attempting to assert this without semantic ascent. She must resort to something along the lines:

If Chairman Mao said that the East is red, then the East is red, and if he said that the East is orange, then the East is orange, and so on.

The problem is that to complete the assertion she needs to replace the 'and so on'. (c) In the latter case, ignorance forces a person into the alternative of attempting an infinitely long conjunction. In others, particularly in logic, that attempt is the inevitable alternative to semantic assent. We can assert each instance of a schema that has an infinite number of instances, thus:

Each instance of that schema is true.

Without 'true' our assertion would be literally endless.

What we need in language is a compact device for referring to many sentences at once. *Our* device is the expression 'is true' and its various cognates. But perhaps that is a relatively accidental feature of English. As Grover, Camp and Belnap (1975) point out, certain quantificational devices would do just as well.

We already have in English devices like

Every drunk is such that he blames everyone but himself for his troubles.

In this sentence, 'he', 'himself' and 'his' are anaphoric pronouns depending for their interpretation on the antecedent quantifier, 'every drunk'; they are like the variables of the logicians (2.4). In natural English, such pronouns are like *nominal* variables; in an instantiation, a name is substituted for them, something that stands in for an individual, in this case an individual drunk. Natural English does not have quantifiers binding terms that are like *sentential* variables; terms for which a sentence is substituted and which stand in for what a sentence says. However, it could have. Indeed, it almost does. Consider:

Every sentence is such that if Mao said it, then it.

That is nearly, but not quite, natural English.

One proposal is that the family of expressions involving 'true' are English's substitutes for this missing quantificational device. Another is that the family is a disguised form of that device. On this view, defended by Grover, Camp and Belnap, the family are *prosentences* (understand 'pro*sentence*' by analogy with 'pro*noun*', each of which are said to be "pro*forms*"): whereas the pronouns, 'he', 'it', and so on are like nominal variables, the prosentences are like sentential variables.

We shall go no more deeply into this matter. Suffice it to say that 'true' plays some logical, quasi-abbreviating role in our language. That is one reason why 'true' is so useful and talk of truth is so pervasive.

9.3 The explanation of behaviour

The possibility that truth is only disquotational should remove any complacency we might have about the need question. We must find something that truth explains. For the reasons we have indicated (9.1), it has been common to seek something about behaviour for truth to explain. The search has proved very difficult.

Putnam's slogan has often recurred in this book: "meaning just ain't in the head" (3.5, 5.1, 7.5, 8.7). The point of it is that nothing in the head can be sufficient to determine reference; reference depends in part on causal links to external reality. This point can be exploited to show that reference and hence truth, which is partly explained in terms of reference, are causally irrelevant to behaviour.

Consider the Twin-Earth fantasy (5.1). When Oscar thinks and talks about water ($=H_2O$), Twin Oscar thinks and talks about Twin water ($=XYZ$). The truth conditions of their thoughts and utterances using 'water' differ. As a result, truth values may differ. Suppose that Oscar and Twin Oscar both token, "Water contains hydrogen". What Oscar says is true, but unless XYZ contains hydrogen, what Twin Oscar says is false. Yet these semantic differences make no difference to the internal psychologies of Oscar and Twin Oscar. Indeed, those psychologies are identical, according to the fantasy. Yet those psycho-logies determine the behaviours of Oscar and Twin Oscar, which are also identical of course. So, the semantic differences are irrelevant to explaining behaviour.

We claimed earlier (7.1) that the causal role of a thought was to be explained partly by its representational content. What the above suggests is that part of that content is irrelevant. The conceptual role of the thought, itself part of the explanation of reference (7.5), is relevant to the explanation of behaviour. But the full-blooded notion of reference, and hence truth, is not.

We can sum up the suggestion in a simple argument.

P1. Reference and truth are irrelevant to the internal psychology of speakers.

P2. The internal psychology of speakers explains their behaviour.

C. Reference and truth are irrelevant to the explanation of behaviour.

Truth and reference are not in the head, but behaviour *is* caused by what is in the head.

This is a powerful argument. It raises difficult and obscure issues. Our discussion of these will be of necessity brief and simplified. The standard responses have seen the argument as having, in one way or another, too restrictive a picture of the explanation of behaviour. We will consider two such responses.

The first links truth to *success* and falsity to *failure*. The idea is that though internal psychology explains the occurrence of behaviour, we must appeal to truth and falsity to explain the success or failure of that behaviour in promoting a creature's goals.

Consider a simple example: a cat fishing from a pond. What explains the trajectory of the cat's paw through the water? The cat receives a pattern of retinal stimulations; this pattern is processed, leading to thoughts; these thoughts cause the cat's behaviour. We have no need to see the cat's thoughts as true or false. That is the point of the above argument. But we do not want merely to explain the behaviour; we want to explain why it succeeded or failed. This suggests a role for truth: the cat will catch the fish if and only if its beliefs about the location of the fish are true.

This suggestion will not do. The truth of an organism's beliefs is not always necessary to explain its success. Its goals may be achieved independently of any of its beliefs and desires: aspects of reality right outside its power may be responsible. A person may campaign diligently to help Marcos win. His goal may be achieved: Marcos wins. Yet Marcos may have won not because of the diligent campaign but because he rigged the election. Even where beliefs are efficacious, they may not be the most important factor in achieving success. It may be more important, for example, to be rich than wise. Reality can intervene in various ways to make a true belief unsuccessful or a false one successful.

The defects of the suggestion are worse still. Talk of truth and falsity is redundant to the explanation of the cat's fishing performance. Suppose the cat misses: misled by the light bending as it moves from water to air, the cat fails to hook its fish. What explains the failure? It is the result of two factors. One is the trajectory of the cat's paw. We have already seen that the internal psychology of the cat explains the trajectory. The second factor is the location of the fish; in particular, the fact that the location is not on the paw's pathway. Jointly, these factors suffice to explain the cat's miss. Nothing more is required. There is no need to invoke the falsity of the cat's beliefs.

The idea that truth explains success must take a different form. A more promising suggestion is that we need to see a belief as true not because it leads to successful behaviour but because it is *conducive* to such behaviour. Similarly, false beliefs are conducive to unsuccessful behaviour. The case of the cat shows that any particular instance of success or failure can be explained without truth. But this case by case treatment misses the fact that some beliefs *tend* to lead to success and others to failure. What is common to the first group is that they are true; what is common to the second is that they are false.

However, even this more promising suggestion faces a formidable difficulty. There is an alternative explanation of conduciveness to success that appeals only to internal psychology. A belief that is *warranted* is conducive to success, and one the negation of which is warranted is conducive to failure. A belief that is well supported by other beliefs and accords with past experiential input is likely to be so also in accord with future input. So behaviour stemming from it is likely to be successful. The relations of a belief to other beliefs and to experience are matters of internal psychology.

To be conducive to success, a belief must simply tend to work at the observation level, it does not have to be true. Thus, a belief in geocentric astronomy is conducive to success, even though it is false, because it tends to work well at the observational level.

Consider the Twin-Earth examples once again. Suppose Oscar were eliminated and Twin Oscar were transported here to replace him. Twin Oscar would be just as successful on Earth as Oscar would have been even though most of his beliefs are about Twin-Earth objects. The reference and truth values of his beliefs are irrelevant. What matters to his success is not whether his beliefs are accurate about Earthly objects, but whether they are "accurate at the level of experience".

Perhaps there is a way to save the idea that we need truth to explain success, but we shall leave it at that and move to the second response.

This response links truth to the special behaviour involved in communication. The idea is that we have to attribute truth and falsity to people's beliefs in order to explain our practices of learning from each other and teaching each other.

We all acquire behaviourally relevant inner states in part from sensory irradiations. We see, hear, smell, touch and taste many things. So, for example, some of the inner states that guide our behaviour are the result of inputs derived from snakes. However, we are advanced organisms. Lots of our snake-directed behavioural patterns are the result of linguistic, rather than snakish, experiences. We may have been told, rather than seen, that snakes are dangerous. We have learnt from others. Similarly, others learn from us. How is this possible?

What happened when young Jake first saw a black thing slithering across the yard? Papa Jake told him that it was a snake and that they were dangerous if molested. As a result, Jake came to believe that snakes are dangerous. So, Jake heard some *noises* – linguistic symbols – and yet acquired an inner state partially controlling his snake-directed behaviour, not just his noise-directed behaviour. How can this connection between linguistic input and a disposition toward apparently unconnected snakish output be mediated? It seems that we must attribute to Jake a certain *theory*. His theory is that the noises his father produced are true if and only if snakes are dangerous; that his father is sincere and so is expressing a belief that is true if and only if snakes are dangerous; finally that his father is reliable about such matters and so his belief is likely to be true. As a result, Jake acquires the belief that snakes are dangerous.

In learning from others we use their beliefs and utterances as guides to reality. Thermometers are instruments we use to tell us about one aspect of reality, the temperature. People are instruments we use to tell us about indefinitely many aspects of reality. In both sorts of case we need to correlate states of an instrument with likely states of the world. The correlation requires a relatively simple theory where the instrument is a thermometer. The claim is that it requires a complicated theory involving truth where the instrument is a language user.

This attempt to motivate truth is essentially one we offered at the beginning of our theory of meaning (2.1. Another, talking of inference, may motivate only disquotational truth). We still think that is along the right lines. However, it also faces a difficulty. We have explained learning behaviour by ascribing to people beliefs that involve the notion of truth. But this alone does not show that truth is an explanatory notion. Consider, for example, the explanation of religious behaviour. The explanation of this may well ascribe to people beliefs that involve the notion of the sacred. That fails to show that the concept of the sacred is needed in a *good* theory of the world; it fails to show that we need to see anything as sacred. What we have shown is that *belief in* truth is explanatory of behaviour not that truth is.

9.4 The explanation of symbols

We think that this objection is a good one. Nevertheless, we think that the discussion of learning and teaching contains many of the ingredients for the answer to our need question. That question must be reoriented and the ingredients put together differently.

The central mistake in the above discussion is that it is focussed on trying to explain behaviour. Truth depends on reference, which is an extra-cranial matter. It is indeed hard to see how any notion depending on extra-cranial matters could be necessary to explain the behaviour, even learning and teaching behaviour. For behaviour is determined by what is intra-cranial.

We rearrange the ingredients as follows. The main point is not the alleged role of people's beliefs about the truth conditions of linguistic symbols in explaining their linguistic behaviour, but the fact that those beliefs are right. For the primary task of linguistics is to explain the symbols not the behaviour (8.2).

It is vital to distinguish these tasks and yet they are usually (always?) confused. Certainly, we ourselves have been guilty of confusing them in the past. And note this from a very recent book by someone completely in touch with the current debate:

> I have been going on for chapter after chapter about semantics' being part of an *explanation of verbal behaviour*, part of psychology. (Lycan 1984: 235–6)

A piece of linguistic behaviour is a series of bodily movements, usually of vocal chords or hands. The symbol is a datable placeable part of the physical world *produced by* the behaviour with the help of the environment. It is usually a sound or inscription. The explanation of linguistic behaviour that has concerned us in this chapter is a psychological description of its *cause*. The explanation of a linguistic symbol which has been the main concern of this book is a semantic description of its *nature*. (In some sign languages, the behaviour is the symbol, but that does not alter the main point: we have a different explanatory interest in it *qua* symbol from *qua* behaviour.)

The nature of a symbol that concerns us is the one that makes it good for the purposes outlined earlier (1.2). What is it about a symbol that makes a person produce it and others respond to it in certain ways? What is it that makes it something we can use to teach and something we can learn from? In brief, what is the nature of its meaning? It is to answer this question that we appeal to truth and reference.

Linguistics is a social science. Like other social sciences, it is dependent on psychological facts. Nevertheless, it is not psychology (8.2). Similarly, economics is dependent on psychological facts but is not psychology. Just as some objects have an economic nature, some have a linguistic nature. Just as it is the task of economics to explain such properties as price and value which go to make up the former nature, it is the task of linguistics to explain such properties as truth and reference which go to make up the latter nature. Just as economics is not concerned primarily with the explanation of economic behaviour, linguistics is not concerned primarily with the explanation of linguistic behaviour.

This is not to say that linguistics is irrelevant to the explanation of linguistic behaviour, anymore than economics is irrelevant to the explanation of economic behaviour. We think that the explanation of learning and teaching sketched above is along the right lines. According to it, people behave linguistically as they do because they have caught on to the semantic properties of linguistic symbols, the properties revealed by linguistics. (Our main doubt about that explanation – a doubt that is very much in the spirit of the last chapter – is that it is over-intellectualized. We think it likely that catching on to semantic properties need not involve having *beliefs* about them.) Explaining behaviour may not motivate truth but, having otherwise motivated it, we use awareness of it to explain behaviour.

Return to the question of our need for truth. We were in great difficulty with this question whilst we were looking for something about behaviour that required truth. The problem was that whenever we seemed to have an answer, it was always possible to come up with another explanation, as good if not better, which did not involve truth. Now that we have focussed on explaining symbols, our position is much stronger. For the truth-conditional explanations of linguistic symbols lacks a rival with comparable plausibility. We see no hint of an explanation of the wide-ranging social use of the rich and variegated array of linguistic symbols that does not appeal to their representational powers. How else can we explain meaning?

We do not pretend that these few remarks, reorienting the need question, should be sufficient to convince the sceptic about truth. The reorientation itself is controversial. We hope that this book as a whole, with its systematic focus on the symbol not the psychology, will help establish the reorientation. Aside from that, clearly more needs to be said in favour of truth's central place in the theory of linguistic symbols. Finally, our discussion in this section applies, in the first instance at least, to the public symbols of our languge. How can we show a need for truth in dealing with the symbols in thought?

Suggested reading

9.1

The need question is raised in the difficult last section of Field's classic paper on truth, "Tarski's theory of truth" (1972); see also part V of his "Mental representation" (1978), reprinted in Block 1981. Stephen Leeds presses the question in his excellent paper, "Theories of reference and truth" (1978).

9.2

For a typically elegant exposition of semantic ascent and its uses, see Quine 1970, *Philosophy of Logic*: chapter 1. The roles of disquotational or redundancy truth are explored in Leeds 1978 and in Grover, Camp, and Belnap 1975, "A prosentential theory of truth", See also Horwich 1982, "Three forms of realism" and Devitt 1984a, *Realism and Truth*: section 3.4.

A germ of the redundancy view is to be found in Frege's 1915 paper, "My basic logical insights", first published in English in Frege 1979, *Posthumous Writings*.

9.3

For a defence of the importance of internal psychology to psychological explanation, see Fodor's paper, "Methodological Solipsism", in his *Representations* (1981a). Pylyshyn 1980, "Computation and cognition", later expanded into Pylyshyn 1984, argues that full-blooded semantic notions are needed in the explanation of behaviour. For different versions of the same general line, see Godfrey-Smith and Sterelny in preparation "Semantic Psychology", and Dennett 1983, "Intentional systems in cognitive ethology".

For the view that we need truth to explain success, see Putnam 1978, *Meaning and the Moral Sciences*: 99–103. The view is criticized in Devitt 1984a: section 6.7.

For the origins of the view that we need truth to explain learning and teaching, see Field 1972: 370–1; 1978; 102–4. The view is developed in some detail in Devitt 1984a: sections 6.8–6.9. Schiffer 1981, "Truth and the theory of content", gives the view a special twist by introducing a principle of reliability, analogous to principles of charity (see chapter 15 in this volume). These issues, and those in 9.2, are discussed in Loar 1981, *Mind and Meaning*, chapter 8. This general approach to motivating truth is criticized in Stich 1983, *From Folk Psychology to Cognitive Science*, chapter 9, section 5; and in Godfrey-Smith in press, "Why semantic notions won't earn their keep".

For a nice account of the problems and discussion of various attempts to solve it, see Lycan 1984, *Logical Form in Natural Language*: 235–42.**

10

Linguistic relativity

10.1 Introduction

Our interest in part II in the meanings of linguistic tokens led to an interest in truth conditions. Our explanation of truth conditions is in terms of structure and reference. Our explanation of those has led, particularly in this part (chapter 7), to an interest in thoughts. For thoughts play crucial roles in the causal history of sentence tokens.

Thought is linguistic. This thesis opens up various relativistic possibilities. If your thought is tied to the *specific* language you speak, and if languages differ in important ways then your thought might be deeply mysterious to the speaker of another language. There are many who argue in this way. Where Chomsky is impressed with similarities between languages (8.8), they are struck by differences. For them, a language is not a neutral medium of communication and thought. Rather, they suppose that to speak a particular language is to adopt a parochial conception of reality.

This sort of relativism has been very popular in recent years. We shall consider it in this chapter. We leave until later (chapters 12–13) a consideration of the related, but much more radical, sort of relativism which holds that *reality itself*, not just thought about it, is relative to language. We start with the ur-spokesman of linguistic relativity, Benjamin Lee Whorf, with occasional reference to his teacher, Edward Sapir.

We can summarize Whorf's thesis as the conjunction of the following claims:

1. All thinking is "in a language – in English, in Sanskrit, in Chinese". (1956: 252)
2. Each language structures a view of reality.
3. The views of reality structured by languages, or at least by families of languages, differ.

There is certainly *something* to be said for these claims, but nothing to warrant the air of excitement and significance, even mystery, with which Whorf surrounds them. We have already discoursed at length on the virtues of 1, if qualified to allow that *some* thinking is not in a public language (7.2-7.3). 2 and 3 are vague. In general, the more excitingly they are interpreted, the less plausible they become. There is no interpretaton of Whorf that is both plausible and exciting.

Sometimes Whorf writes as if language simply *influences* the views we come to have. Language is "the shaper of ideas, the program and guide for the individual's mental activity" (p. 212); it *imposes* on experience (Sapir 1931: 128). As a result of this influence or imposition, differences between languages lead to "incommensurable" (p. 128) world views: views that are "widely divergent" (Whorf 1956: 247) or "mutually unintelligible" (p. 246). At other times he suggests the stronger claim that a language *forces* people to think in certain ways and *constrains* their world view; it has "unbreakable bonds" (p. 256), a "tyrannical hold" (Sapir 1931: 128), which prevent them from having certain thoughts (Whorf 1956: 213-14). Differences between languages lead to *insurmountable* incommensurability. What is to be said for these views?

The question divides in two. The first concerns the influence/constraint of *vocabulary*; the second, that of *syntax*. The first is easier to discuss, but the second seems to be what Whorf has chiefly in mind. We shall consider the first in the next section, the second in section 10.3.

10.2 The tyranny of vocabulary

Clearly the *vocabulary* a language provides does influence thought. It is much more difficult to coin concepts than to use ones already available. And language makes many concepts available. Consider thoughts about unobservables; for example, about genes. It is very hard to have thoughts about genes unless one has been introduced to the word 'gene' (or a translation of that word). Darwin's own writing on evolution and inheritance is confused in places precisely because he lacked this concept. But it is not impossible to have the thoughts without the word. If Mendel had not had thoughts about genes without benefit of the word 'gene', the convention of using that word to refer to genes would never have been invented. So the absence of a word does not prevent or constrain, in any strong sense, thought about unobservables. Even less does it constrain thought about observables. Captain Cook had thoughts about kangaroos without having any word for them simply on the strength of observing them. So also does a dog have thoughts about bones.

In effect, this issue of the relation between word and concept has already been discussed in our consideration of Grice (7.5-7.6). There was a respect in which the existence of a word with a certain conventional meaning was dependent on the existence of a concept (=part of a thought meaning) and a respect in which the reverse was the case. We could sum up these dependencies as follows: the existence of a concept in some people creates the convention for a word; this convention explains the existence of the concept in many others.

This view acknowledges the influence of language on thought whilst giving ultimate priority to thought. And language does not prevent thought at all.

Whorf does write sometimes as if language constrains and prevents thought. If it did it would lead to an incommensurability between linguistic communities that was insurmountable. How *could* language be that influential? It seems that it would have to be *prior* to thought. But if it were, there could be no plausible explanation of the origin of language. How could the Chinese have come to have their particular linguistic conventions? It would be as if their language sprang miraculously out of nothing. The plausible view is that our distant ancestors were, like other higher animals, thinkers but not talkers; talking evolved from thinking.

So we reject prevention or constraint but accept lesser forms of linguistic influence. Let us explore the extent of that influence.

It helps to avoid exaggerating the influence to note how different are the views that can be expressed in the one language. Language provides us with conceptual resources, but it does not determine how those resources are to be used. The world 'Earth' helps us to think about the Earth but does not tell us whether it is flat. Once we have words like 'god' and 'sacred' we can think religious thoughts, but we can still end up atheists. The radically different philosophies of Descartes and Derrida were both written in French.

Consider next the effect on thought of the differences between languages. The number of Eskimo words for snow is legendary; doubtless the contemporary Eskimo thinks thoughts about snow that the typical English speaker does not. This is certainly a sign of the influence of language but not of any prevention or constraint. Nor does there seem to be any incommensurability here. English speakers can catch up with the Eskimo because (we assume) all the Eskimo words for snow can be translated into English. Of course, each Eskimo word is likely to require a complex English phrase, thus discouraging thought. But discouragement is one thing, prevention another.

The ultimate explanation of this difference in thought between the Eskimoes and the English is obvious enough and has nothing to do with language: they live in different natural environments. It is that difference that accounts for *both* the difference in language and the difference in thought. In some other cases the key difference is in socio-economic conditions or religious beliefs; a popular example of such a difference is in the kinship relation. As we move from community to community, natural and social conditions change and so does thought and language. There is nothing surprising nor mysterious about this and certainly no basis for imbuing language with any deep power over thought.

Some differences between language defy translation and accompany more radical differences in thought than those between Eskimoes and English. These are cases of genuine incommensurability. The language of Plato could not express the ideas of quantum physics and nobody who spoke it had any such ideas. These absences from Classical Greek strongly influenced the thought of Plato and his contemporaries. However, the case also provides striking evidence of the influence of thought on language. We have the language of quantum physics because some scientists thought up quantum physics and passed on the benefits to others. Plato did not have the language because those scientists did not have their thoughts until two millennia after his death.

We have mentioned one way for a community to gain a concept and a word that expresses it: some people think up the concept and establish the convention of using the word for it. Another way is common and easier: borrow the concept and word from another community. A person comes across aliens using a word he cannot translate. He masters the use of the word and adopts it, thus introducing the concept into his community.

In sum, we reject entirely the idea that vocabulary forces or prevents thought. Hence we reject the idea of linguistic differences leading to an insurmountable incommensurability. Ultimately, thought is prior to vocabulary. However, vocabulary does influence, perhaps even impose on, thought. Weak influence, involving no incommensurability (as in the Eskimo case), is doubtless quite common. Even where the influence does involve incommensurability, and so is strong (as in the Plato case), the conceptual differences can be readily removed by modifying the vocabulary.

10.3 The tyranny of syntax

It seems that Whorf is more impressed with the way syntax structures a view of reality than with the way vocabulary does. The role of syntax is much more difficult to discuss than that of vocabulary. The problem is that we lack clear and convincing examples of significant syntactic differences between languages.

To avoid exaggerating the influence of vocabulary, we indicated the range of views expressible within the one vocabulary. The same point applies to syntax. It is possible to express fundamentally different conceptions of reality in the one syntax. Our picture of the world, and of our place in it, has changed enormously in the last few thousand years. We have gone from the primeval animist conception, regarding the forces of nature as agents, to the Aristotelian purpose-governed picture; from there to Newton's mechanical picture; finally, to contemporary physics. These fundamentally different views can all be expressed in English. The syntax of English pushes us neither towards seeing the wind as an agent, as a being with desires or plans, nor as a vast cloud of particles whose aggregate movement is a vector of many physical forces. *Qua* English speakers, we could believe any of these alternatives, or many others. Of course, it is possible that these world views are brothers under the skin compared to some radical alternative inexpressible in English, but we need powerful reasons for thinking so.

It is going to be impossible to produce such reasons if all languages are, at bottom, syntactically similar, as Chomsky thinks (8.9). For if they are similar, we must lack any way of *expressing* that radical alternative! What we need in the first place, therefore, is evidence that languages are syntactically different in a way that influences or constrains world views.

Whorf has several suggestions about the syntactic differences between "Standard Average European" (SAE) languages like English and American Indian languages like Hopi. These are mostly brief and obscure. We shall consider his main suggestion, which concerns *time*.

Whorf argues that SAE languages thrust a certain conception of time on us. We see it

> as a smooth flowing continuum in which everything in the universe proceeds at an equal rate, out of a future, through a present, into a past; or, in which, to reverse the picture, the observer is being carried in the stream of duration continuously away from a past and into a future. (1956: 57)

Whorf's key point is that SAE languages make us see time as an objective quantifiable kind of stuff like space. We *reify* time. How does language work this trick?

(a) We quantify time in exactly the same way that we quantify physical aggregates: 'ten days' has exactly the same linguistic form as 'ten men'.

(b) Most crucially, our tense/aspect system has a tripartite distinction of past/present/future which encourages this view of time.

(c) Metaphor is spatialized and reified. Thus Whorf writes:

> all languages need to express durations, intensities, and tendencies. It is characteristic of SAE . . . to express them metaphorically. The metaphors are those of spatial extension, i.e. of size, number (plurality), position, shape, and motion. We express duration by 'long, short, great, much, quick, slow,' etc.; intensity by 'large, great, much, heavy, light, high, low, sharp, faint,' etc.; tendency by 'more, increase, grow . . .'; and so on through an almost inexhaustible list of metaphors that we hardly recognize as such, since they are virtually the only linguistic media available.

It is clear how this condition "fits in." It is part of our whole scheme of OBJECTIFYING – imaginatively spatializing qualities and potentials that are quite nonspatial . . . (1956: 145).

According to Whorf, things are different in Hopi. In that language, physical and temporal aggregates have distinct linguistic structures. Metaphors for duration, intensity, and duration are not spatial. Most importantly, their tense/aspect system does not map onto our past/present/future trichotomy. Whorf claims that their "tense" markers are validity forms; they have *epistemic* interpretations. One form indicates *direct report*: it applies roughly to occasions in which we use simple past or present. Another indicates *expectation*: it is roughly equivalent to our future, though it can be used to describe an event distant from but simultaneous with the utterance. Finally, there is a *nomic* form: it is roughly equivalent to the English generic present, as in 'A man lives and dies in sin'. In addition, there are temporal conjunctions. These link clauses and translate approximately as 'earlier than' and 'later than'.

Whorf is suggesting that SAE influences/constrains us to one conception of time, Hopi influences/constrains the Hopi to another. It is "gratuitous" (p. 57) to attribute our concept of time to them.

There are serious problems with this line of thought. First, his gloss on the Hopi language is controversial (Lenneberg 1953). However, let us suppose, for the sake of argument, that he is near enough right about the differences between SAE and Hopi.

Second, it is not obvious from these differences in language whether we do differ from the Hopi in our conception of time. Indeed, it is not obvious what our conception of time is, let alone what the Hopi's is. These are not matters that can be simply read off language, particularly since most talk that is directly about time seems straightforwardly metaphorical (how *could* time flow?). Whorf's own accounts of the metaphysics of the Hopi (pp. 57–64) cast more darkness than light. Further, his claim that the Hope conception of time is operationally equivalent to ours (p. 58) – so that it is just as useful for daily life – is evidence *against* the conceptions being different. However, let us suppose again that Whorf is right and that the two conceptions are different.

Third, the supposition that we differ from the Hopi in language and thought is quite compatible with the view that we have urged: that thought is ultimately prior to language. On this view the linguistic difference between Hopi and English has arisen from the conceptual difference, not vice versa. Of course once the linguistic difference exists it will influence the thought of those that come after. That is the full extent of the influence of language. There is no constraint. Indeed, the supposition that there is constraint seems absurd because it would make the origins of language miraculous.

Granting the differences between us and the Hopi, we have allowed some influence to language. How extensive might it be?

We have already seen in discussing vocabulary that the extent of influence depends on translatability. If Hopi syntax could be translated into SAE, albeit clumsily, then the influence would be slight. SAE could express the Hopi conception of time, but would not encourage its adoption. There would be no incommensurability between SAE and Hopi. The situation would be analogous to the Eskimo case.

Whorf does seem to think that Hopi cannot be translated into SAE, but his evidence for this is weak, and his own glosses on Hopi (for the most part) give it the lie. Indeed, it seems doubtful that the *syntax* of any known language prevents its translation into any other.

It is only if the Hopi syntax did defy translation into SAE that we would have incommensurability. We would be in a situation analogous to the Plato case: a situation of strong linguistic influence (but still no constraint). However, the incommensurability might be more serious in our situation. It seems likely that it would be more difficult for us to learn the Hopi's conception of time than it would be for Plato to learn our quantum conceptions. But, as we have said, we lack any persuasive reason for supposing that Hopi syntax is untranslatable.

We have been supposing, for the sake of argument, that languages do differ significantly in their syntax. Yet that is just what Chomsky and his followers deny. They think that there is a rich set of "linguistic universals" common to all languages (8.9). Further, they argue that the tense-aspect system – the syntactic feature most emphasized by Whorf – is part of the surface structure. The tense markings on verbs are determined by relatively superficial transformation rules, together with the morphology of the language. The tense-aspect system is not, therefore, one of the structural fixtures of the language. If this is right, the underlying form of the auxiliary verb system will be similar across languages. So, linguistic influences on conceptions of time are likely to be fairly trivial.

In sum, syntax no more forces or prevents thought than did vocabulary. Hence syntax gives rise to no insurmountable incommensurability. Indeed it is doubtful that it gives rise to any incommensurability at all. If Chomsky is right there are unlikely to be metaphysically significant syntactic differences between languages; the influence of syntax on thought is trivial. Even if there are significant differences between languages, the determining influence is from world view to syntax, not vice versa.

Whorf's remarks are interesting and suggestive, but the argument for an important linguistic relativity evaporates under scrutiny. The only respect in which language clearly and obviously does influence thought turns out to be rather banal: language provides each of us with most of our concepts.

In their exaggeration of the influence of language over thought, and their consequent relativism, Sapir and Whorf exemplify important parts of structuralist thinking, as we shall see (13.3–13.4).

10.4 The scientific Whorfians

Whorf argued that linguistic communities can be opaque to each other. In the last 20 years or so, some philosophers of science, led by Thomas Kuhn and Paul Feyerabend, have argued that scientific communities can be so also. They claim that the languages of different theories in the one area are not inter-translatable and hence the theories are "incommensurable". This claim is part of a radical critique of orthodox views about science.

Twentieth-century orthodoxy has two sources: the logical positivists and Karl Popper and his followers. As a result it is not homogeneous. The positivists hold an accumulationist and evolutionary view of science. Science consists in a steady accummulation of data punctuated at intervals by its theoretical reorganization as theories became more general and precise. Thus, Newton made Kepler's laws of planetary motion more general (Newton's applied to other celestial and all terrestrial objects) and more precise. Popper disputes this picture: theory change is not an elaboration but a replacement; it is a revolution rather than a reform.

Nonetheless, underlying this disagreement are many common threads. In particular, both groups took science to have a common language. That language is the language of *observation*. However much theories may differ from one another, they share a language in which reports of experiment and observation can be given. This common language has great epistemic and semantic significance for the orthodox.

This language is epistimically prior to theoretical language in that statements in it – observation statements – settle the fate of theories. Popper emphasized the role of these statements in falsifying theories. The positivists emphasized their role in confirming theories. In both cases, observation rules.

This language is also semantically prior, for the positivists at least. It was held that ultimately the meaning of the special theoretical language of a science depends on the meaning of the observation language shared by all sciences. Much ink was spilt attempting to explain this dependence.

Kuhn and Feyerabend and the other radicals reject the whole orthodox picture. We shall be concerned only with their Whorfian rejection of the commensurability of theories.

First, they deny the existence of any common scientific language that is neutral between all competing theories. When the theories are comprehensive ones within an area – what Kuhn calls *paradigms* – there is no way of translating the language of one theory into the language of another. This failure of translation stretches even to the observational consequences of the theories; the theories do not share a neutral observation language.

Many of the most important episodes in the history of science are clashes between relatively comprehensive theories: Ptolemaic *versus* Copernican astronomy; Newtonian *versus* relativistic physics; special creation *versus* Darwinian views of life. In such situations, according to the radicals, the competitors cannot be compared. Each theory is a complex intellectual structure which creates its own language; the meaning of a term is determined by its place in that structure. Consider, for example, the term 'species'. In Darwinian biology, species are conceived of as changing and evolving, with characteristics that are the relatively accidental product of selection and chance. In creationism, species are fixed and immutable, created for some purpose from a template in the mind of God. These different conceptions result in different meanings for 'species'. Even when a term in one theory is of the same physical type as one in another, it is of a different semantic type (4.2); it expresses a different "concept".

Second, as a result of this lack of shared concepts, the radicals think that comprehensive theories cannot be compared in the ways dear to the heart of the orthodox. Because there are no shared concepts there can be no logical relations between the theories. So the idea of one theory being reduced to, or included in, another must go: it requires that the statements of one theory entail the statement of another. That requires a common language, which is precisely what is lacking here. Worse still, there can be no question of one theory refuting another. That requires that statements be inconsistent, which again requires a common language. Theories become as different as chalk and cheese.

This incommensurability thesis has drastic consequences for the picture of science. Science is not a steady accumulation of knowledge. It is not the replacement of one theory by another that refutes it, but nevertheless takes over many of its findings. Rather, science is a succession of incommensurable theories. The whole idea of progress in science becomes problematic.

10.5 The rejection of scientific Whorfianism

The incommensurability thesis talks of meaning, a very broad notion. The first point to make in assessing the thesis is that the comparison of theories does not require that terms share meanings; it is sufficient that they share *referents*. Thus, to take a simple example, we can compare the "theories", 'the evening star is closer than the Earth to the Sun' and 'the morning star is not closer than the Earth to the Sun', even though the terms, 'the evening star' and 'the morning star', differ in meaning. We can do so because the terms are co-referential. Given this fact, we can see that the two theories cannot both be true; one refutes the other. So we can set aside talk of meaning and concentrate on reference.

It is clear that Kuhn and Feyerabend think that incommensurability survives this point. For they think that theory change involves reference change, not just meaning change. Indeed, they seem to think that *reality itself* changes when theories change. We are setting that sort of view aside until the next part of the book (12.3, particularly). Meanwhile, we shall adopt a robust realism and assume that view of reality false. In so doing, it is only fair to add, we are seriously undermining the plausibility of the incommensurability thesis. With reality "fixed", it turns out that there is only a little to be said for a radical view of reference change; for a view that undermines theory comparison.

1   Some terms in discarded theories that were once thought to refer are now thought to be empty. 'Witch', 'phlogiston' and the 'humours' of the blood are cases in point. Yet these are not cases of reference change. There never were witches, phlogiston and humours and so the terms in question never did refer. What has changed is not their reference but our view of their reference. And this change poses no problem for theory comparison. From our theoretical perspective, these discarded theories are thoroughly misguided. Statements in such a theory implying the existence of, say, witches, are perfectly intelligible – we still have the word 'witch'; they are just plain false.

2   Sometimes there really are cases of reference change. A theory takes over a term from an old theory and uses it in a new way. We are told that this happened to the term 'atom' in the nineteenth century. However, the reference change need not be problematic for theory comparison. Suppose, first, that from the perspective of the new theory, the term in its old use referred (which was the case with 'atom'); from the new perspective, the entities referred to by the old use are still thought to exist. So there is no problem comparing what the two theories say about those entities. Suppose, next, that from the new perspective the term in its old use does not refer; there has been a change in view about what exists. Provided the past theory is dismissed as thoroughly misguided, there is again no trouble with theory comparison. It would be as if physicists called some newly discovered fundamental particles "witches".

3   There is one genuinely problematic sort of reference change. It is the one where, from the new perspective, a term in its old use does not refer *and yet the old theory is not dismissed as thoroughly misguided*. Consider the change from classical physics to relativistic physics. Terms like 'mass', 'force' and 'gravitation' were taken over by Einstein from Newton and given a new reference. Further, from the relativistic perspective, those terms in their classical use, lack reference altogether. The problem is that we do not dismiss classical physics the way we dismiss the theory of witches. We see that physics as more or less true, within certain limits, and give or take an error or two. Though Einstein made a major advance, we think of him as

having retained much of Newton. This is seen as a typical example of accumulation in science. But how can it be since the crucial terms in Newton's theory fail to refer?

So Kuhn and Feyerabend have raised a problem. We think that the problem is not beyond solution, though the solution is technical. The key idea is to replace reference and truth in our semantic theory with *partial reference* and *partial truth* (4.3, 5.2). The contrast between classical physics and the theory of witches can then be brought out as follows: the terms in the former, unlike those in the latter, partially refer; as a result the former theory, unlike the latter, is partially true.

We agree that there is a problem of reference change but think it arises rarely. Kuhn and Feyerabend, in contrast, think it utterly pervasive. In a really revolutionary change like that to relativistic physics, *all* terms are affected. Not even terms like 'flask', 'ruler' and 'pointer', referring to the paraphernalia of the laboratory, are exempt. Why do they exaggerate in this way?

The answer is that they subscribe to versions of the description theory of reference. On that theory, if we change the descriptions associated with a term we are likely (barring accidental co-reference) to change its reference, for the term applies to whatever is picked out by those associated descriptions. In a radical theory change, our whole view of the world changes. Different descriptions are associated with all the terms taken over from the old theory. This is true even of the observational terms. The result is wholesale reference change.

We have, in effect, already given our response to this. The description theories of reference that Kuhn and Feyerabend rely on are false. Indeed, the implausibility of the view that reference of words like 'pointer' change with the move from Newton to Einstein, is an extra reason for rejecting those theories of reference. We allow that there may be a place for description theories of some sort for some terms (5.4). But reference is ultimately determined by causal links to reality that are, unlike associated descriptions, importantly independent of theory. As a result, the terms of a false theory can still refer. Without description theories there is no plausibility to the view that theory change leads to wholesale reference change.

There is a deeper reason for the exaggeration by Kuhn and Feyerabend. They do not approach the problem of reference change with a firm view of the reality to which reference is to be made. Rather they allow their preconceptions about reference to form their views of reality. We shall have much to say about this mistake, and about the realism that underlies our response to the incommensurability thesis, in the next part.

Suggested reading

10.1–10.3

For Whorf's views see *Language, Thought, and Reality* (1956), particularly, "An American Indian model of the Universe", "The relation of habitual thought and behaviour to language", and "Science and linguistics". His most famous paper is "Language, mind, and reality", but it bears more on the concerns of chapter 12.

McCormack and Wurm 1977, *Language and Thought*, part II, is a useful anthology of some of the Sapir–Whorf material. Hook 1969, *Language and Philosophy*, part I, consists of essays on Whorf.

See Fishman 1960, "A systematization of the Whorfian analysis", for a sympathetic overview of Whorf. See Black's paper, "Linguistic relativity: the view of Benjamin Lee Whorf" in *Models and Metaphors* (1962), for a less sympathetic one.

Rosch 1977, "Linguistic relativity", argues that the strong form of the Whorfian hypothesis is empirically untestable, and that even the weaker form lacks much empirical support. Lenneberg 1953, "Cognition in ethnolinguistics", criticizes Whorf's handling of Hopi.

10.4

See Nagel 1961, *The Structure of Science*, for a detailed discussion of the positivist viewpoint. Suppe's introduction to *The Structure of Scientific Theories* (1977) is a good overview of positivist philosophy of science. Popper's famous work is *The Logic of Scientific Discovery* (1959), first published in German in 1934.

Kuhn's views were first set out in his very influential, *The Structure of Scientific Revolutions* (1962); see particularly, chapters 10 and 12. Feyerabend's views appeared in a series of articles from 1962 on. Perhaps the most helpful is "Against method" (1970b), later expanded into a book (1975). See also Kuhn 1970, "Reflections on my critics", and Feyerabend 1970a, "Consolations for the specialist", both in Lakatos and Musgrave 1970, *Criticism and the Growth of Knowledge*.

10.5

Scheffler 1967, *Science and Subjectivity*, particularly chapter 3, makes the point that reference, not meaning, is the crucial notion for theory comparison. Incommensurability has generated a storm of responses. See Newton-Smith 1981, *The Rationality of Science*, chapters 5–8, for a nice survey of Kuhn, Feyerabend, and the incommensurability debate.

Devitt 1979, "Against incommensurability" criticizes the incommensurability thesis. Devitt 1984a, *Realism and Truth*, chapter 9, includes these criticisms within a critique that is relevant to chapter 12 of this volume.

PART IV

LANGUAGE AND REALISM

11

Verificationism

11.1 Realism

It is hard to talk about language without talking about the world. We have made no attempt: this book is replete with claims about sentient life and its place in an impersonal world. A theory of language is bound to be influenced by a theory of the extra-linguistic world. Should a theory of that world be influenced by a theory of language? One would think not. Language, after all, is a local phenomenon, probably confined to humans. It is hard to see why our ideas of the stars, of biochemistry and geology, should be influenced by our ideas of language.

Surprisingly, current orthodoxy goes against this obvious thought. The literature is full of arguments seeking to illuminate the structure of the world on the basis of considerations about language. We think that these arguments are wrong-headed. In this part of the book we aim to analyse and rebut some representative samples.

The main target of these arguments has been *realism*. This is a metaphysical doctrine with two dimensions. First it is a doctrine about what exists, and second it is a doctrine about the nature of the existence. Concerning the first, it holds that such physical entities as stones, trees and cats exist ("are real"). Concerning the second, these entities do not depend for their existence or nature on our minds, nor on our awareness, perception or cognizance of them. Realists thus speak of these entities as being "independent" of and "external" to the mind. They say that an entity exists "objectively" in that its existence does not depend on anyone's opinion; nor does it arise from the imposition of our concepts or theories. Universal disbelief in the existence of stones does not lead to stonelessness. Neither do theories that make no mention of stones.

Realism has traditionally been opposed by idealism. Idealists typically did not reject the first dimension of realism; they did not deny the existence of the ordinary furniture of our environment (Hume was one notable exception). What they typically rejected was the second dimension: mind independence.

An example of this is captured in Berkeley's famous slogan: "*esse est percipi*", "to be is to be perceived".

The realism we are interested in should be distinguished from another called "scientific realism". That doctrine is concerned with the *unobservable* entities posited by science – such entities as electrons, muons and curved spacetime. Our realism is concerned with *observable* entities, particularly those of common sense, but also those of science (e.g. the moons of Jupiter). So, perhaps our doctrine would be more aptly called "common-sense realism". The two doctrines have obvious affinities, but they are independent: it is possible to hold either without the other. One might accept common-sense realism but reject scientific realism on the ground that unless we can observe an entity we can have no strong reason for supposing that it exists. A scientific realist might reject common-sense realism on the ground that science shows that our folk view of the world is hopelessly wrong and that nothing exists but swarms of quarks and gluons. In general, however, the two doctrines tend to go together.

Realism about the ordinary observable physical world is a compelling doctrine. It is almost universally held outside philosophical circles. Indeed, it is regarded as too obvious to be worth stating. Yet within philosophy the doctrine has enjoyed little popularity. Anti-realism is an occupational hazard of philosophy.

Traditional philosophical arguments against realism start from a thesis in epistemology: from an assumption about the nature of knowledge. In one way or another it was then argued that we could have knowledge only if we gave up realism. For knowledge to be possible, "the gap" between the object known and the knowing mind must be closed; the object must, in some way, be made dependent on our way of knowing. In the twentieth century, in contrast, arguments against realism typically start from a thesis in the philosophy of language. For reference to be possible, "the gap" between the object referred to and the referring mind must be closed; the object must, in some way, be made dependent on our way of referring, dependent on our language. With this recent change has gone another which is decidedly unwelcome: the anti-realist nature of conclusions is often only implicit and is nearly always shrouded in mystery. Attention has centred so heavily on language that the metaphysical issue has tended to disappear; or to be redefined in linguistic terms; or, worst of all, to be confused with linguistic issues. In general, the philosophy of language has become too big for its boots (1.1).

In this chapter we shall discuss two examples of anti-realist positions stemming from *verificationist* views of language.

11.2 Logical positivism and the elimination of the realism dispute

Logical positivism began in central Europe in the early 1920s with the forming of a group known as "the Vienna Circle". Membership was not limited to philosophers, but included scientists and mathematicians. The members were all scientifically minded people who were shocked by what was happening in philosophy, particularly in German philosophy of that period. An example they were fond of disparaging was the following from Heidegger's *What is Metaphysics?*

> What is to be investigated is being only and – *nothing* else; being alone and further – *nothing*; solely being, and beyond being – *nothing*. *What about this Nothing?* . . . *Does the Nothing exist only because the Not, i.e. the Negation, exists?* Or is it the other way around? *Does Negation and the Not exist only because the Nothing exists?* . . . We assert: *the Nothing is prior to the Not and Negation* . . . Where do we seek the Nothing? How do we find the Nothing . . . We know the Nothing . . . *Anxiety reveals the Nothing* . . . That for which and because of which we were anxious, was "really" – nothing. Indeed: the Nothing itself – as such – was present . . . *What about this Nothing? – The Nothing itself nothings.* (Quoted in Carnap 1932: 69)

The positivists felt that such philosophical talk was literally meaningless and they sought a way to show this.

They found their way in the *Verifiability Principle*: at its simplest, "Meaning is method of verification". A corollary is that if a sentence has no method of verification – if it does not have associated with it a *way of telling* whether it is true or not – then it is meaningless. With this weapon, the positivists hoped to *eliminate* metaphysics.

One metaphysical dispute that had to go, according to the positivists, was that between realists and idealists. Whether there was a reality external to the mind, as the realists claim, or whether all reality is made up of "ideas", "sense data" or "appearances", as idealists claim, is a "meaningless pseudo-problem" (Schlick 1932–33: 86). For, both parties to the dispute agree on the "empirical evidence" (Ayer 1940: 16) – the "given" (Schlick: 83). The given is what verifies statements and hence is all that can provide meanings. Agreement on the given leaves nothing substantive to disagree on. All there is to the dispute between realists and idealists is a pragmatic dispute "about the choice of two different languages" (Ayer: 18): whether to choose a material-thing language defined in terms of the given or a sense-datum language defined in terms of the given. There is no fact of the matter about one choice or the other being right.

The positivists dismissed metaphysical issues and replaced them with linguistic ones. The philosophical task was to analyse what statements mean, in terms of the given, and thus prepare them for testing. The move from metaphysics to language was known as the "linguistic turn" in philosophy.

The Verifiability Principle ran into massive problems and has long since been abandoned. In particular, it proved impossible to frame it in a moderate enough form to save much of our cherished knowledge; the weapon eliminated not only German metaphysics, but just about everything else as well. Further, it cast doubt on its own status. How was *it* to be verified.

Our whole approach to language is at odds with the Principle, as we shall bring out later (11.4). In this section, we shall consider another matter. Suppose the Principle were true. Would the positivists then have succeeded in eliminating metaphysics? They would not.

On the basis of the Principle, the positivists claim that there is no substantive question about whether there are material things, sense data, and so on. It is all just a matter of choosing a convention for language. This choice does not concern a matter of fact; it is simply pragmatic. What then *are* matters of fact? The answer is clear: those that concern the given. For it is the given alone that verifies any true statement. The given is what stops us saying *absolutely anything* in our theories: it is the reality we must accurately describe. In fact, all statements, insofar as they have meaning, are translatable into statements about the given. When the chips are down, the positivist must talk only of the given.

So, at the same time that the positivists are rejecting the metaphysical dispute about the nature of reality, they are making a strong metaphysical assumption about reality: it consists only of the given. What exactly *is* the given? The positivists find it very hard to say. However, a certain view of it always comes through in their writings: it is *the indubitable content of experience*. In other words, the given is indistinguishable from the ideas and sense data of traditional idealists. The positivists are closet anti-realists. Despite their disavowals, they are committed to a powerful and, we claim, thoroughly false metaphysics.

One cannot theorize about anything, least of all language, without implicit commitment to a view of the world. As a result, attempts to eliminate metaphysics lead not to its elimination but to its mystification; the philosopher has to hide or deny his own metaphysical assumptions.

11.3 Dummett and the misidentification of the realism dispute

Though the Verifiability Principle of the positivists has been abandoned, verificationism has recently been reborn under the influence of the Oxford philosopher, Michael Dummett. We have seen that the positivists used verificationism in an attempt to *replace* the metaphysical issue of realism with an issue about language. Dummett attempts to *identify* realism with such an issue and then use verificationism to show that realism is false.

Dummett's discussion of realism is voluminous, repetitive and difficult. It is aimed not only at the realism that concerns us – realism about common-sense physical entities like stones, trees and cats – but also realism about scientific entities, about mathematical entities, about the past, and so on. He identifies each realism dispute with a dispute about the *truth conditions* of the relevant set of statements. In the present case, these would be common-sense physical statements containing words like 'stone', 'tree' and 'cat'. So his argument begins:

> The common-sense realism dispute is the dispute about whether these statements have realist or only verificationist truth conditions.

Dummett goes onto argue that the statements have only verificationist truth conditions, and so realism is false.

"Realist" truth conditions involve a "realist" notion of truth. A notion of truth is realist, for Dummett, if it does not make the truth of a statement dependent on the *evidence* we have or might have for the statement. So a statement could be true even though we had no effective way of *telling* whether it was. Clearly the notion of truth that we have been using to explain meaning is a realist one: it is explained in terms of reference and structure without any mention of the evidence for truth. In contrast, a notion of truth is verificationist if it takes a statement to be true only if it is, or could be, *established* to be true.

The distinction is brought out nicely by one of Dummet's favourite examples: the person who died without ever having been put in danger. Consider the following statement about that person:

> The person was brave.

Is it true or false? If the statement has only verificationist truth conditions, this question amounts to: Can we discover whether it is true or false? Very likely we cannot discover any information about this person that is relevant to the statement. In which case, the statement is neither true nor false. On the other hand, if the statement has realist truth conditions, its truth or falsity transcends this evidential matter. There was something about that person, whether we can discover it or not, that makes the statement true or false.

The idea that truth conditions are verificationist is clearly a relative of the discarded Verifiability Principle. Oversimplifying, if meaning is truth conditions and truth conditions are verificationist, then meaning is method of verification.

Set aside the rest of Dummett's argument until the next section and consider the premise displayed above. Dummett identifies the realism dispute with one in semantics. Moreover, that identification is neither covert nor abashed: Dummett thinks it is his main contribution.

> The whole point of my approach to [the various disputes concerning realism] has been to show that the theory of meaning underlies metaphysics. If I have made any worthwhile contribution to philosophy, I think it must lie in having raised this issue in these terms. (1978: xl)

Dummett is an enthusiast for the linguistic turn (11.2).

We could summarize our description of realism in section 11.1 as follows

> Common-sense physical entities objectively exist independently of the mental.

This says nothing about language at all: it contains no semantic or grammatical term like 'mean', 'true' or 'noun'; it says nothing about linguistic items like sentences or words. It is a doctrine about what there is and what it is like. It is about the largely impersonal and inanimate world. In contrast, a theory of language has its place within a theory of people. (Of course realism is stated *in* language. *How else* could it be stated? But it is not *about* language. Using language is one thing, talking about it another; 2.7.)

Given that the doctrine we have called "realism" seems to have nothing to do with language, it is appropriate to wonder whether Dummett is using the term 'realism' in some other way. If so, our disagreement with him would be only verbal. However, it is clear that Dummett sees himself as reinterpreting and rejecting the traditional metaphysical doctrine of realism.

What licenses this reinterpretation? On Dummett's view, a metaphysical thesis by itself is only a metaphor or picture. Such a thesis is only "a picture which has in itself no substance otherwise than as a representation of the given conception of meaning" (1977: 383).

A metaphor has to be made literal if it is to be more than suggestive. Dummett's view, very much in the spirit of positivism, is that a metaphysical metaphor can be cashed only by a theory of meaning. Central to his identification of realism with a semantic thesis is his view that *without* that identification, realism has no genuine content, however irresistible an image it might represent.

We think that this "metaphor thesis" should be rejected and that the above premise is false.

To start with, note that the metaphor thesis could only seem plausible if one *already* thought that metaphysical views were special in some way. Doubtless this thought is encouraged by the allegedly *a priori* nature of metaphysics, and by Heideggerian excesses. From our naturalistic perspective (1.3), metaphysics is empirical and not special.

Nobody should think that the view that there are stones is just a metaphor; nor the view that there are trees; nor the view that there are cats. The first dimension of realism is just a generalization of such thoughts and so is not the least bit metaphorical. It is harder to keep a metaphorical element out of the second dimension. Anti-realist characterizations of the alleged dependence of objects on the knowing mind – the attempts to close "the gap" – often strike us as metaphorical, as will become apparent in the next two chapters. However, removing these metaphorical elements does not reduce the realism dispute to one about meaning; it remains a metaphysical dispute about the nature of reality.

Nor are Dummett's reasons for the metaphor thesis compelling. They rest on an analogy with a dispute in the philosophy of mathematics. In that discipline there has been disagreement over mathematical entities. Some philosophers have denied that there are any such entities; cf. denying our first dimension above. However, if the existence of the entities is accepted, then the dispute becomes analogous to one over our second dimension. Given that there are numbers, what are they like? Do they exist independently of us? Do mathematicians *discover* their properties and relations, just as a biochemist discovers the structure of a virus? Or are numbers rather our own creations? Do we construct the number system and so invent the properties of numbers rather more than discover them?

These are deeply puzzling questions. Suppose that numbers are real and independent of us. No naturalistic account of their nature has so far been successful, so the result is *platonism*: numbers are real but not physical nor even spatiotemporal at all. Thus their nature is deeply mysterious. And how could we come to know about these strange and causally isolated objects?

The alternative, known as *constructionism* or *intuitionism*, is no more appealing. If we have invented mathematics in somewhat the same way that we have invented the game of chess, it is very odd that it is so useful, indeed indispensable, in our investigation of the world.

In the face of these puzzles, Dummett proposes that we should treat the platonism–intuitionism dispute over entities as a metaphorical version of a dispute over the conditions on mathematical proofs. This turns quickly into an issue about the truth conditions of mathematical statements.

Dummett's proposal has some plausibility, but the extension of this approach beyond the mathematical dispute to common-sense realism does not. For the plausibility of Dummett's proposal in mathematics comes precisely from the *contrast* between mathematical entities and familir physical entities. Numbers (if there are any) contrast with stones, trees and cats in their strange non-spatiotemporal properties, their causal isolation, and their inaccessibility to experimental investigation. That is what makes the mathematical dispute seem so metaphorical.

In sum, we think that Dummett's premise is false. *Prima facie*, realism is a metaphysical dispute – a dispute about the nature of reality. Dummett needs a strong argument to show that, despite appearances, it is about language. His attempt to show this by establishing the metaphorical nature of the realism dispute fails. It rests on a mistaken analogy with mathematics. It is precisely the *dis* analogy between numbers and ordinary things that makes the metaphor thesis seem plausible for the mathematical dispute.

It follows from this that whatever the strengths of the rest of Dummett's argument, that argument alone does not establish anything about realism.

11.4 Verificationism

We have argued that verificationism does not eliminate metaphysics as the positivists claim, nor does it establish anti-realism as Dummett claims. In this section we shall assess verificationism itself, and consider what relation it does have to realism.

Let us start by considering the rest of Dummett's argument. This seeks to etablish that statements have only verificationist truth conditions. In its most prominent form it attempts this by arguing that these are the only sort of truth conditions that the competent speaker could *know*. Suppose that the truth conditions of a statement are: it is true if and only if certain circumstances hold. Dummett claims that the speaker could not know these truth conditions if those circumstances transcend those in which the statement could be verified. The main problem with this argument is that it presupposes a "propositional assumption" about competence: that competence consists in propositional knowledge of truth conditions. We have argued that competence does not consist in propositional knowledge (8.4, 8.7). If we are right then Dummett's claim that the speaker could not know realist truth conditions is irrelevant to realist truth. We shall therefore say no more of this prominent form of the argument.

It is possible to discern another form of the argument that does not depend on the propositional assumption. It takes competence as simply a practical ability that does not require any knowledge about the language. Dummett argues that statements can have only verificationist truth conditions because a statement that had truth conditions that transcended its conditions of verification could not be understood. For, a speaker must be able to manifest her understanding in behaviour, and all she can manifest is her ability to associate the statement with the conditions that verify it. Most simply, she can show that she *recognizes* a certain situation as conclusively justifying the assertion of the statement.

The details of this argument are very complicated and need not concern us. But, in summary, Dummett argues that understanding must be verificationist and so truth conditions must be also.

We indicated earlier (11.2) that verificationism is at odds with our whole approach to language. We can bring this out by moving from sentences to words; the truth conditions of sentences depends on the reference of words. Our approach is inconsistent with verificationism because *verificationism requires description theories of the understanding and reference of words*. To understand a name it will be necessary to be able to describe or recognize its bearer; and the referent will be the object, if any, recognized or described. So, it is no surprise that Dummett does subscribe to a description theory of names. Causal theories of reference and understanding were born out of the rejection of description theories and are essentially anti-verificationist. *If the arguments from ignorance and error offered against description theories (3.3–3.4) are correct, then verificationism is false*. A person can use a term to refer though almost entirely wrong or ignorant about its referent.

So we think that verificationism is basically implausible. However, we think that there are deeper considerations against it. These emerge from a consideration of its relation to realism.

Dummett identifies realism with realist truth. We must avoid this mistake. The issues are quite distinct. Nevertheless, they are related. We need to consider how they are related. What conclusions can we draw from a position on realism about truth and understanding? And what conclusions can we draw from a position on truth and understanding about realism? These questions give rise to another. Where should we start? Should we start with a position on realism and see what follows from that about truth and understanding, or vice versa? Those, like Dummett, who are part of the linguistic turn in philosophy, think that we should start with truth and understanding.

Suppose that Dummett were right – that we should be verificationist about truth and understanding. Then this starting place is sufficient to establish anti-realism (even without Dummett's mistaken identification). The verificationist position is that a statement is true if and only if it is verifiable. (By "verifiable" we mean verifiably true, not, as the positivists usually meant, verifiably true or false). For example:

'Caesar had five moles' is true if and only if 'Caesar had five moles' is verifiable.

Now it is a relatively trivial fact about truth, captured in the *disquotation principle* (9.2), that a sentence in the form of

'Caesar had five moles' is true

is equivalent to another in the form

Caesar had five moles.

If we are entitled to assert one of these two sentences then we are entitled to assert the other. So we can substitute the latter for the former in the earlier sentence to get:

Caesar had five moles if and only if 'Caesar had five moles' is verifiable.

This claim relates a state of the world – Caesar having five moles – very closely to our abilities. The world can *be* a certain way only if we can *verify* a certain statement. In contrast, realists think that there are indefinitely many facts about the world that could never be discovered. The world could be related to our verifying abilities in the above way only if it were somehow dependent on us for its existence or nature; it must be, in some way, our creation. Such a world is not the objective independent one that the realist believes in. Thus:

verificationism → anti-realism.

The '→' here does not represent an entailment. Rather it represents an inference to the best explanation. So there is no *inconsistency* in being a verificationist and a realist. The point is that once verificationism has been accepted, the most plausible view of the world is an anti-realist one.

We think that this procedure of arguing from a view of language to a view of the world is all wrong. We have garnered a theory of the extra-linguistic world through arduous years of living. We think that there are stones, trees, cats, and so on: a huge impersonal universe that does not depend on us for its existence or nature; indeed, a universe often singular impervious to us. That is, we are committed to realism. It is not a mysterious doctrine. It causes no mystical glow. It is dull and familiar. But that is not to its discredit. On the contrary, it indicates that realism is as firm a starting point as we can expect to find. Certainly it is a much firmer one than speculations in the largely unknown areas of truth and understanding. This is not to say that realism is unquestionable; perhaps our common-sense ontology is largely false. However, what is scarcely conceivable is that realism could be shown to be false by discoveries about language and understanding.

Our attitude here reflects our naturalism (1.3, 14.1). For us, a theory of language is just one empirical theory among many others of the world we live in. As such it does not compare in strength to realism, which is an overarching ontological doctrine abstracted from our most secure common-sense and scientific theories of physical reality. To think otherwise is to take an *a priori* view of the theory of language. Speculating from the comfort of our armchairs, we are supposed to be able to decide what truth and understanding *must* be like, and hence what the world *must* be like, without concerning ourselves with empirically established theories of extra-linguistic reality. In our view, such speculations are baseless.

We started this section by indicating the clash between verificationism and the arguments from ignorance and error used against description theories. The case against verificationism is deeper. If we start thinking about language from a firmly realist perspective, as we have just urged we should, then it seems that truth cannot be verificationist. In effect, the point is one that we have already made in claiming that description theories of reference cannot be true for all terms (3.5, 4.2). For, verificationism requires description theories. All that description theories can do is relate some words to other words, some concepts to other concepts. If we are ever to relate words and concepts to a mind-independent reality, we need causal theories for some words and concepts. With causal theories goes the abandonment of verificationism. So, the inference to the best explanation that we favour is:

realism → anti-verificationism.

In conclusion, the realism dispute cannot be eliminated in favour of an issue about language, nor can it be identified with such an issue. Further, it is not appropriate to base an argument against realism on largely uncertain and *a priori* speculations about language. Rather, we should speculate about language from a firm realist base. From that base, we can see that verificationism must be rejected.

Suggested reading

11.1

See Devitt 1984a, *Realism and Truth*, chapter 2 for a more detailed account of realism, and chapter 5 for a defence of realism.

11.2

The most persuasive defense of the classical logical positivist position on realism is in Schlick 1932–33, "Positivism and realism", reprinted in Ayer 1959,

Logical Positivism. The latter is a very helpful collection of articles from the heyday of positivism.

Ayer 1940, *The Foundations of Empirical Knowledge*, particularly chapters 1, 2 and 6, is a nice example of the positivist approach to realism. Ayer 1946, *Language, Truth and Logic*, was the very successful introduction of positivism to the English-speaking world.

Carnap 1950, "Empiricism, semantics and ontology", and Hempel 1950 "Problems and changes in the empiricist criterion of meaning", both reprinted in Linsky 1952, *Semantics and the Philosophy of Language*, are more recent statements of the positivist position. Hempel's paper is also reprinted in Rosenberg and Travis 1971.

11.3–11.4

The great quantity and difficulty of Dummett's writing on realism make suggestions difficult. However, we think that a fairly good idea of his views can be obtained from "Realism" and "Preface" in *Truth and Other Enigmas* (1978). **For more details of his verificationist views of language, see "What is a theory of meaning?" (1975), particularly pp. 105-25, and "What is a theory of meaning? (II)", particularly pp. 68-111.**

For a more detailed criticism of Dummett see Devitt 1983, "Dummett's anti-realism", which contains many references to appropriate parts of Dummett's work. That paper appears, in modified form, as chapter 12 in Devitt 1984a. Chapters 3 and 4 are also relevant to the discussion. George 1984, "On Devitt and Dummett", is a response to Devitt 1983.

** Quine's scepticism about meaning involves a holistic verificationism; see the suggested reading for 1.3.**

Neo-Kantianism

12.1 Kant

The approach of this book has been uniformly naturalistic. Philosophy is just part of the empirical attempt to understand nature. Neither philosophy in general, nor philosophy of language in particular, has any special status. Such a view has been unappealing to the philosophically inclined. Overtly or covertly, most have practised "first philosophy": Philosophy thought of as anterior to science in particular, and empirically based knowledge in general. The *a priori* armchair approach to the philosophy of language criticized in the last chapter (11.4) is an example of first philosophy.

Traditional epistemology is another example. It tried to show how scepticism could be refuted and knowledge claims justified. Since these claims include science, it would be circular to place epistemology within science. Science itself needs justification. That justifiction can only be given by a discipline that is conceptually and epistemically prior to science. Thus epistemology got its traditional role.

In this chapter and the next we shall be concerned with various first philosophers who draw metaphysical conclusions about the nature of reality from reflections on language. To understand these conclusions, which are usually inchoate and obscure, it is important to have some acquaintance with the view of the great German philosopher, Immanuel Kant. Acquaintance is not easy because Kant is deep, dark and difficult. His concern is not with language but with knowledge. Kant's views on realism are a result of his struggles with the traditional epistemological problem of scepticism.

There is a view of the mind and of perception that makes the sceptical worry acute. It is sometimes called, anachronistically, "the movie-show model" of the mind. The mind, the conscious self, does not have direct access to the external world: its access is via the sense organs. That much is obvious. So what is immediately presented to the mind, the model concludes, is not the world but perceptual impressions ("ideas", "sense data"): images, sounds, tastes, touches and smells, channelled to the mind from the appropriate organs. The mind is like a person sitting in a movie theatre watching these perceptual impressions play on a screen. However, there is one crucial difference. The person can leave the theatre and look outside, but the mind cannot; it is forever confined to the action on the inner screen.

If we are guided by this model, it is no wonder that sceptical worries obtrude. What grounds has the person who never leaves the theatre for thinking that he is watching a documentary? If he never compares the external reality with the images on the screen, then he can never know if any of the images are accurate. No more can the mind know if its images are accurate. The perceptual impressions cohere, of course, but so do most movies, however fictional. Perhaps the mind is entitled to think that *something* must be causing the inner show, but what? There is no warrant for assuming that what causes the picture is *like* the picture. The world is forever shrouded behind the "veil of ideas".

We have mentioned earlier "the gap" between the object known and the knowing mind (11.1). The movie-show model makes that gap seem unbridgeable. At least, it seems unbridgeable if the object is independent of the mind, as the second dimension of realism requires.

Kant closed the gap with his view that the object known is in part constituted by the knowing mind. Objects as we know them – stones, trees, cats, and so on – are not to be confused with objects as they are independent of our knowledge. Kant calls the former "appearances" and the latter "things-in-themselves". Appearances are obtained by our *imposition* of *a priori* concepts; for example, causality, time and the Euclidian principles of spatial relation. Only things-in-themselves have the objectivity and independence required by realism. Appearances do not, as they are partly our construction. And, it must be emphasized, the familiar furniture of the world is appearances not things-in-themselves.

This deeply mysterious metaphysics has fascinated philosophers for two centuries. Reality as it is in itself is mysterious in being forever inaccessible. Reality as we know it is mysterious in being somehow the result of our own handiwork. How could we, literally, have made the stars?

Many contemporary anti-realisms combine Kantianism with relativism. Kant was no relativist: the concepts imposed to constitute the known world were common to all mankind. Contemporary anti-realisms tend to retain Kant's ideas of things-in-themselves and of imposition, but drop the universality of what is imposed. Instead, different languages, theories and world views are imposed to create different known worlds. Such relativistic Kantianism is extraordinarily popular. We shall now consider some examples.

12.2 Whorfian relativism

The contemporary route to Kantian metaphysics starts not with the theory of knowledge but with the theory of language (which is why we are concerned with it in this book). Passage along the route is aided and abetted by a persistent vacillation between talk of theory and talk of the world. This vacillation is of enormous help to the anti-realist because, of course, *theories really are mind-dependent*. So, if the distinction between theories and the world is blurred, an anti-realist position will seem much more plausible.

It is obvious that people construct their theories of the world, and that they do so on the basis of experiential stimuli that they receive. And we accept Whorf's point that the theories they construct are influenced (but not constrained) by the language of their community (10.2–10.3). So we can go along with Whorf's claim that a language

is a classification and arrangement of the stream of sensory experience; (1956: 55)

and that

the world is presented in a kaleidoscopic flux of impressions which has to be organized by our minds – and this means largely by the linguistic system in our minds. (p. 213)

For the sake of argument, let us also go along with the following exaggeration by Sapir:

No two languages are ever sufficiently similar to be considered as representing the same social reality. (1949: 162)

However, none of this has anything directly to do with the world. It is *experience* of the world that we are organizing, not the world itself; it is a *theory* of the world that language helps us construct, not the world itself. Yet Whorf and Sapir slip quickly from talking of experiences and theories to talk of the world. Whorf's "classification and arrangement" of experience "results in a certain world-order". The worlds in which Sapir's linguistically different societies live "are distinct worlds". How could anything a person does to his experience – how could any of his modes of representation – affect stones, trees, cats and stars? In one breath, Whorf runs together the ideas of imposition on the world and imposition on experience:

different languages differently "segment" the same situation or experience. (p. 162)

We are frequently told of our handiwork on reality: "We dissect nature"; "we cut nature up" (Whorf 1956: 213); "the 'real world' is to a large extent built up on the language habits of the group" (Sapir 1949: 162).

It is plausible to claim that our minds, concepts and languages construct theories out of experience. It is wildly implausible to claim that our minds, concepts and languages construct the world out of experience. Imposition on experience is one thing, imposition on the world is another. Are Sapir and Whorf simply conflating the two (cf. Dummett's identification: 11.3)? If so they are seriously confused. If not, they must think that their claims about world construction *follow from* their claims about theory construction. Yet this is an inference of such startling badness that only its apparent popularity excuses anyone bothering to reject it.

Are we being uncharitable? Perhaps the talk of different worlds is just a careless way of talking about different world views. We think not. First, it would then be hard to accommodate the claims of Sapir and Whorf about the incommensurability of different world views, for reasons to be brought out in the next section. Second, we suspect that only by taking their views literally can we explain the breathless excitement – the aura of *significance* – with which they are presented and received.

We do not suggest that claims about language and mind have *no* implications for metaphysics. We have already allowed that some do (11.4). What we insist is that Whorf's particular claim *has no metaphysical implications at all*. Furthermore, we think that the procedure of arguing from theories of language or mind to metaphysics is generally wrong-headed: it puts the cart before the horse (11.4).

In the passages quoted from Sapir and Whorf, and many others, we find two central Kantian ideas: first, the idea of the known world being partly created by an act of human imposition; second, the idea of there being something, "nature", independent of us and beyond our ken. Whorf describes the latter with mystical fervour

the unknown, vaster world – that world of which the physical is but a surface or skin, and yet which we ARE IN, and BELONG TO. (p. 248)

We shall criticize these Kantian ideas in the next section.

The passages quoted, and many others, add relativism to these Kantian ideas. Studies by Sapir and Whorf of different linguistic communities lead them to the conclusion that the communities have different world views (10.1). These different views are imposed to yield different realities; the world that each community lives in is relative to its language and theory.

We concluded earlier that Whorf exaggerates the differences in world views (10.2–103). Nonetheless, there are real and important differences. What is the proper response to these differences? Not to come to the conclusion that each community "lives in its own world". There is only one world. Rather, we should examine these differences and see what we can learn from them. Sometimes we will discover a people that has learned about things we know nothing of. Their theories of the world will be complementary with ours, and we can borrow from them. Sometimes, though, their views and ours will be inconsistent. Then we must decide who is right. Perhaps the aliens are right; in which case we should change our own theory. Perhaps we are right and the aliens wrong. To grant this possibility is not cultural chauvinism; it is taking the aliens seriously. It would be condescension to refuse to apply to their views the same critical standards that we apply to our own. The people that believe that they gain the strength of their enemy by eating his liver and drinking his blood are simply mistaken. Similarly, the people that think that every Sunday they eat the body, and drink the blood, of God.

12.3 Scientific relativism

Radical philosophers of science like Kuhn and Feyerabend are also, we think, relativistic Kantians. Once again, it is hard to be certain of an interpretation. Like their arch-rivals, the positivists, the radicals are ontologically coy.

The vacillation we have complained of between talk of theory and talk of the world is to be found in the writings of the radicals. Consider the following example taken from Kuhn's account of the discovery of the planet Uranus:

> That scrutiny disclosed Uranus' motion among the stars, and Herschel therefore announced that he had seen a new comet! Only several months later, after fruitless attempts to fit the observed motion to a cometary orbit, did Lexell suggest that the orbit was probably planetary. When that suggestion was accepted, there were several fewer stars and one more planet in the world of the professional astronomer. (1962: 114)

Charity dictates that we should take the last sentence as a harmless metaphor used to emphasize the radical shift in theory that had taken place. After all, how could the acceptance of a suggestion by a few astronomers literally destroy stars and create planets?

However, consider the following from his account of the discovery of oxygen:

At the very least, as a result of discovering oxygen, Lavoisier saw nature differently. And in the absence of some recourse to that hypothetical fixed nature that he "saw differently", the principle of economy will urge us to say that after discovering oxygen Lavoisier worked in a different world. (p. 117)

Here the difference between claiming that things *look* different as a result of a theory change and claiming that they *are* different as a result of the change is acknowledged, and still the latter claim is made. And it is made for a very Kantian reason: "fixed nature" is beyond our ken; it is the other side of "the gap"; it is a mere thing-in-itself. There is little room for charity here.

Quite apart from many such passages in Kuhn and others – passages that talk of the different worlds of different thinkers – there are good reasons for taking the radicals to be deeply anti-realist.

First, there is their forthright rejection of a correspondence view of truth. By itself, this is not decisive evidence of anti-realism. It is possible to be a realist and accept any theory of truth, or none. But, as we have attempted to show in this book, a correspondence theory of truth is the natural semantic side salad to a realist metaphysics. The sharpness with which the radicals reject it is certainly some evidence for their anti-realism.

Much more decisive evidence comes from the radicals' enthusiasm for the incommensurability of theories (10.4). This incommensurability requires that theory change be accompanied by extensive reference change. But if the world remains the same through theory change, it is not plausible to think that there is extensive reference change; most terms will continue to refer to entities in that unchanging world. Indeed, we have earlier found it easy to argue against incommensurability by presupposing, in effect, that theories referred to a theory-independent world (10.5).

To accommodate the incommensurability thesis, and what goes with it, we must take literally the idea that theories do create their own worlds: the Kantian idea, once again, of human imposition on reality. However, these worlds do not exist "absolutely" but only "relative-to-theory". All that exists "absolutely" is a "nature" beyond reach of knowledge or reference: a Kantian thing-in-itself. Throughout the writings of the radicals, there are references to this independent reality which, in some ineffable way, theories are constrained by and must conform to. It is dough awaiting the cookie cutter of theory.

It would be nice to find a clear statement of this unappealing metaphysics in the writings of the radicals. Understandably, we do not; for their metaphysics, no news is good news.

The main weakness of this metaphysics lies in the whole idea of imposition on an external reality. The act of imposition is internal to the mind. So also is the material on which we impose: what Kant calls the "raw material of sensible impressions". So the result of this imposition can only be internal to the mind. Talk of imposing on the world should be just a metaphor. Yet the metaphysics of the radicals requires that we take this metaphor literally. If we do, then we still seem to have the familiar external world. This illusion is heightened by the idea that an object "exists-relative-to-theory", which should be just a metaphorical way of saying that the theory has a *concept* of the object. Once these metaphors are recognized for what they are, we are left with only the organizing mind and its experience together with the unknowable, and gratuitously assumed, thing-in-itself. There are not really any stones, trees and cats at all.

And there are other problems for this metaphysics. Despite much labour by Kuhn, Feyerabend and others, it has not yielded a satisfactory account of the confirmation of scientific theories, of their conflict, or of scientific progress.

What drives the radicals to this metaphysics? First, they start with a theory of language, in particular a theory of reference. Second, the theory they subscribe to is a description theory, as we have already indicated (10.5). Applying this theory, they conclude that, from our present perspective, none of the terms of past theories refer. For, from that perspective, the description associated with those terms do not pick anything out. So, still from that perspective, the purported referents do not exist. This applies across the board to observables and unobservables alike: even the flasks, rulers, pointers, stones, trees and cats talked of in Newtonian times do not exist from our perspective. To sugar this bitter pill, we are told that those entities all do exist-relative-to-the-Newtonian-perspective.

We have urged an opposite procedure. We start with metaphysics. As theories have changed, have we abandoned our belief in entities that we previously thought to exist? First, consider observables. Theoretical progress certainly results in the addition of new observables, terrestrial and celestial, to our catalogue. But there have been very few deletions. Cases like witches and Vulcan (it was once thought that there was a planet, Vulcan, between Mercury and the Sun) are relatively rare. There have been some mistakes, but there is nothing in our intellectual history to shake our confidence that we have steadily *accumulated* knowledge of the make up of the observable world. We have been wrong often enough about the *nature* of those entities, but it is *their* nature we have been wrong about. We have not been wrong about the fact of their existence. In brief, theory change is no threat to common-sense realism.

Furthermore, we should be sufficiently confident of this metaphysics to reject any theory of language that fails to fit it. It is not that the historical facts of theory change, together with a description theory of reference, show realism to be false. Rather, those facts, together with realism, show description theories to be false. The main significance of the radicals' argument at the observable level is to put another nail in the coffin of description theories of reference.

It is less easy to rebut Kuhn and Feyerabend on unobservables. It is plausible to suppose that we have often been wrong in supposing that an unobservable exists. Even there, the radicals' commitment to the description theory leads them to exaggerate our degree of error. Without these exaggerations, scientific realism is not in much trouble. While our views of, say, the subatomic particles have changed and evolved, we still believe in the entities posited by Bohr and Rutherford. *At most*, the history of science should make us cautious in our commitment to unobservables. It should not lead us into Kantianism and talk of relative existence.

Relativistic neo-Kantianism is to be found way beyond the influence of Whorf, Kuhn, and company. It is endemic to the structuralist movement, to be discussed in the next chapter. Indeed, it has some claim to being the dominant metaphysics of our time, at least among intellectuals.

12.4 The renegade Putnam

We will finish this chapter with a surprising example of a philosopher led into Kantian idealism by considerations of language. Hilary Putnam was a founder of causal theories of reference and was, at that time, a staunch realist. He now finds his former position, which he calls "metaphysical realism", incoherent. Putnam's route to his present position is complex and difficult; part of it depends on one of the paradoxes of modern logic. We shall deal briefly with what we take to be the two main elements.

(1) We have mentioned "the gap" between the object known and the knowing mind, and the sceptical problem that this gives rise to (11.1, 12.1). Given the gap, how do we know that our senses are not deceiving us? Descartes made this problem vivid by raising the possibility that there was a Deceitful Demon interfering with our senses; from the point of view of our senses, it was exactly *as if* there were the familiar external world, but there wasn't really. This worry has been translated into modern idiom. Perhaps you are a brain in a vat, nourished and deceived by Superscientist. The realist makes a sharp distinction between what could *be* the case and what we could *discover* to be the case (11.4). So the realist is committed to the view that you could be a brain in a vat even though you could never discover you were (because Superscientist was too clever to let you discover). That is an admission that worries many: How, then, do you know you are not a brain in a vat?

The sceptical problem is not the concern of this book. What is our concern is Putnam's argument to show, contra realism, that you could *not* be a brain in the vat. For the realist thinks that you could be; it's just that you aren't. The argument is as follows:

> If you were a brain in a vat, you could not think that you were.
> So, you could not be a brain in a vat.

The premise is sound. It is an application of the causal theory of reference. Ultimately, reference is determined not by what is in the head but by appropriate causal links to objects. A brain in a vat is not appropriately linked to any object; it lacks the perceptual links that are neccessary for reference. None of its thoughts are *about* anything. So, though the words 'I am a brain in a vat' could run through its mind, that would not amount to thinking that it was a brain in a vat. We, who are not brains in vats, can think that thought only because we are appropriately linked to brains and vats. It is not enough to be a brain to think about brains, nor to be in a vat to think about vats.

The premise is true, but the argument is fallacious: the conclusion does not follow from the premise. Putnam wants to show that a certain kind of illusion is impossible. But all that his argument actually shows is that, were we suffering from that illusion, we could not even conjecture that we were. This the realist can, and we do, grant. Indeed, how *could* anything follow from what you can *think* to what you can, thoughts aside, *be*. That line of reasoning could be sound only if we *already accepted* that nature itself (in this case, human nature) was not independent of our thoughts. There is nothing in Putnam's argument to threaten realism.

The following analogous argument may help to make this clear:

> If everything were red, you could not think that it was.
> So, everything could not be red.

The premise is plausible. You cannot have thoughts about redness without the concept *red*; and people need to be struck by the difference between red things and non-red things to introduce and sustain that concept. Yet the conclusion obviously does not follow from the premise.

(2) We think that we have the bones of a satisfactory theory of language consonant with realism. That confidence is largely based on a causal theory of reference. Putnam thinks that the confidence is misplaced and offers the earlier-mentioned argument from logic to prove it. Underlying this argument is a certain picture of our referential situation. We start from scratch, locked in our minds, wondering how a thought can fasten onto objects outside the mind. Can the causal theory provide an answer? According to Putnam, all that theory does is add further thoughts *in the mind*; for example, the thought that *a* refers

to *x* in virtue of causal link L. What makes *that* thought reach outside the mind to "grasp" *x* and the causal link L? To suppose it does is to have a "magical theory of reference" (1981: 51). It is to suppose that we can get outside our minds and have a "God's Eye View" of the correspondence between mental signs and mind-independent things (pp. 73–4).

Putnam's solution is a Kantian one that makes the world we wish to refer to immediately accessible to our minds. He offers the following as "the metaphor" for his position: "the mind and the world jointly make up the mind and the world" (p. xi). He cashes the metaphor as follows:

> "objects" do not exist independently of our conceptual schemes. *We* cut up the world into objects when we introduce one or another possible scheme of description. (p. 52)

This is, once again, the Kantian idea of imposition on reality, which we have already dismissed (12.3). Putnam talks in a Kantian way also of things-in-themselves, but ultimately seems to regard such talk as "nonsense", even if psychologically irresistible (pp. 61–2, 83). So far, then, his metaphysics is like those discussed earlier in this chapter. However, his differs from those by avoiding any interesting relativism. He avoids this with the aid of the "principle of charity", which we shall criticize later (15.4).

The picture that leads Putnam to this desperate metaphysics is wrong-headed. We are not hermetically sealed in the prison of our minds, trying to push our thoughts through the bars of perception. The causal theorist does not think that it is our *thought*, "*a* refers to *x* in virtue of causal link L", that makes *a* refer to *x*. What makes it do this is the fact that *a is* so causally linked to *x*. It is not our thoughts about causal links, but our having of those links, that welds our thoughts onto the world.

Putnam proceeds in the wrong direction. In theorizing about language, we do not start with the mind locked up and innocent; we start with what we already know. Reflection on our best science has committed us to many entities of the largely inanimate and impersonal world. We go on, naturalistically, to seek an explanation of that small part of the world which exhibits the phenomenon of reference: people and their words. The result is a theory of no special status. It is, of course, *possible* that the formulation of theory might lead us to revise our views of what exists in other areas. But great changes are unlikely: the theory is narrow in scope and, for the foreseeable future, tentative. It is particularly unlikely to change our view of the independence of what exists from theorists and theories. Finally, semantic relations are no more inaccessible than other relations. Theorizing about the relation between a thought or expression and an object no more requires a God's Eye View than does theorizing about the relation between, say, Margaret Thatcher and Ronald Reagan.

In sum, we reject the views of the various neo-Kantians considered in this chapter. Their talk of imposition is simply a comforting metaphor, giving the illusion of commitment to the familiar world. Their talk of things-in-themselves is simply comforting nonsense, as Putnam points out: it adds a fig leaf to the nakedness of Kantian idealism. Their relativism arises from exaggerating the differences between languages. Finally, their metaphysics all exemplify a deep mistake: that of inferring what the world is like from a theory of language. Any theory of language is less secure than most others from common sense and science. If an implausible world view is a consequence of a theory of language, then we should unhesitatingly reject that theory not accept the consequences. The philosophy of language is exactly the wrong place to start metaphysics.

Suggested reading

12.1

The most accessible of Kant's accounts of his metaphysics is *Prolegomena to Any Future Metaphysics* (1953; first published, 1783). **His great work is *Critique of Pure Reason* (1929; first published, 1781), but this is very long and very difficult. Strawson 1966, *The Bounds of Sense*, is about as readable an account of the *Critique* as can be had.**

12.2

The most helpful papers in Whorf 1956, *Language, Thought, and Reality*, for the concerns of this section are: "Science and linguistics", "Languages and logic", and his most famous paper, "Language, mind, and reality". For general reading on Sapir and Whorf, see suggestions for sections 10.1–10.3.

12.3

See the readings concerned with Kuhn and Feyerabend suggested for 10.4 and 10.5.

12.4

The best place to find Putnam's views is *Reason, Truth and History* (1981), particularly chapters 1–3. For a a more detailed criticism along the lines of the text, see Devitt 1984a, chapter 11.

13

Structuralism

> To be human ... is to be a structuralist.
> (Hawkes 1977: 15)

13.1 Introduction

A book on language should not fail to discuss the extremely influential movement known as *structuralism*, an approach to the theories known sometimes as *semiotics* and sometimes as *semiology*. Elements of that discussion would have been appropriate enough in each of the previous two parts as well as in this part. However, we have preferred to gather the discussion together in one chapter. And we have put that chapter here because most of the excitement generated by structuralism has come not from its views of language but from what it is thought to show about the world in general.

The term 'structuralism' refers to a certain theoretical approach; briefly, it is an approach that sees the objects of study as defined relationally. 'Semiology' and 'semiotics' both have their roots in the Greek word for a sign and refer to the "science of signs". The first term was invented by the Swiss linguist, Ferdinand de Saussure, and is preferred in Europe. The second was invented by the American philosopher, C. S. Peirce, and is preferred by English speakers. For most purposes, the three terms can be treated as equivalent: the science of signs has been almost the only home of the structuralist approach; and everything done under the banner of semiotics or semiology has been structuralist, or deeply influenced by structuralism.

It is usual to see structuralism as beginning with Saussure's *Course in General Linguistics* (1966), published posthumously in 1916. It is the movement arising out of that work, particularly in France where it has dominated intellectual life, that we shall be considering in this chapter. However, it should be noted that a different but related movement known also as structuralism arose independently in America. This started with Edward Sapir and was made prominent by Leonard Bloomfield's *Language* (1933), a landmark in American linguistics. The structuralist influence remains in transformational grammar, as we have pointed out (6.4, 8.7). Structuralist ideas are also to be found in the movement known as "Russian Formalism", which began in Moscow and St Petersburg during the First World War.

Saussure saw linguistics as only part of his concerns, for he thought that there were many signs other than linguistic ones. The structuralist approach he found appropriate in linguistics was to be projected into human culture in general. Structuralism has been taken to span anthropology, social theory (particularly Marxian), psychology (particularly Freudian), literary criticism, philosophy, the history of ideas, and much else besides: the structuralizing of everything. Key figures in this movement have been Claude Levi-Strauss, Louis Althusser, Jacques Lacan, Roland Barthes and, perhaps, Michel Foucault. (In his later years, Barthes moved to "post-structuralism". That is also the position of Jacques Derrida, who introduced the idea of *deconstruction*. We shall not discuss post-structuralism. However, in our view, it shares the central weaknesses of structuralism in its approach to reference and realism.)

13.2 Saussure's linguistics

Saussure's linguistics is the way into structuralism. We shall begin our characterization of that linguistics with its most important thesis: that a language is constituted by its *internal relations*.

(1) A language can be decomposed into a number of elementary units that appear and reappear. Thus the sound type /t/ would be tokened four times in any pronunciation of the immediately preceding sentence; the letter type 't' is tokened five times. In virtue of what are such sounds or letters tokens of the one type? We shall concentrate on the case of sound types, since the primary form of language is speech not writing. Sound types are called *phonemes*. So our question becomes: when are different sounds tokens of the same phoneme?

Saussure and the linguists following him think that we cannot define phonemes in terms of their *acoustic* properties: the physical properties of the sound wave. For one thing, the phonetic environment of a sound affects the way it is pronounced and hence its acoustic properties: /t/ pronounced in the middle of a word is acoustically different from /t/ pronounced at the end. For another, speech is a continuous stream; it does not break into discrete units. Finally, differences between speakers are also considerable. For instance, the pitch – the frequency of sound waves – is typically higher for women than for men. There must be some limits, but the degree of variation of the physical signal is considerable.

What determines the amount of allowable variation? According to Saussure, it is the linguistic system itself. Some differences are *marked*: they correspond to a difference in sign. Others are not. In English, consonants may be *voiced*: their pronunciation involves the rapid vibration of the vocal chords as air is expelled past them. The phonemes /d/ and /t/ differ only in that /d/ but not /t/ is voiced. Thus English distinguishes /bed/ from /bet/. Not every language marks every distinction English does, and English does not mark distinctions other languages do. It is notorious, for example, that some Asian languages do not mark the distinction between /l/ and /r/. For sounds, it is the linguistic system itself that defines typehood, for the linguistic system determines what physical similarities and differences between sounds count as important.

This approach to phonology was developed into "binary feature analysis". The essential idea was to define phonemes as clusters of articulatory features: features like voice (vibrating *versus* non-vibrating vocal chords); nasality (open *versus* closed nasal passages); front *versus* back tongue position; upper *versus* lower tongue position; and so on. These features are binary: they are present or not present. This involves ignoring some aspects of the pronunciation process (for example, there are many different tongue positions that are classified as front), while highlighting others. The linguistic system plays its role in determining which features are to be highlighted. Thus round *versus* non-round lips is a difference that makes a difference in standard English (between /cot/ and /caught/, for example), but not in a number of American regional accents. The contrasts marked by the linguistic system determine which articulatory features are relevant to the definition of phonemes.

A central idea of structuralism has been to extend this approach to defining phonemes to *all* categories of linguistic theory; to extend it from the phonetic and phonological to the morphological, syntactic and semantic. The linguistic contribution of each item is given by its *differences from other items* in the language; "each linguistic term derives its value from its opposition to all other terms" (Saussure 1966: 88). This exemplifies the structuralist approach. An item is defined not by what it is in itself – not by its essential properties – but by its relationship in a *structure*.

> that the world is made up of relationships rather than things, constitutes the first principle of the way of thinking which can properly be called "structuralist". (Hawkes 1977: 17–18)

In applying the approach to words, Saussure distinguishes two sorts of relationships that words have to each other: *syntagmatic* and *associative* or *paradigmatic*. Syntagmatic relations are those a word holds to other words, typically of other syntactic categories, with which it can be conjoined in well-formed strings called *syntagms*. Thus the relation between 'Zanzibar' and 'explodes' is syntagmatic; the two can be conjoined to form a syntagm, in this case the sentence, 'Zanzibar explodes'. Paradigmatic relations are those a word holds to other words which are possible alternatives to it in the well-formed string – i.e. to words that could be substituted for it. Thus the relation between 'explodes' and 'approves' is paradigmatic; the latter could replace the former in the above sentence.

It is a central tenet of structuralism that *all* of a word's syntagmatic and paradigmatic relations go into its meaning – its linguistic identity. Thus Philip Pettit, in his commentary on structuralism, writes of the paradigmatic ones:

> if a word lost some such relationship or gained others it would lose its old formal identity: . . . [it] would become a . . . different word. (1977: 9)

In the same vein, Jonathan Culler writes that we cannot grasp the meaning of 'brown' until we have grasped its relation with all other colour words (1976: 25).

Furthermore, syntagmatic and paradigmatic relations *exhaust* the meaning of a word. So, Culler claims, there is nothing more to the meaning of 'brown' than these relations; our concepts of colour "are nothing but a product or result of a system of distinctions" (p. 25).

> Language is a system of interdependent terms in which the value of each term results solely from the simultaneous presence of the others . . . (Saussure 1966: 114)

From our perspective, this is the most surprising and objectionable feature of structuralism, for it *omits reference*. Part of the meaning of 'brown' is given by the fact that it refers to brown things. A word's relations to others in the language – *internal* relations – are undoubtedly important to its meaning, but so also are its relations to the world outside the language – its *external* relations. We shall return to this criticism in the next section.

(2) The relationism that we have described leads straight to the next feature of Saussure's linguistics: its *holistic* view of language. The meaning of each term is defined by its place in the entire structure; it has no identity except in that structure. Change the structure and the term's meaning changes. So the introduction of one new term changes all terms. And there is no question of the new term "bringing a meaning with it". We cannot coin a term, giving it a meaning, and simply add it with its meaning to the language. We cannot borrow a foreign word with its meaning; once borrowed, its old meaning is irrelevant:

> it exists only through its relation with, and opposition to, words associated with it, just like any other genuine sign. (Saussure 1966: 22)

This holism is a direct consequence of ignoring reference. For the reference of a word will be dependent, at most, on that of only a few others and may be independent of all others, as we have seen (chapters 4 and 5). Reference is a part of a word's meaning that can persist through changes in its paradigmatic and syntagmatic relations.

(3) With relationism and holism goes the view that a language is an *autonomous* system, to be explained entirely in its own terms without any reference to anything outside its structure:

> the structure is *self-regulating* in the sense that it makes no appeals beyond itself ... The transformations act to ... "seal off" the system from reference to other systems. A language ... does not construct its formations of words by reference to the patterns of "reality", but on the basis of its own internal and self-sufficient rules. (Hawkes 1977: 16–17)

It is "self-defining" and "self-contained" (p. 26).

In this regard, Saussure's often-used analogy with chess is instructive:

> In chess, what is external can be separated relatively easily from what is internal ... everything having to do with its system and rules is internal. (Saussure 1966: 20)

> But just as the game of chess is entirely in the combination of the different chesspieces, language is characterized as a system based entirely on the opposition of its concrete units. (p. 107)

Saussure is clearly right about the autonomy of chess. The notion of check is defined only *within* the rules of chess; it has no content independent of that rule system. Change the relevant rules – as for example in "blitz" chess, which allows the king to be taken – and you change or eliminate check.

Chess is indeed a good model for Saussure's view of language, but it is a poor one for language itself, as we shall emphasize (13.3).

(4) If the elements of a language depend on the linguistic system, it is plain that linguistics must be concerned with that system itself. The structuralist is therefore not interested in particular linguistic acts. No set of acts can be more than a partial and inexact reflection of the system. Saussure distinguishes the linguistic system he is studying, *langue*, from its manifestations in the behaviour of speakers, *parole*. This distinction is an ancestor of Chomsky's much discussed one between competence and performance (6.1, 8.2).

(5) If the study is of a self-contained system then it is ahistorical. How the system originated is beside the point. Thus Saussure distinguished himself from his predecessors in arguing for the importance of a *synchronic* approach in linguistics. Prior to that, linguistics had been entirely concerned with the historical and causal development of languages: it had been *diachronic*. Saussure did not deny a place for diachronic linguistics, but he did want to keep it sharply distinct from synchronic. History creates the interrelations and structures that constitute the system. However, the story of this creation is irrelevant to our understanding of that system. Thus it is of no consequence to synchronic linguistics how English came to mark the distinction between /t/ and /d/ as significant, but not that between mid-word and word-final /l/. What matters is just that the one difference is part of the structure and the other is not. Finally, Saussure thought that "the synchronic viewpoint predominates" (p. 90).

13.3 The rejection of reference

The rejection of reference is central to the relational, holistic and autonomous view of language that is definitive of structuralism. We shall now consider that rejection.

At first sight it may seem that the structuralist does take some note of reference. For, he sees a sign as a composite entity made up of the *signifier*, that which signifies, and the *signified*, that which is signified. However, the signified is not a language-independent referent. Rather, it is a *concept*, the nature of which is entirely determined by relations internal to the language, syntagmatic and paradigmatic relations of the language. In this way the linguistic system imposes on thought:

> our thought – apart from its expression in words – is only a shapeless and indistinct mass . . . without the help of signs we would be unable to make a clear-cut, consistent distinction between two ideas. Without language, thought is a vague uncharted nebula. There are no pre-existing ideas, and nothing is distinct before the appearance of language. (Saussure 1966: 111–12)

We have, in effect, already rejected this structuralist idea in discussing Whorf (10.2–10.3).

Talk of concepts need not involve denying reference, of course, if a concept is thought of as something that *determines* reference. This would be to treat it like our notion (following Frege) of *sense* (2.6). However, there is no suggestion in Saussure of this role for the signified. Indeed his rejection of reference is clear, even if rather more implicit than explicit.

The emphasis [in Saussurean linguistics on the relationship between the signifier and the signified] tended . . . to exclude any consideration of the thing itself, of the object of reference in the "real world". (Jameson 1972: 105–6)

Other structuralists have been quite explicit.

The word 'dog' exists, and functions within the structure of the English Language, without reference to any four-legged barking creature's real existence. (Hawkes 1977: 17)

From our perspective, this rejection of reference makes structuralism fundamentally implausible. For reference has been a central notion in our theory of language. With its rejection must go the rejection also of a place for notion of truth in linguistics.

We can bring out the main basis for this charge of implausibility by considering the structuralists' favourite analogy: chess. For chess is like language *as the structuralists view it*, but it is importantly different from language *as it really is*.

Chess is a game. It is something we indulge in "just for fun". It is "valuable in itself". None of these things is true of language, in its central uses at least. Language has something to do with life in general. The point of language is not simply to have fun, but to further non-linguistic purposes (1.2); a word game is not communication. The theoretical notion that is crucial to capturing this difference between chess and language is reference, the very notion that the structuralists ignore. Chess pieces and chess moves do not refer to the world. No consideration from outside the game can validate or undermine anything within the game. In contrast, linguistic symbols do refer to the world and are open to external assessment; most notably, they can be true or false.

There are other implausibilities consequent on the rejection of reference. First, the resulting holism makes it difficult to give a natural account of developmental facts about language. Linguistic items cannot be identified across systems. How then are we to explain language acquisition? We want to say that a child begins by learning a minimal vocabulary and a few rudimentary syntactic rules. The child continues by extending these rules. On a structuralist picture of language, we cannot say this. Vocabulary does not remain constant across changes in the system. Each time the child changes the system, *everything changes*. Language learning cannot be represented as a cumulative process.

Second, what goes for development goes also for linguistic change. Consider the simplest change, lexical borrowing. It is natural to claim that the word is borrowed because its meaning fills a gap in the language. Not infrequently that gap will be referential: the borrowed term will name a natural kind or artefact only recently encountered by the speakers of the borrowing language. The structuralists can make sense of neither elements of this claim. Talk of "gaps" is subversive of the idea that a language system is autonomous, complete in itself. / Plugging a gap with a borrowing implies that meaning can be constant over systems.

What drives structuralists into this implausible rejection of reference? They are not very explicit on this matter but we have unearthed two possible reasons.

First, they seem to think that the *arbitrariness* of linguistic signs tells against reference. Thus Jameson claims that the construction of the sign = signifier + signified –

> strikes down . . . the apprehension of language as names and naming. There can no longer be any question of such an intrinsic relationship once the utterly arbitrary character of language has been made clear. (1972: 30)

Consider also the way structuralists typically move directly from arbitrariness to their relational view:

> The fact that the sign is arbitrary . . . means that [it] require[s] ahistorical analysis . . . Since the sign has no necessary core which must persist, it must be defined as a relational entity, in its relation to other signs. (Culler 1976: 36)

This move could seem appropriate only if arbitrariness undermines reference. If reference remains, the sign need not be defined solely by its internal relations.

What has arbitrariness got to do with reference? Jameson's use of 'intrinsic'; is a clue. The structuralists seem to think that the only possible theory or reference is a naive picture theory. If signs were "pictures" of things then, the thinking goes, they would not be arbitrary: they would be constrained by what the things were like. Yet signs are arbitrary. So, they are not "pictures". So, reference must be rejected. Some such line of thought seems necessary to make sense of the structuralists' remarks about reference. And consider this revealing passage:

> The overall characteristic of this relationship is . . . arbitrary. There exists no necessary "fitness" in the link between the sound-image, or signifier 'tree', the concept, or signified that it involves, and the actual physical tree growing in the earth. The word 'tree', in short, has no "natural" or "tree-like" qualities . . . (Hawkes 1977: 25)

The mistake here is obvious. Reference does not depend on picturing, as any causal theory shows. Arbitrariness and reference are perfectly compatible.

Second, there is a suggestion of an argument against reference in some curious and overstated remarks by Culler – already alluded to (13.2) – about teaching someone the meaning of 'brown' (1976: 24–6). It is alleged that the person cannot be taught this by the presentation of brown objects.

It is only when he has grasped the relation between brown and other colours that he will begin to understand what brown is. (p. 25)

A little later Culler claims that

the signifieds of colour terms are nothing but the product or result of a system of distinctions. (p. 25)

So, the signified of those terms does not include their references.

The premise about learning needs to be taken with caution. The concept of brown, and hence a word for it, would probably not be aquired by an organism that could not discriminate brown from other colours (11.4). But the possibility of reference borrowing undermines the claim that 'brown' cannot be learnt without making those discriminations. In any case, even if it were necessary to discriminate brown to learn the reference of 'brown', it would hardly follow that it had no reference. Nor, as a matter of interest, would it follow that the reference of 'brown' was in any way dependent on that of other colour words that featured in the learning process. What is required to learn a reference is one thing, what reference is is another.

In sum, structuralism's rejection of reference is not well based and is thoroughly implausible.

13.4 The rejection of realism

The rejection of reference not only leads to an implausible theory of language, it has very serious consequences for metaphysics. It encourages anti-realism.

Reference is the link between language and independent reality. Deny reference, and reality is likely to seem problematic. Indeed how can reality be made relevant at all to an *autonomous* system? Jameson brings out nicely this "contradiction within structuralism":

its concept of the sign forbids any research into the reality beyond it, at the same time that it keeps alive the notion of such a reality by considering the signified as a concept *of* something. (1972: 106)

The structualist solution is to take the language system as creating its own reality.

> Language . . . allows no single, unitary appeals to a "reality" beyond itself. In the end, it constitutes its own reality. (Hawkes 1977: 26)

> Writing . . . can be seen to *cause a new reality to come into being*. (p. 149)

If taken literally, this talk of language's power over the world is mysterious and inexplicable, if not absurd. Taken metaphorically, it seems to leave us without a world at all (cf. 12.3). Certainly, a world created in this way cannot be the realist's world of "independently existing objects" (p. 17).

Given the structuralists' view of a system of signs, any reality created by one must, it seems, be "made up of relationships rather than things" (p. 17). This relational view of the world has some plausibility in linguistics and the social sciences in general. It is reasonable to think, for instance, that in economic explanations we should abstract from the nature of particular capitalists and workers, focussing instead on the relations between them imposed by the capitalist system. But what about the world of the natural sciences, the *natural* world? The world of stones, trees, cats and so on cannot be merely relational. Indeed, it is this natural world of objects – particularly people and their output – that stands in the relations that are the focus of those social sciences. Moreover, the properties of those objects centrally constrain those relations. To take an utterly banal example, the fact that people need to eat is of no small significance to social science.

Structuralist discussions of reality contain several other unappealing features of a sort already criticized in the last two chapters.

First, anti-realism is made easy by a swift move from talk of the language-dependence of theories to talk of the language-dependence of reality (12.2–12.3):

> since [language] . . . constitutes our characteristic means of encountering and of coping with the world beyond ourselves, then perhaps we can say that it constitutes the characteristic human structure. From there, it is only a small step to the argument that perhaps it also constitutes the characteristic structure of human reality. (Hawkes 1977: 28)

A small step indeed! Constituting theories of the world is one thing, constituting the world, a very different thing.

Second, the structuralists' metaphysics is a form of Kantianism. One aspect of this is apparent already: the world we know is one created, constructed, etc., by our language. This world is like Kant's world of appearances. Do the structuralists also believe in a world independent of our knowledge, a world of things-in-themselves (12.1)? It has been claimed so:

> all the Structuralists: Levi-Strauss with his idea of nature, Barthes with his feeling for social and ideological materials, Althusser with his sense of history, *do* tend to presuppose, beyond the sign-system itself, some kind of ultimate reality which, unknowable or not, serves as its most distant object of reference. (Jameson 1972: 109–10)

Thus independent reality becomes mysterious and inaccessible, scarcely to be mentioned without scare quotes; "a formless chaos of which one cannot even speak in the first place" (p. 33). This is completely unacceptable (12.3–12.4).

Third, the neo-Kantianism of the structuralists is like that of Whorf and Kuhn in being relativistic (12.2–12.3). This is an inevitable result of the view that a system of signs is both autonomous and the creator of its own reality. As we change cultures and hence systems, we change worlds.

> all societies construct their *own realities* in accordance with mental or psychological principles that determine form and function . . . they then covertly project these upon whatever the real world may in fact be . . . this is what *all* societies do, not just "primitive" or "savage" ones. (Hawkes 1977: 56)

On the face of it, this relativism should make translation across languages *impossible*. That is a nettle that the structuralists do not grasp, preferring the much more defensible claim that translation is often difficult (Saussure 1966: 116; Culler 1976: 21–2).

Finally, the structuralists exemplify the mistake that we have been emphasizing throughout this part of the book: the mistake of attempting to derive a world view from a theory of language (11.4, 12.1). This is the deep cause of their obscure and implausible metaphysics. The right procedure, we have argued, is to start with a world view and attempt to derive a theory of language. And the plausible world view to start with is realism.

Suggested reading

Saussure 1966, *Course in General Linguistics* (first published in 1917), is the *locus classicus* of structuralist linguistics and is quite readable. Aarsleff 1982, *From Locke to Saussure*, is a good survey of the ideas leading up to structuralism. Lyons 1981, *Language and Linguistics*, pp. 219–23, is a neat summary of the main ideas.

See also Culler 1976, *Saussure*. Akmajian, Demers and Harnish 1979, *Linguistics*, has a good introduction to the basic ideas of phonology.

Nearly all the works of the key figures in contemporary structuralism are very difficult. De George and de George 1972, *The Structuralists from Marx to Levi-Strauss*, is a good collection of articles from the key figures. A recent work, widely taken to be a classic, is Eco 1984, *Semiotics and the Philosophy of Language*.

Amongst commentaries, Hawkes 1977, *Structuralism and Semiotics*, particularly chapters 1-2, is the best to start with. It contains an excellent annotated bibliography. See also Jameson 1972, *The Prison-House of Language*, and Pettit 1977, *The Concept of Structuralism*. Sturrock 1979, *Structuralism and Since*, is a useful introduction to significant structuralist and post-structuralist figures. Eagleton 1983, *Literary Theory*, contains excellent material on the place of semiotics in literary theory.

John Searle, a prominent American philosopher of language, has engaged in a number of vigorous debates on the merits of post-structuralism. See particularly the debate on deconstruction: Derrida 1977a, "Signature event context"; Searle 1977, "Reiterating the differences: a reply to Derrida"; Derrida 1977b, "Limited Inc abc . . ."; Searle 1983b, "The word turned upside down"; Searle and Mackey 1984 "An exchange on deconstruction". Derrida 1986, *The Archeology of the Frivolous*, is a recent post-structuralist work treating philosophy in a typically tantalizing way.

PART V

LANGUAGE AND PHILOSOPHY

14

First philosophy

14.1 Philosophy naturalized

In part IV we were concerned with the relation between the study of language and realism. In part V, we are concerned with the relation between that study and philosophy.

Philosophers ask many difficult questions. Amongst the most difficult are questions about philosophy itself. What is it? Our answer must reflect a major theme of this book: naturalism. We advocate *philosophy naturalized*.

Philosophy, we say, is not an *a priori* discipline. It is not a subject that can be developed apart from other areas of human knowledge. Its results form no body of knowledge against which the lesser breeds are to be tested. It is not an intellectual police force. It is empirical and fallible. Indeed, it is mostly less secure than common sense and mature science. Philosophy is continuous with science.

Briefly, and roughly, we can divide philosophy's role in three.

1. Philosophy's most basic task is to reflect upon, and integrate, the results of investigations in the particular sciences to form a coherent overall view of the universe and our place in it.
2. Philosophy is concerned with certain problems in particular sciences, for example, in physics, biology, psychology, and mathematics. These problems arise in the most speculative and conceptually difficult parts of the sciences.
3. Some sciences, or areas of science, are traditionally done in philosophy, in some cases, but certainly not all, because they are not mature enough to go out on their own: epistemology, logic, morals, politics and aesthetics. (We confess to having only the dimmest of ideas about how to accommodate some of these within our naturalistic viewpoint.)

Our part-II discussion of word meaning and reference comes much under 3. Our discussion of syntax, and part III as a whole, falls mostly under 2.

However, part III also exemplifies the integrative concerns of 1. Those concerns dominate part IV.

Our naturalistic view of philosophy underlies all these discussions. The view is controversial. The book is not the place to attempt a detailed defence of it, but we can say something in its favour.

To a degree, the book itself is a defence. A theory of philosophy, like any other theory, should be judged on its results. We have outlined some of the results of naturalism in this book. We hope to have provided the beginnings of a coherent and plausible account of language. If we have, that is a positive argument for philosophy naturalized.

A central aspect of defending a theory is criticizing its rivals. That will be the concern of the rest of this book. Our choice of rival philosophies to discuss, and our discussion of them, is influenced by the dominant concern of this book: language. So we shall be particularly concerned with rivals that tie philosophy, in one way or another, to the study of language. And we shall continue theorizing about language and its relations to other matters even while considering the general question of the nature of philosophy.

In this chapter we will consider some forms of *first philosophy* (12.1). Much of the history of philosophy is the history of first philosophy. We shall start with the traditional form of this, particularly as it is exemplified in a problem that we think stems from one in language: the "one-over-many" problem. We shall then consider some recent manifestations of first philosophy, all of them part of the linguistic turn in philosophy. In the next chapter we shall consider some philosophers who reject naturalized philosophy less directly. They claim that important parts of human knowledge - parts concerned with humans themselves - are *ascientific*. This knowledge is not worse than scientific knowledge; it is just irreducibly different. Folk psychology and folk linguistics are given a special status outside science.

14.2 Traditional first philosophy; the one-over-many problem

A first philosophy stance was natural for the rationalist tradition. For, according to that tradition, knowledge in general was *a priori*: rationalists thought that important truths about people and the universe were discoverable through reflection and reason. However, interestingly enough, the same stance was taken by the rival tradition, that of empiricism. Empiricists thought that all knowledge of the world was derived ultimately from perceptual experience. There is therefore a tension between their philosophical stance and their view of knowledge. How can the *a priori* method that they practised in philosophy yield knowledge if all knowledge is empirical? This tension was never satisfactorily removed. The favoured response was to see philosophy as yielding *analytic* truths like those in logic and mathematics. The problem with this response is that it seems to make philosophy trivial; its truths should hold simply "in virtue of the meanings" of words. Yet philosophy does not seem trivial, particularly not to those who practice it. (There are analogous problems for the views that logic and mathematics are analytic.)

We have already mentioned one of the major concerns of traditional first philosophy: scepticism (12.1, 12.4). *A priori* reflections about what is required for knowledge – epistemological reflections – make all ordinary knowledge seem open to doubt. How, Descartes asked, could he be certain even that he was sitting by the fire? Perhaps his senses were deceiving him. Perhaps he was dreaming. Perhaps there was a Deceitful Demon misleading him into thinking that he was by the fire. Attempts to solve this problem have typically led to implausible and mysterious anti-realist metaphysics; Kant's metaphysics is a famous example (12.1, 12.3). Such implausible consequences of first philosophy's treatment of scepticism alone count against that approach. However, worst of all, despite the aid of metaphysical systems designed to provide a solution to the sceptical problem, first philosophy has never produced a convincing solution. We would argue that the approach should be abandoned in favour of the naturalistic one. This does not so much solve the sceptical problem as set it aside as uninteresting; it is a problem so framed as to be insoluble.

What we will discuss is another central problem of traditional first philosophy: the one–over–many problem. It is obvious that the world is full of individual things; stones, trees, cats and so on. But in addition to these "particulars", are there "universals" shared by many particulars?

Recently, a number of philosophers have argued that there are theoretical advantages in positing the existence of universals. But historically they were posited because of the one–over–many problem. That leads to universals as follows. Here is a red rose. There is a red house. That is a red sunset. Now surely, it is claimed, there must be something that all these things have in common that makes them red. That something is the "attribute" redness. So argued Quine's adversary, McX, in Quine's classic paper, "On what there is" (1961: 9–10). Each thing must partake of the "form" redness. So argued Plato two millenia ago. These things have the same nature, the "property" redness. So argues David Armstrong (1978). This attribute, or form, or property, is "the one" that spreads itself over, or runs through, "the many". It is a universal shared by many particulars. In this way first philosophers through the ages have convinced themselves of the existence of universals.

The conviction has generated a host of bizarre metaphysical problems. What is a universal? Where does it exist? Is there a universal for every predicate, even empty ones? What is a particular? How is a universal related to particulars? Universals are said to "inhere in" particulars and the particulars to "partake of" the universals, but how is that achieved? By metaphysical glue ("Plato's grip")? Even particulars begin to look mysterious, for what are they when stripped of their clothing of universals? Philosophers have been driven to think of them as "bare particulars", "mere thisnesses", or propertyless "substrata". Struggles with these problems have led some to say that there are, instead of, or as well as, properties, property-instances: "abstract particulars" or "tropes".

Controversy has raged over these problems for centuries. If we can dissolve them, we should. In particular, we should not believe in the existence of universals unless we really have to. We should favour here, as in science, simple and economical theories. In ontology, the less the better.

Does the one-over-many argument really require us to posit universals? We think not. Certainly there are red roses, houses and sunsets. We are *tempted* to say that there is something, redness, that they all share, but we need not say that. We do just as well saying that they are all red. What we are tempted to say is a mere manner of speaking, to be avoided when the ontological chips are down. There is nothing about the situation that requires us to talk of redness. To suppose that there is redness as well as red things clutters the landscape without explanatory or descriptive gain.

The friend of universals will object. "You have failed to say in virtue of what all these things are red." Our failure here could be a scientific one: we have not said what it is, physically, about a thing that makes it red. However, this is not the failure the friend of universals has in mind. Suppose we removed the failure, pointing out that it is in virtue of being P that things are red, where 'P' is the appropriate physical predicate. The friend would still not be satisfied. "In virtue of what are the things P?" He does not want a scientific explanation, he wants a *metaphysical* explanation.

At this point, the naturalistic philosopher demurs: there is nothing further to explain. "Things just are P. What more could you want to know?" The first philosopher will insist that a metaphysical explanation is needed. We seem to be at an impasse. However, the naturalistic philosopher has one more card to play. If there really were something requiring a metaphysical explanation here, we would expect to find some sign of progress in the 2000 years that philosophers have struggled to provide the explanation. Yet there is no sign of progress: Armstrong is no closer to a solution than Plato. This is strong evidence that there is no problem: the one-over-many is a pseudo problem; the explanations prompted by it are pseudo explanations.

We have chosen to discuss the one-over-many not only because it is a major example of first philosophy, and one of its most conspicuous failures, but also because we suspect that the reason philosophers are beguiled by this pseudo problem is to be found in their theory of language. Though some of them deny it, we suspect that underlying their response to the one-over-many is an implicit commitment to the "'Fido'-Fido" theory of meaning.

This theory has a persistent hold over the minds of philosophers and many others. According to the theory, the meaning of a term *is* its role of naming something. It will be remembered that on the Millian view (2.5) the meaning of the name, 'Fido', is its role of naming Fido. The 'Fido'-Fido theory generalizes this view of meaning to all terms.

Consider:

That rose is red.

This sentence, like all others, has a certain complexity. It has two terms, the singular term 'that rose' and the general term 'red', playing quite different roles (2.2, 2.4). How can the 'Fido'-Fido theory cope with this complexity? It has to see the two types of term naming two types of entities: the different roles of the terms require different types of entities. The entity named by 'that rose' is a particular rose; that named by 'red' is the universal, redness, which can be shared by many particulars. The one-over-many begins to look like a real problem.

The 'Fido'-Fido theory is false. Our part-II discussion exemplifies a quite different way of coping with the complexity of sentences. It is not that each term stands in the one semantic relation of naming to different kinds of entities. Rather, the terms stand in different semantic relations to the same kinds of entities, neither "particulars" nor "universals" but just plain objects. Thus 'that rose' *designates* a certain object, a rose, while 'red' *applies to* many objects, including many roses. Where the 'Fido'-Fido theory catches the complexity with different sorts of entity, we catch it with different sorts of relation. The only entities we need are objects of the familiar sort.

If we are right in these speculations, the one-over-many is not only an example of the failure of traditional first philosophy, but also another example of a bad theory of language leading to a bad theory of the world (part IV).

14.3 The linguistic turn: ordinary language philosophy

When the naturalistic philosopher points his finger at reality, the linguistic philosopher discusses the finger.

The linguistic turn has dominated Anglo-American philosophy in the twentieth century (much to the astonishment of many laymen). According to this movement, briefly, philosophers should be concerned simply with language. It is characteristic of the movement, therefore, to be concerned not with morals, but with the language of morals; not with science, but with the language of science; and so on. Philosophy of language becomes the centre, if not all, of philosophy.

What is the explanation of this turn? One factor has already emerged (11.2): a dissatisfaction with the metaphysical excesses of much nineteenth-century philosophy, particularly that emanating from Germany. Such dissatisfaction became common in Britain and America. The dissatisfaction encouraged the turn because philosophers thought that a close attention to language would prevent the excesses. This certainly seems to be true of G. E. Moore, who was very influential in determining the path of philosophy in Britain. Beyond this dissatisfaction, it is hard to account for the turn. We conjecture that it is partly a response to the earlier mentioned tension between first philosophy and empiricism (14.2). If philosophy is prior to science it cannot be part of science. Yet empiricism seems to rule out any role for philosophy outside science. The favoured response, as we mentioned, is to see philosophy as yielding analytic truths, truths holding "in virtue of the meanings" of words. So meanings, and hence language, become the concern of philosophy.

Within the linguistic movement, philosophers can be distinguished by the degree to which their focus on language makes them negative about philosophy. The various positions tend to shade into each other because most philosophers in the movement – positivists excepted – were not explicit about their metaphilosophy.

The very influential philosopher Ludwig Wittgenstein, who was certainly explicit enough, was probably the most negative of all about philosophy. He thought that the study of language would dissolve all philosophical problems: he saw philosophy as grammatical therapy and encouraged those for whom the therapy was successful to give it up. We shall call this negative wing *ordinary language philosophy*. (This name is reasonably in accord with history, though it is sometimes used more broadly.) We shall consider it in this section.

The logical positivists, whom we have already discussed in connection with realism (11.2), were less negative. Though they argued for the elimination of metaphysics, they thought that it should be replaced by significant philosophical problems about language. Less negative still is Michael Dummett, whom we have also discussed in connection with realism (11.3–11.4). He identifies philosophical issues with problems about language, and has a very positive view of the role of philosophy in solving them. In this he is typical of the most common version of the linguistic turn in recent years: philosophy as *conceptual analysis*. We shall consider this positive wing of the movement in the next section.

Wittgenstein's concern with language in his famous *Philosophical Investigations* (1953) is explicit: "our investigation is . . . a grammatical one" (#90). However, he does not see the investigation as concerned with genuine intellectual problems. The problems arise from "misunderstandings concerning the use of words" (#90); we are entangled in our own rules (#125); we are in the grip of "confusions" (#132) and "plain nonsense" (#119). "Philosophy is a battle against the bewitchment of our intelligence by means of language" (#109). "A philosophical problem has the form: 'I don't know my way about'" (#123).

What we should attempt to do is free ourselves of these problems by close attention to how language is actually used. The problems arise "when language is like an engine idling, not when it is doing work" (#132). We need a rich diet of examples to help us from the bewitchment (#593). The result we hope for is not "any kind of theory" or "explanation" (#109). Philosophy "leaves everything as it is" (#124); its problems should *completely* disappear (#133). What we look for is a cure of the philosopher, not a piece of philosophical knowledge. Philosophy "is like the treatment of an illness" (#255). In a characteristically vivid metaphor, he describes the aim of philosophy as: "to shew the fly the way out of the fly bottle" (#309). Interestingly enough, one of the main targets of his therapy was the 'Fido'-Fido theory of meaning (14.2).

In sum, philosophical problems are pseudo-problems, arising from the misuse of language. Philosophers should study language not to come up with theories, even ones about language, but to dissolve problems.

If this book is close to being right, then ordinary language philosophy is mistaken. We have been urging solutions to genuine problems in the philosophy of language and the philosophy of mind. And we have alluded to others in metaphysics and epistemology. Nevertheless, we do think that there is *some* truth in this view of philosophy. It is likely that some philosophical problems are pseudo-problems, and we have nominated one that we think is: the one-over-many problem. And we have suggested, in a Wittgensteinian way, that this problem arises from the bewitchment of language. In general, however, philosophy's task is constructive.

Wittgenstein taught at Cambridge until 1947, but it was at Oxford in the 1950s that ordinary language philosophy had its heyday. Two Oxford philosophers, to a degree independently of Wittgenstein, were very influential: Gilbert Ryle and J. L. Austin. Wittgenstein set out the ideology of ordinary language philosophy in its starkest form and, to a considerable degree, conformed to that ideology in his philosophical practice. Ryle and Austin were less explicitly negative in ideology and in practice. Thus they were closer than Wittgenstein to the conceptual analysis wing of the linguistic movement.

14.4 The linguistic turn: conceptual analysis

The conceptual analysis view of philosophy is ordinary language philosophy gone positive. The conceptual analysts come not to bury philosophy but to do it.

They take philosophy to consist in the investigation of the structure of our concepts, especially the important ones for our understanding of the world. G. J. Warnock characterizes their views as follows:

> Political philosophy involves the study of political concepts, but says nothing of the rights or wrongs of political issues. The moral philosopher examines the "language of morals", but does not as such express moral judgements. The philosopher of religion may be, but by no means need be, a religious believer. . . . philosophy is the study of the concepts that we employ, and not of the facts, phenomena, cases, or events to which those concepts might be or are applied. (1958: 167)

Since all the concepts that the analysts are interested in are ones for which we have words, their method is hardly distinguishable from the ordinary language philosophers' investigation of the use and misuse of words.

An analysis is necessary and knowable *a priori*. It is not, of course, always known by all who have the requisite concepts; it is implicit rather than explicit in the structure of concepts. Conceptual analysis is characterized not only by the kind of truths sought, but even more by its method. It proceeds by thought experiment. The analyst considers a range of imagined situations, both actual and possible (in the widest sense) and asks, "What would we say?". Our intuitions about these situations are generalized to construct an analysis, which is then tested against further cases.

Consider a famous example of analysis, that of the concept knowledge. Is knowledge true belief? No: we imagine a situation where someone has a true belief accidentally and so we would not say that he *knew*. Is knowledge true belief for which the believer has good reasons? This won't do either: we imagine situations in which the believer has the reasons, but they are psychologically inert. Someone who correctly guesses the answer to a mathematical problem does not know the answer even if she has the information from which the answer can be deduced. And so on, until we come up with an analysis of knowledge that resists these imagined counter-examples.

What sort of "fact" makes an analysis true? It must be something implicit in the concept being analysed. How can we come to know this fact *a priori*? It must be inside the mind, for if it were outside the mind, we would have to look outside to know of it. We would have to depend on experience for knowledge of it and hence our knowledge could not be *a priori*. What could there be in the mind that we come to know in analysis? The popular answer is the only plausible one: facts about meanings. Our ordinary understanding of a word is thought to be in the mind. *Analysis probes the associations between words implicit in the very understanding of those words*, associations established in learning them. These associations are the facts implicit in our concepts. A likely example of the fruits of such an investigation would be the discovery that all bachelors are adult unmarried males, a fact that holds in virtue of the fact that 'bachelor' is associated with 'adult unmarried male'. Clearly, the links must be more subtle, and about more philosophically significant topics than this, if conceptual analysis is to have a central role in philosophy.

We think that there are two reasons for doubting that conceptual analysis has any role in philosophy. First, conceptual analysis is tied to a description theory of understanding; it requires that understanding a word does associate it with certain other words. We think that this is a plausible theory for some words. For example, it is plausible to think that the reference of 'bachelor' is determined by the reference of 'adult', 'unmarried' and 'male' (5.4); and that a person understands 'bachelor' only if she relates it to the other words so that they do determine its reference (7.5, 8.8). And we think that it may be appropriate to say that such associations yield *a priori* knowledge (5.5). Certainly, we do not know enough about meaning and understanding to rule out these proposals. Nevertheless, the description theory is very implausible for many other words. The understanding of proper names and natural kind terms is primarily a matter of being appropriately related to the causal networks for those terms (4.1, 5.2, 8.8). Analysis is useless with such terms because little if any knowledge *is* implicit in our understanding of them (5.5). To that extent, Putnam is right: "meanings just ain't in the head" (3.5, 5.1). This raises the possibility that no philosophically interesting knowledge is implicit in understanding. Perhaps the only sort of knowledge that can be got by analysis is the sort illustrated by the claim about bachelors.

Second, conceptual analysis is supposed to yield knowledge about such areas as the mind, semantics, morals and epistemology. But compare these areas of knowledge with others, for example, physics. It would be absurd to say that physics was knowable *a priori*. Why suppose that the correct theory of the mind is any more to be discovered by examining our ordinary mental concepts than the correct theory of physics is to be discovered by examining our ordinary physical concepts?

Despite these doubts, we do not insist that conceptual analysis has no role in philosophy. We allow that it may yield philosophical knowledge. However, what we do reject totally is the conceptual analysis view of philosophy, the view that *all* philosophy is conceptual analysis. We suspect that little if any is.

Where do mental, semantic, moral and epistemic terms come from? From our theorizing, or our ancestors' theorizing, about the mind, semantics, morals and knowledge (7.6). Just as we gain an economic vocabulary from economic theorizing, a biological one from biological theorizing, a physical one from physical theorizing, so also do we gain the vocabularies that interest the conceptual analyst. Where links between words are implicit in our understanding of them, these links must have been established by theorizing about the area in question. Presumably, the links in meaning must have facilitated the theorizing.

Take a humdrum example from our discussion of the Eskimos (10.2). Suppose that there is an Eskimo word, '*F*', which, as a result of links to other words, means "light fluffy snow that has fallen recently". Presumably those links were set up because it aided Eskimo theorizing to have one word for this concept.

This suggests a couple of points. First, the *a priori* parts of the theory, reflecting meaning links that can be revealed in analysis, will surely be less interesting than the empirical parts of the theory facilitated by those links. Return to our humdrum example. Perhaps analysis can discover that something could be *F* if and only if it were light and fluffy snow that had fallen recently. This would explain why a certain piece of *F* is light and fluffy. But the more interesting explanations of the Eskimo theory of snow will come from applying its empirical generalizations to the many other properties of *F* that make it noteworthy.

Second, it seems likely that the *a priori* parts of a theory will be a relatively small part of the theory. Most of the theory will surely be empirical generalizations and hence not to be revealed by mere analysis.

In the light of this, the fruits of conceptual analysis should be small and boring. Yet it will be objected, the fruits do not seem so poor. In the philosophy of mind, for example, analysis seems to have provided extensive and interesting theories (e.g. Armstrong 1968).

Our explanation of this is that, despite what they think, analysts are not mostly doing conceptual analysis. The concepts that interest the analyst come from *folk theory* or, less pretentiously, *folk opinion* (1.3). What the analysts are mostly doing from their armchair, we suggest, is generalizing perfectly empirical folk opinion into what can truly be called a theory. When they ask "What would we say?" about this and that imagined situation, their answer is guided not by their implicit understanding of the terms in question but by their folk opinions. Analysts bring to their armchairs not only their understanding of a language but also much hard-won empirical theory and opinion – the wisdom of the ages. Certainly, there is no way that mere introspection can distinguish persuasively between knowledge based on linguistic understanding and that based on folk opinion.

We conclude that the conceptual analysis view of philosophy is wrong. The study of language, and the concepts it expresses, is important but it should not be identified with philosophy or even made central to it. The linguistic turn is a mistake and does not re-establish first philosophy.

Some further remarks are appropriate about the consequence of subscribing to the conceptual analysis view. We have seen that the practice associated with this view results in the systematization of folk opinion, part *a priori* conceptual analysis perhaps, but largely empirical. This is a result worth seeking. In the areas that concern the analysts – areas like mind and meaning – folk theory is often just about all we have got to start with. However, discovering folk theory can be only the beginning of the theoretical task. That theory then needs to be critically examined against the phenomena it is supposed to explain.

How right is folk theory? It reflects the wisdom of the ages and so is likely to be not bad so far as it goes. But some folk theories in the past have been spectacularly wrong (1.3). So it should always remain an open question how correct the folk theory is. (Note that if it is largely wrong, the *a priori* bits revealed by analysis will be simply uninteresting. There is no interest in discovering by analysis that something could be a witch if and only if it cast spells since there are no witches or spells.)

How adequate is the theory? As a folk theory it is certain that it will not go far enough in explaining the phenomena. We will need to introduce a range of new concepts and make new connections between old ones. We must make moves undreamt of by folk. Even when the folk theory is right, the task is not to enshrine it but to improve it.

Unfortunately, the conceptual analysis view works against the critical examination of folk theory. For, if a person holds the view, he takes his results to be necessarily true, because known *a priori*, and to be completed by the mining of ordinary concepts. So, though the conceptual analysis view can lead to useful results, it also leads to a complacency about those results. It discourages attention to the phenomena which led to the folk opinions in the first place and which it is the task of the theory to explain.

In this chapter, we have defended our naturalistic view of philosophy by criticizing various versions of *a priori* first philosophy. Our criticism of traditional first philosophy focussed on one of its central and perennial problems: the one-over-many. This is a pseudo problem, arising, we suspect, from an implicit commitment to the false 'Fido'–Fido theory of meaning. The linguistic turn has dominated Anglo–American first philosophy in this century. At its most negative, this turn sees all philosophical problems as pseudo problems, arising from linguistic confusions. Mostly, it has the more positive view that the problems are soluble by linguistic or conceptual analysis. Philosophical problems are not, in general, pseudo problems, and analysis has little if anything to do with solving them.

Suggested reading

14.1

The focus of arguments for naturalism in philosophy has been on epistemology. The major figure has been Quine: see "The scope and language of science" in

The Ways of Paradox (1966), "Epistemology naturalized" in *Ontological Relativity* (1969), and "The nature of natural knowledge" in Guttenplan 1975, *Mind and Language*. The second of these essays is reprinted in Kornblith 1985, *Naturalizing Epistemology*, which is a good collection of essays with a helpful introduction and a massive bibliography. See also Devitt 1984a for a detailed defence of the naturalistic approach to philosophy. Millikan 1984, *Language, Thought, and Other Biological Categories*, is an extended defence of a naturalistic approach to the philosophy of language and epistemology.

The relationship of language to philosophy is considered in Hacking 1975, *Why Does Language Matter to Philosophy?*

14.2

Quine's "On what there is" in *From a Logical Point of View* (1961) is the classic rejection of the one-over-many problem. Armstrong 1978, *Nominalism and Realism*, takes the problem seriously and critically examines all known attempts to solve it. Armstrong describes the Quinean position as "Ostrich Nominalism", which led to a symposium: Devitt 1980b, " 'Ostrich Nominalism' or 'Mirage Realism'?"; Armstrong 1980, "Against 'Ostrich' Nominalism"; Quine 1980, "Soft impeachment disowned". Campbell 1976, *Metaphysics*, contains a clear treatment of this question.

14.3–14.4

Wittgenstein's views are expounded in his classic, *Philosophical Investigations* (1953). Useful introductions are Pears 1971, *Wittgenstein*; Kenny 1973, *Wittgenstein*.

Two classics of ordinary language philosophy/conceptual analysis are Ryle 1949, *The Concept of Mind*; Austin 1962b, *Sense and Sensibilia*. The former is much more positive in its view of philosophy and has been very influential. It founded philosophical behaviourism.

Warnock 1958, *English Philosophy Since 1900*, is a very sympathetic survey. Gellner 1959, *Words and Things*, is a biting and unsympathetic assault. Passmore 1966, *A Hundred Years of Philosophy*, Chapter 18, is a short readable survey. Rorty 1967, *The Linguistic Turn*, is a collection of classic papers with a useful but difficult introduction.

Lewis 1969, *Convention*, is an example of the conceptual analysis approach at its positive best.

The debate on analyticity is central to the possibility of conceptual analysis, since a correct analysis is alleged to be necessary and known *a priori*. See the suggested reading for section 5.5.

Two nice examples of works from philosophers following the practice of conceptual analysis, but viewing the results as articulations of folk opinions (and hence not known *a priori*) are: Stich 1982, "On the ascription of content", in Woodfield 1982, *Thought and Object*; and Dennett 1985, *Elbow Room*.

Rational psychology

15.1 Rational psychology *versus* protoscience

In this chapter, we shall consider a theory of persons that challenges both our naturalistic approach to philosophy and the theory of language that we have urged in this book.

We all gain an apparatus for thinking about people, if not with our mother's milk at least with our play lunch. Early in life we gain folk psychology. This psychology ranges over sensations (e.g. pain), emotions (e.g. envy), character (e.g. bravery) and thought (e.g. belief). It is the last of these that concerns us: folk cognitive psychology.

We use folk cognitive psychology to explain behaviour. Why is Otto eating candied ants? We take Otto to have a certain desire: he craves something sweet and crunchy. We take him to have a certain belief: that candied ants are sweet and crunchy. So we can explain Otto's behaviour.

We use folk cognitive psychology to explain non-cognitive mental states. Why does Otto hate Felix? We know that Otto believes Felix deliberately humiliated him. We know that people frequently hate those they believe humiliated them. So we can explain Otto's mental state.

We use folk cognitive psychology to explain cognitive mental states. Why does Otto believe that Felix humiliated him? Otto believes that Felix snickered and giggled when beating him at chess and told others that he, Otto, was an idiot. Further, Otto believes that anyone who does such things humiliates those to whom they are done. So we can explain Otto's mental state.

What is the status of folk cognitive psychology? There are two very different answers to this question.

The answer dictated by our naturalism is that folk psychology, like all folk theories, is a *protoscience*. It differs from a science proper in being immature: it is imprecise, inexplicit and unsystematic; it is held uncritically; it is not associated with a methodology for its development (1.3). Nonetheless, it has the same general characteristics as a science. It contains, or yields, empirical lawlike generalizations that enable explanation and prediction. It is open to scientific revision.

The alternative answer rejects this naturalistic view. It does not take folk psychology to be inferior science, but rather takes it not to be science at all. It is a different category of knowledge that is incommensurable with science. Two prominent defenders of this view are Daniel Dennett and Donald Davidson. They argue for what we shall call the *rational psychology* approach to folk psychology.

This approach does not differ from the naturalistic one in its ontology. Both Dennett and Davidson think that the subject matter of folk psychology – people – are physical objects subject to physical law. They certainly do not think that folk psychology differs from science in being concerned with ghostly mind-stuff. It differs in that what it says about this part of the physical world is outside science. Folk psychology is methodologically different from science. There are four related aspects to this difference.

1   *The no-replacement thesis*. Folk psychology is not replaceable by science, in particular by scientific psychology. There are two ideas here. First, science could not show folk psychology to be wrong, to be making deeply mistaken claims about human nature. Second, a scientific theory could not serve the same functions in our lives as the folk theory. It is, Dennett suggests (1981a), a different tool for a different job. The task of folk psychology is to *rationalize* people; it is to *understand* people in a special non-scientific way; it is to *impose an interpretation*.

2   *The no-reform thesis*. Folk psychology is not open to scientific reform; it cannot become science-like. Folk explanations are necessarily loose, imprecise, and laced with escape clauses and hence are different from those in science (Davidson 1980: 221–3; though Dennett does seem to think it can be made like mathematics by reforming it into decision theory; 1981a).

3   *The no-integration thesis*. Folk psychology cannot be integrated with science; the two cannot be joined to form a single seamless theory of people. Dennett is enthusiastic about scientific psychology, but thinks that there is no prospect of reducing beliefs and desires to that psychology. Davidson seems to leave no room for a scientific psychology at all, and rejects the possibility of a reduction of folk psychology to physics.

4   *Principles of charity*. Finally, folk psychology involves principles that have no place in science. In ascribing beliefs and desires, we have to be charitable: we have to see people as rational and believers of the truth. These surprising principles are central to rational psychology and are thought to underpin the other ways in which folk psychology is marked off. It is because we must apply them that folk psychology is thought to be ascientific; in applying

them we impose an interpretation. The principles will be the concern of sections 15.4 and 15.5.

Rational psychology's challenge to naturalism (and hence to naturalistic philosophy) is clear: it places some of our knowledge outside the realm of empirical science.

What are the consequences of rational psychology for the theory of language? Dennett draws no conclusions about language. Indeed his work does not include a systematic discussion of language. Davidson's certainly does, but the bearing of his rational psychology on that discussion is not clear, as we shall see (15.3). On almost any plausible view, the theory of language will have close links with cognitive psychology (8.2, 9.4). Certainly, on our Gricean view, the speaker meaning of a linguistic symbol is to be identified with the content of a thought (7.4). Rational psychology places the folk view of content outside science and so should place folk semantics outside it also. Explanations of symbols in terms of meaning, truth and reference should also be ascientific. There would still be a place, presumably, for scientific linguistics, but it would not include the truth-referential semantics that we have placed in the centre stage.

The rational psychology of Davidson and Dennett is reminiscent of a tradition that has been well established in continental Europe since the turn of the century through the work of Wilhelm Dilthey (1976) and Max Weber (1949). The tradition takes a "humanist" view of the social sciences, insisting that they differ from the natural ones in requiring *Verstehen*, a sort of empathetic understanding. Indeed, Graham McDonald and Philip Pettit (1981) have derived a *Verstehen* view from an explicitly Davidsonian perspective. They also claim that this is the only good route to *Verstehen*. If they are right about this, our arguments against rational psychology will count also against the continental tradition.

Dennett and Davidson are not philosophical twins. We shall briefly characterize their rather different philosophies of mind before turning to the principles of charity.

15.2 Dennett

Dennett distinguishes two stances: the *intentional stance*, which is the one of folk cognitive psychology; and the *design stance*, which is the one of scientific cognitive psychology.

Suppose that we are confronted by a chess player – a person or a computer – and wish to predict its next move. We adopt the intentional stance when we attribute to it certain desires, including that to win, and certain true beliefs, and then try to work out the *best* move. What, given those thoughts, would it be most rational to do? Something whose behaviour can be predicted like this – or approximately predicted, because some slippage is allowed – is called an intentional system. In treating something as an intentional system, we are not supposing that it really embodies thoughts which cause it to behave as it does. It is just that it is convenient for prediction to treat the object *as if* it embodied them. In other words, the intentional stance is not realist but *instrumentalist* about beliefs and desires: they are mere instruments for prediction.

The design stance, in contrast, is thoroughly realist. It is concerned with what is really going on in the object that causes it to behave as it does. What are its internal states, and what sort of structure do they operate in? These are the concerns of scientific psychology. Like any science it will introduce a range of theoretical entities, but none of these will be beliefs and desires.

Dennett does consider an "engineering hypothesis": to each thought in the behaviour-predicting intentional network there corresponds a functionally salient inner representation. He regards this as a possible but not mandatory explanation of how there could be intentional systems. Two of his reasons for rejecting it are fairly clear. One is the potential infinity of thoughts; a person has too many thoughts for it to be possible for them all to be represented. Thus, we can rightly attribute to Ron indefinitely many beliefs that he has never entertained; for example, the belief that rabbits don't lay eggs. Secondly, Dennett thinks that the identity conditions for thoughts are too loose for this hypothesis to be right. People can be computationally very different and yet still have the same beliefs (1978: chapters 1–3, 6; 1981a).

We do not find either of these reasons persuasive. The first can be met by distinguishing actual from potential thoughts or, equivalently, explicit from tacit thoughts. Only explicit thoughts are identified with inner representations; implicit thoughts are mere dispositions to form representations. The second underplays the extent to which systems that are computationally different can be similar at a higher level of abstraction.

Suppose that the engineering hypothesis is right. Could we not then *identify* thoughts with the representations explaining the behaviour that led us to attribute the thoughts in the first place? Dennett appears to think not. His view rests on an obscure distinction he inherits from Gilbert Ryle (1949). He distinguishes between causal and constitutive questions about belief. The engineering hypothesis is not a constitutive one about what thoughts *are*, but only a hypothesis about how natural objects can be complex and subtle enough for the intentional strategy to work. So Dennett views the hypothesis as a candidate answer to this causal question. As such it is an empirical hypothesis. The constitutive question, he thinks, must be settled by conceptual analysis and hence must be *a priori* (14.4). This analysis reveals that *all there is* to being a true believer is being a system whose behaviour is reliably predictable via the intentional strategy, and hence *all there is* to really and truly believing that *p* (for any proposition *p*) is being an intentional system for which *p* occurs as a belief in the best (most predictive) interpretation. (1981a: 68)

We reject the view that constitutive questions are to be answered only *a priori* (14.4). Beliefs may *be* causes of behaviour.

15.3 Davidson

Davidson's view of the mind is obscure. He has much to say about what psychological states are not, but is rather coy about what they are. He calls his position *Anomalous Monism*. His monism is clear enough: each token mental state or event is simply a physical state or event; in humans, it is a brain state or event. The difficulty comes with the alleged anomalousness of the mental.

Anomalousness is the denial that there can be any psychological laws, and hence that beliefs and desires are scientific kinds:

there are no strict deterministic laws on the basis of which mental events can be predicted and explained. (Davidson 1980: 208)

This view depends in some way on the denial that there are psycho-physical laws (pp. 209, 224): there are no laws linking the psychological to the physical. These two denials are not accompanied by any clear statement of what, as a result, mental states are. What are psychological explanations and what are they for? How do mental facts relate to physical facts?

If there are no psychological laws, if psychological kinds are not natural kinds, then folk cognitive psychology cannot be protoscience. We have mentioned that principles of charity play a central role in this view of Davidson. But there is another important strand in Davidson's thought: his views on the nature of science are deeply conditioned by the model of physics. He argues that intentional explanation is irredemably loose. Any psychological explanation must be "holistic" (p. 217), in the sense that it involves implicit reference to the agent's entire belief–desire system. Furthermore, psychological phemomena do not constitute a closed system. Both militate against there being genuine psychological laws.

Consider some piece of behaviour: Tommygun Marsala's voting for Reagan. Why did Tommygun so vote? It will obviously be very difficult to have a complete and accurate story here. We may cite various desires of Tommygun: his opposition to gun control, his dissatisfaction with street crime, and the like.

We may cite some of his beliefs: that Reagan too is opposed to gun control and mugging. However, this explanation remains somewhat loose. If Tommygun had had various additional beliefs and desires, he would have voted for Carter or stayed home. These interfering factors must be guarded against in the explanation; it is implicitly holistic. Yet, according to Davidson, it is impossible to specify all these factors so that anyone who had that complex of thoughts would have voted for Reagan. The best we can expect are generalizations that embody "practical wisdom", and that "are insulated from counterexample by generous escape clauses" (1980: 219).

To qualify as a scientific law, Davidson thinks generalizations must be tight, precise, quantifiable, and near enough deterministic. These conditions are satisfied only by a "comprehensive closed theory" (p. 219). The psychological realm is not a closed system. Psychological processes are constituted out of, and hence depend on, neural and other biological processes. Psychological prediction and explanation assume the normal functioning of our internal machinery. Hence, an explanation can fail, not because of a psychological error, but because the machinery is not functioning normally. "Too much happens to affect the mental that is not itself a systematic part of the mental" (p. 224).

We can grant Davidson's premises, yet deny his conclusions. Such a paradigm science as biology manifests the same characteristics as folk psychology. Consider, for example, the processes involved in meiosis, fertilization, and development; the processes by which genotype is translated into phenotype. There is no closed system here either. The non-biological affects the biological: radiation induces mutations; chemicals induce development abnormalities. Thalidomide is a tragic example of the latter. Yet nobody, we take it, denies that genetics and embryology discover laws. These laws are "loose" in the same way as psychological laws. Consider the phenotypical consequences of the presence of some gene. (a) The specification of consequences is holistic: the effect of a given gene depends on which others are present (this is called "epigenesis"). (b) We assume the process is normal: there is no interference from trauma, unusual chemicals, radiation, and so on. "Generous escape clauses" are allowed.

On Davidson's view of laws, the only laws would be those of physics and physical chemistry.

Implicitly at least, Davidson sees his theory of language as stemming from his Anomalous Monism. However, it is very hard to see how it does. He urges a theory of meaning based on Tarski's theory of truth. Truth itself is left unexplained. In particular, he rejects the need for, and possibility of, explaining truth in terms of reference. As a result, he sees no need for causal theories of reference. But why does Davidson need a theory of meaning at all? If folk semantics is outside science, why do we need to supplement it – as Davidson does so enthusiastically – with a theory based on Tarski's theory of truth (2.2,

2.4)? Reference is just as much part of folk semantics as meaning and truth. Why then is reference discriminated against? We do not know the answers to these questions.

15.4 Principles of charity

It needs emphasizing that any principle of charity strong enough to mark off folk psychology from science must be a *constitutive* one: one that must apply to an object if it is to be a believer–desirer. Constitutive principles are very different from epistemic or heuristic ones. A good epistemic principle may be: we are justified in assuming that a person is, for the most part, rational or a believer of the truth. A good heuristic principle may be: start your explanation of a person with the assumption that she is rational and a believer of the truth. But such principles would not distinguish folk psychology from science. Being an object of charity must be of the very essence of an intentional system.

Dennett holds a constitutive principle of charity. And it is easy to see why Dennett thinks that such a principle divides folk psychology off from natural science. He explicitly takes the principle to be *normative* and *idealizing* rather than descriptive. Intentional psychological explanation then inherits this characteristic. In deploying the intentional stance, we predict of some *well-designed* beast that it believes what it *ought* and does what it *should*. Hence the analogy between psychology and formal theories like game and decision theory.

We believe that the fact/value gap is not a chasm, and that values are a kind of fact. We also think that the formal sciences are ultimately empirical too. Nonetheless, if belief–desire psychology is rather like decision theory, and ought eventually to become more like it, then folk psychology is not proto-science in the relevant sense. However, we shall argue (15.5) that folk psychology does not deploy any principle of charity that is nearly strong enough to warrant separating it from science.

It is much less clear why Davidson thinks that a principle of charity demarcates the mental from the physical. It is clear that he endorses a constitutive principle:

in inferring this system [of beliefs and desires] from the evidence, we necessarily impose conditions of coherence, rationality, and consistency. These conditions have no echo in physical theory, which is why we can look for no more than rough correlations between psychological and physical phenomena. (1980: 231)

There is a *prima facie* puzzle here. Davidson goes straight from the claim that the mental has a different nature or essence from the physical, to the denial of psychophysical laws. But from the fact that what, constitutively, makes something food "has no echo" in physical theory, it hardly follows that digestion is not a lawlike process.

We will see that there is no single principle of charity, but rather a cluster of related ones varying on two dimensions. Some of these principles sustain the demarcation in that, were they true, folk psychology could not be protoscience. But that is not the case for all the principles. Some of them can be seen plausibly as capturing part of the *scientific* essence of an intentional system. As such they are part of empirical science.

The *first dimension* of principles of charity concerns *topic*: principles may be of true belief, rational belief, or rational action. Those, like Dennett and Davidson, who urge a principle of charity tend to run these together. Yet they are very different, with very different degrees of plausibility.

(1) *Charity-as-true-belief*. Charity sometimes appears as the thesis that most of the beliefs of an intentional system must be true. False beliefs are comparatively rare and require a special explanation. Thus Davidson writes:

> it cannot be assumed that speakers never have false beliefs. Error is what gives belief its point. We can, however, take it as given that *most* beliefs are correct. (1984: 168)

In a similar vein, Dennett writes:

> A species might "experiment" by mutation in any number of inefficacious systems, but none of these systems would deserve to be called belief systems precisely because of their defects, their nonrationality, and hence a false belief system is a conceptual impossibility. (1978: 17)

Assigning beliefs to a system so that they come out true amounts to assigning ones that agree with ours, for our beliefs represent our best view of what is true. So, "a good theory of interpretation maximizes agreement" (Davidson 1984: 169).

Charity, as they say, begins at home. A striking consequence of the principle of charity-as-a-true-belief is that most of our own beliefs must be true.

It is this version of the principle which most clearly threatens the naturalistic view of folk psychology. There is no scientific basis for linking beliefs to truth in this way.

(2) *Charity-as-rational-belief*. Charity sometimes requires the rationality of beliefs given other beliefs; the inferential connections among beliefs must be

rational. There are signs of this in the above passage from Dennett. Consider also:

> The assumption that something is an intentional system is the assumption that it is rational . . . the animal . . . must be supposed to *follow* the *rules* of logic. (1978: 10–11)

Davidson talks of rationality and consistency of the system (see above and 1984: 159).The intentional system must apply good rules of deduction. If Igor believes that one million volts kills any vampire, and if Igor believes that Yorga is a vampire, then Igor must believe that one million volts will kill Yorga. The system must apply good rules of induction. It must not, for example, argue counter-inductively. If Igor believes that all previous vampires were stake-proof, he will not infer that Yorga will perish from stake insertion.

It is not obvious that commitment to this principle would show that folk psychology is ascientific. It is an open scientific question what sort of structure a system must have to have beliefs and desires. Perhaps the system has to operate according to certain rules. Perhaps those are the rules of logic that we think exemplify rational inference. Whether or not this is so is a matter for scientific investigation and no threat to naturalism.

(3) *Charity-as-rational-action*. Finally, charity sometimes requires that the connection between an intentional system's beliefs and desires and its actions be rational. Davidson puts it as follows:

> The belief and desire that explain an action must be such that anyone who had that belief and desire would have a reason to act in that way. (1984: 159)

Dennett has a similar view (1978: 59). If a piece of behaviour is to be treated as something the agent *does* – as an action – and not as a mere bodily movement, then it must be rational given the agent's beliefs and desires. The basic pattern of belief–desire explanation is: an agent desires that p, believes that doing A will bring it about that p, and so does A. Igor desires that Yorga be dead, believes that this can be achieved by electrocuting him, and so electrocutes him.

This principle is certainly plausible: most behaviour that we explain by appeal to an agent's beliefs and desires is rational in just this way. But perhaps not all: we explain the verbal behaviour of someone with a bad stammer, of a compulsive spoonerizer, in part by appeal to their beliefs and desires even though their actual behaviour is not rational given those beliefs and desires. In any case, commitment to this principle does not make folk psychology in the least bit non-scientific. It is an entirely empirical question how much of an agent's behaviour is to be explained in this way.

The *second dimension* of principles of charity concerns *strength*. Some qualifications are already apparent; charity-as-true-belief, for Davidson, requires only that *most* beliefs be correct. Dennett has a similar view (1978: 18). Both philosophers also accept lapses from perfect rationality (Dennett 1978: 11; Davidson 1984: 159). These qualifications increase plausibility at the cost of introducing vagueness.

Davidson sometimes suggests a further qualification: that we can be uncharitable provided that the error we attribute is *explicable* (1984: 196). If this were simply the requirement that we should minimize the inexplicable, then it would not distinguish folk psychology from science. It would just be an instance of a general principle of scientific methodology. The general principle of minimizing the inexplicable applies, of course, as much to the attribution of true beliefs as to the attribution of false ones. A rational reader does not interpret the ramblings of Nostradamus as expressing advanced knowlege of our times, because there could be no explanation of Nostradamus' acquisition of that knowledge. So it is an important feature of this further qualification that it applies only to error: falsity and irrationality require explanation, but truth and rationality do not. This asymmetry is necessary if the principle of charity is to distinguish folk psychology from science.

15.5 Against charity

We think that there is no truth in the principle of charity-as-true-belief, some truth in that of charity-as-rational-belief, and perhaps more in charity-as-rational-action. Since it is only charity-as-true-belief that really threatens naturalism, we shall concentrate on it.

From our naturalistic perspective, the task in ascribing beliefs and desires to a person and truth values to his utterances is the usual one of explanation. The canons of good explanations we use here are just the same as those (largely unknown) ones we use elsewhere. A good explanation is likely to see the person as often agreeing with us, but it is likely also to see him as often disagreeing. Thus our best explanation of many of our fellows may take an uncharitable view of opinions on religion, semantics, politics, the weather, etc. It remains an entirely empirical question how true a person's beliefs are.

We reject, therefore, Davidson's frequently stated claim (e.g. 1984: 199–200) that the possibility of error and disagreement depends on general correctness and agreement. Davidson thinks that some error is possible. Why does disaster suddenly strike our explanation if we suppose that error goes beyond the Davidsonian limit? We have heard the suggestion that though we can ascribe error in a few areas we cannot in most. But what difference does it make to our attempt to explain a person uncharitably in, say, semantics that we have already explained him uncharitably in, say, religion and politics? Why does accumulation of error make a difference?

Prima facie it is implausible to commit folk psychology to any principle that demarcates it from the rest of our knowledge. There is only one world, so our knowledge of it should be unified. It ought to be possible to construct a single, integrated picture of nature, including our place in it. Furthermore, Davidson and Dennett do not offer any persuasive reasons for thinking otherwise. We shall now consider their reasons.

(1) Talk of "the principle of charity" was begun by N. L. Wilson in the process of urging a description theory of names (1959: 532). The description theory does indeed require charity. At one point, Davidson appeals implicitly to that theory as support for charity:

> how clear are we that the ancients – some ancients – believed that the earth was flat? *This* earth? Well, this earth of ours is part of the solar system, a system partly identified by the fact that it is a gaggle of large, cool, solid bodies circling around a very large, hot star. If someone believes *none* of this about the earth, is it certain that it is the earth he is thinking about? . . . It isn't that any one false belief necessarily destroys our ability to identify further beliefs, but that the intelligibility of such identifications must depend on a background of largely unmentioned and unquestioned true beliefs. (1984: 168)

We think that the answer to Davidson's rhetorical question is clear. The ancients believed that *this* earth was flat. What other earth is there? Indeed, the fact that the description theory leads to the paradoxical view that the ancients did not have that belief gives us a very good reason for rejecting it (3.3, 10.4, 12.3).

(2) Dennett has argued that natural selection underwrites charity ("Intentional Systems" in 1978). A creature that is irrational or largely in error will not survive to reproduce. We have three comments.

1   The argument might show that it is reasonable to be charitable about any creature we confront simply because it has survived to be confronted. But that is an epistemic principle. To establish the constitutive principle, it needs to be established that we should be charitable also about the creatures we do not confront because they have not survived. Evolutionary con-

siderations do not establish this. Indeed, they suggest exactly the opposite: *the best explanation of non-survival may be error and irrationality*. Abandoning charity may be central to explaining evolutionary failure.

2 We can imagine environments that systematically mislead creatures with a certain perceptual equipment. On some accounts of perceptual properties (like colours), *our* environment is one such. There is nothing incoherent in the claim that our common-sense picture of the world is radically mistaken. So, not only is the constitutive principle false, but the epistemic one has to be taken with caution.

3 Natural selection does not favour true beliefs but rather ones that work in the creature's limited environment. Thus, it will not matter to the survival of a mouse that it is mostly wrong when it thinks, "Look out, a predator". What matters is that it is always right when it thinks, "All clear".

In sum, evolution gives some support, but very far from conclusive support, to the epistemic principle that creatures that survive are likely to be believers of the truth and rational. It helps to refute the constitutive principle that concerns us here.

(3) Both Dennett and Davidson advocate a *holistic* theory of belief and desire. A belief is identified relationally, in virtue of its role in the intellectual system of the believer. This requires that the belief have some systematic connections with other beliefs. These connections, the suggestion runs, yield charity-as-rational-belief.

First, this holism is too extreme: beliefs are partly identified by their causal links to the external world. This is similar to a point we made earlier against structuralism (13.23–13.3). Second, this holism alone does not require that the connections be rational, only that they be systematic. Perhaps an intentional system could be systematically overconfident in its inductions (as a result of living in a very uniform environment). Or perhaps one could be systematically underconfident. There is no reason to suppose, as Dennett does (1978:21), that lapses from optimal rationality are arbitrary, accidental and unsystematic. It is an empirical question how well people infer. The answer emerging from cognitive psychology is that they often infer rather badly. Finally, as we have pointed out, even if some degree of rationality is required in an intentional system, that alone does not place folk psychology outside science.

In sum, charity needs to be split into various distinct principles. One of these is near enough true, one false, and one probably half and half. Such truth as there is in charity is no threat to naturalism. Folk psychology is rough and unsystematic, but there is no reason to suppose that it cannot be suitably modified and developed into a scientific theory.

Suggested reading

15.1

For Dilthey's views, see a recent collection, *Selected Writings* (1976). For Weber's, see *The Methodology of the Social Sciences* (1949).

See McDonald and Pettit 1981, *Semantics and Social Science*, chapter 2, for a nice discussion of the *Verstehen* tradition and of its relationship to Davidson's view.

15.2

Dennett's view of folk psychology is to be found in *Brainstorms* (1978), part I, particularly "Intentional systems"; see also, "Three kinds of intentional psychology" (1981a); and "True believers" (1981b).

Sterelny 1981, "Critical notice of Dennett 1978", is a discussion of Dennett's philosophy of mind.

15.3

For Davidson's views, see *Essays on Actions and Events* (1980), pp. 207–60. For Davidson's theory of language, see *Inquiries into Truth and Interpretation* (1984). Platts 1979, *The Ways of Meaning*, is a Davidsonian introduction to the philosophy of language.

Lycan 1981a, "Psychological laws", is a good critical discussion of Anomalous Monism.

For a discussion of the Davidsonian position on reference, see the suggested reading for section 2.2.

15.4–15.5

The best place to find Dennett's principle of charity, though not under that name, is "Intentional systems", chapter 1 of *Brainstorms* (1978). Davidson discusses charity in many places in the two collections of his essays cited above; see references in the indexes.

McGinn 1977, "Charity, interpretation and belief", is a critical treatment of Davidson on charity.

Cohen 1981, "Can human irrationality be experimentally demonstrated", argues for charity-as-rational-belief in a different way. Stich 1985, "Could man be an irrational animal?", in Kornblith 1985, *Naturalizing Epistemology* argues against Cohen and also Dennett. Stich's paper has a nice summary of some of the psychological literature allegedly demonstrating human irrationality.

For discussions with a similar perspective to that in the text, see Devitt 1981a, section 4.8, and 1984a, section 10.6.**

Glossary

A posteriori or **Empirical**   Primarily applied to knowledge. *A posteriori* or empirical knowledge is knowledge depending for its justification on our experience of the world. Empirical methods are those of observation and experiment. Cf. *A priori*.

A priori   Primarily applied to knowledge. *A priori* knowledge is knowledge independent of and prior to our experience of the world. That independence and priority is not causal and temporal, but logical or inferential. Our experience of the world is not required to *justify a priori* knowledge. Logical and mathematical knowledge provides favourite examples. *A priori* methods are those of armchair reflection. Cf. *A posteriori* or Empirical.

Analytic   Primarily applied to sentences. An analytic sentence depends for its truth value only on the meaning of its elements, not on meaning together with extra-linguistic reality. Hence such sentences are trivial: they carry no information about the world. 'Bachelors are unmarried' is a standard example. Cf. Synthetic.

Anaphor (Anaphoric)   A word or phrase that depends for its interpretation on some other word or phrase in the discourse. Pronouns are typical anaphors. For example, 'he' and 'himself' in 'Max is he who hates himself' are anaphors that depend for their interpretation on 'Max'. 'Max' is said to be the *antecedent* of the anaphors. Antecedents typically, but not always, precede the anaphors they interpret. In 'That he lost the election upset Peacock greatly', 'he' may be an anaphor whose antecedent is 'Peacock'. Cf. Deictic.

Application   In this work, a species or mode of reference. The relationship between a predicate and the object it refers to.

Attributive   In this work, the use of a singular term, or a token of that use, to refer (without any particular object in mind) to whatever is alone in having a certain property. An attributive term depends for identifying reference on denotation. Cf. Designational.

Compositionality   A constraint placed on semantic theories. It is the requirement that the semantic properties of complex expressions (phrases, clauses, sentences) be a function of the semantic properties of the elements composing those complexes.

Constituent   An element of a sentence. Elements may be words or larger groups like phrases or clauses, but not every sequence of words within a sentence is a constituent. 'Every dog chases' is not a constituent of 'Every dog chases some man'. The grammar of a language reveals the constituent structure of each sentence in the language.

Contingent truth   A true sentence that might not have been true. It is not true "in all possible worlds". Cf. Necessary truth.

Conventional meaning   The meaning of an expression determined by the established linguistic conventions of the speaker's language. Cf. Speaker meaning.

d-chain   Short for "designating chain". A causal chain between an object and person consisting of groundings, reference borrowings, and abilities to designate. A singular term can designate an object only if there is a d-chain connecting the user of the term to the object.

Deep structure   A level of structure distinguished from surface structure by transformational generative grammar. It displays the fundamental organization of a sentence: its organization into main and subordinate sentences; the subject and object; the application of modifying words and phrases, and the like. Cf. Surface structure.

Definite description   A species of singular term whose basic form is 'the F', where 'F' stands in for a general term. However, superlatives like 'the tallest mountain', and expressions like 'her father' (='the father of her') are also definite descriptions.

Deictic   A use of a pronoun or demonstrative that is not anaphoric. A use that is out of the blue and directly indicates an object. Cf. Anaphor.

Denotation   A species or mode of reference. It has a general use as the relation between a singular term and its referent. In this work, it is used more narrowly: the mode of reference of an attributive term. So it is the relationship between an attributive term and the unique object the term's asociated description applies to. Cf. Designation.

Designation   A species or mode of reference. It has a general use as the relation between a singular term and its referent. In this work, it is used more narrowly: the mode of reference of a designational term and the object in which the d-chains underlying it are grounded. Cf. Denotation.

Designational   In this work, the use of a singular term to refer to a particular object in mind. A designational term depends for identifying reference on designation. Cf. Attributive.

Eliminitivism   To be eliminitivist about a theory is to believe that the objects posited by it simply do not exist; thus atheists are eliminitivists about religion.

Empirical   Cf. *A posteriori*.

Epistemology   The theory of knowledge.

First philosophy   The branch of, or view concerning, philosophy in which philosophy is seen as prior to any empirical or scientific enterprize. Philosophy's role is to discover important truths *a priori*. Sometimes used to cover that part of philosophy which investigates what there is (cf. Ontology) prior to finding out *about* what there is. Cf. Naturalism.

General term   A term that can apply to each severally of any number of objects; e.g. 'cat'. Cf. Mass term and Singular term.

Grounding   In this work, a perception (or quasi-perception) of an object that begins a reference determining causal chain for a term.

Idealism   An ontological doctrine: the entities that make up the world are dependent for their existence or nature on minds, or are themselves mental. Cf. Realism.

Idiolect   The variety of language spoken by a single speaker.

Mass term   A term that refers cumulatively: thus 'gin' refers to any sum of parts which are gin. Cf. General term and Singular term.

Natural kinds   The kinds required for the explanation of the natural universe.

Natural language   A natural language is one that has developed naturally and has, or has had, native speakers (speakers who acquired it as their first language).

Naturalism   An approach to philosophy: philosophy is part of a broadly empirical and scientific enterprise, not epistemologically prior to science. Naturalism rejects the view that philosophical knowledge is *a priori*. Cf. First philosophy.

Necessary truth   A sentence that must be true. It is true "in all possible worlds". Its falsity is "inconceivable". Favourite examples are the truths of logic and mathematics; more recently and controversially, identity statements like 'water is H_2O'. Cf. Contingent truth.

Ontology   The theory of what there is; i.e. of the basic kinds of entities that comprise the universe, and of their general nature. Derivatively, the ontology of a theory is the set of entities posited by the theory.

Opaque, or Intensional, context   A place within a sentence where the substitution of a singular term for a coreferential term may change the truth value of the sentence. Cf. Transparent, or Extensional, context.

Ostension (Ostensive definition)   The act of pointing out an object or property. Hence, an ostensive definition is an explanation of the meaning of a term by pointing out (examples of) its referent. Cf. Groundings.

Phrase-structure trees   Displays of syntactic structure. The trees show how a unit (typically a sentence) is organized into its immediate sub-units; how the sub-units in turn decompose into smaller units, and so on down to the primitive elements, words or morphemes. Both deep and surface stucture are typically displayed as phrase structure trees. Cf. Transformational generative grammar.

Physical type   In this work, a type of entity identified by overt physical characteristics and used as a medium of language; for example, a certain type of sound. Cf. Semantic type.

Physicalism   The doctrine that the only entities are physical entities and that, ultimately, physical laws explain everything (in some sense).

Primitive   A word or concept is primitive if it cannot itself be analysed into more basic words or concepts. Primitive words or concepts are definable only ostensively, if definable at all.

Qua-problem   A problem for the theory of reference fixing by grounding. It is the problem of discovering in virtue of what a term, particularly a name or natural kind term, is grounded in the cause of a perceptual experience *qua* -one-kind and not *qua* -another. For that cause will always be an instance of many kinds; e.g. the one object may be an echidna, a monotreme, a mammal, a vertebrate, and so on.

Quantifier   an expression that binds, i.e. determines the interpretation of, what are called "variables" in logic. The variables of natural language are typically pronouns or other proforms. For example, in 'Every gunman who says he wants to die with his boots on hopes he will die in bed', the quantifier 'every gunman' binds the two tokens of the pronoun 'he' and the relative clause proform 'who'. These proforms are variables. Some other examples of quantifiers in English are 'all', 'some', 'most', 'a few'. Thus a variable is an anaphor.

Realism   An ontological doctrine. In this work, common-sense realism is the doctrine that most of the observable entities posited by common sense objectively exist independently of the mental. Scientific realism is the parallel doctrine about the unobservables posited by science. Cf. Idealism.

Reference   In this work, the genus of which all referential relationships - for example, application, designation, denotation - are species. Often used more narrowly for the relationship between a singular term and its referent.

Reference borrowing   A person's acquisition or reinforcement of an ability to use a term as a result of the exercise of such an ability by another person in an act of communication.

Semantic type   A type of entity identified by semantic characteristics; thus, a sound token and an inscription token can be of the same semantic type. Cf. Physical type.

Semantics   The theory of meaning. Sometimes contrasted with syntax: semantics is seen as the study of the relations between symbols and the world, whereas syntax is the study of the relations between symbols. The contrast is overdrawn: the semantic properties of complex expressions depend in part on their structure, i.e. on their syntactic properties. Cf. Syntax.

Sense   The semantic properties of an expression which determine its reference.

Singular term   An expression purporting to refer to just one object; examples are names, definite descriptions and demonstratives. Cf. General term and Mass Term.

Speaker meaning What the speaker means by an expression on a particular occasion of its use. This meaning is determined by the content (meaning) of the thought that the speaker is expressing. Cf. Conventional meaning.

Structuralism An approach to language and other systems that holds them to be autonomous, and hence to be explained by appeal to the relations between the elements in the system rather than by extra-linguistic reality. There are two, somewhat similar, structuralist movements: one which began in France early in the century, and one which began in the USA somewhat later.

Surface structure A level of structure distinguished from deep structure by transformational generative grammar. It determines how the sentence is pronounced or written by displaying the superficial organization of the elements of the sentence into words, phrases and clauses. Cf. Deep structure.

Syntax The theory of the principles determining the formation of complex symbols from simple ones; in particular, of the formation of sentences from words and phrases. Cf. Semantics.

Synthetic Primarily applied to sentences. A synthetic sentence depends for its truth value not only on the meaning of its elements, but also on extra-linguistic reality. Such sentences are, therefore, genuinely informative (if true). Cf. Analytic.

Thoughts or **Propositional attitudes** Mental states that differ in two dimensions. One is in the kind of attitude: belief, hope, desire, fear, etc. The other is in content: that Reagan is wrinkled, that Thatcher is tough, that Andropov is dead, etc.

Transformational generative grammar A generative grammar for a language is a system of rules for that language that shows how an indefinitely large number of sentences may be constructed from a finite number of basic elements of the language, the words or morphemes. Transformational generative grammars recognize two kinds or rules. Base rules assemble the primitive elements into deep structures. These structures are mapped onto surface structures by transformational rules.

Transparent, or **Extensional**, **context** A place within a sentence where the substitution of a singular term for a coreferential term never changes the truth value of the sentence. Cf. Opaque, or Intensional, context.

Truth conditions That property of a sentence in virtue of which it is true if a certain situation in the world obtains and not true if that situation does not obtain.

Variable Cf. Quantifier.

Bibliography

Aarsleff, H. 1982: *From Locke to Saussure: Essays in the Study of Language and Intellectual History*. Minneapolis: Minnesota University Press.

Akmajian, A., Demers, R. A. and Harnish, R. M. 1979: *Linguistics: An Introduction to Language and Communication*. Cambridge, Mass.: MIT Press.

— and Heny, F. 1975: *An Introduction to the Principles of Transformational Syntax*. Cambridge, Mass.: MIT Press.

Aqvist, L. 1965: *A New Approach to the Logical Theory of Interrogatives*. Uppsala: Filosofiska Institutionen, Uppsala University.

Armstrong, D. M. 1968: *A Materialist Theory of the Mind*. London: Routledge and Kegan Paul.

— 1971: Meaning and communication. *Philosophical Review*, 80, 427–47.

— 1978: *Nominalism and Realism: Universals and Scientific Realism, Vol..1*. Cambridge: Cambridge University Press.

— 1980: Against 'ostrich' nominalism: a reply to Michael Devitt. *Pacific Philosophical Quarterly*, 61, 440–9.

Austin, J. L. 1962a: *How to do Things with Words*. Oxford: Clarendon Press.

— 1962b: *Sense and Sensibilia*. Oxford: Clarendon Press.

Ayer, A. J. 1946: *Language, Truth and Logic*. 2nd edn (with a new introduction). London: Victor Gollancz. [1st edn, 1936.]

— 1940: *The Foundations of Empirical Knowledge*. London: Macmillan.

— (ed.) 1959: *Logical Positivism*. New York: The Free Press.

Bach, K. 1981. What's in a name. *Australasian Journal of Philosophy*, 59, 371–8.

Baker, C. L. 1977: *Introduction to Generative-Transformational Syntax*. Englewood Cliffs: Prentice-Hall.

Belnap, Nuel D. and Steel Jr, Thomas B. 1976: *The Logic of Questions and Answers*. New Haven: Yale University Press.

Bennett, J. 1976: *Linguistic Behaviour*. Cambridge: Cambridge University Press.

Bertolet, Rod 1979: McKinsey, causes and intentions. *Philosophical Review* 88, 619–32.

— 1980: The semantic significance of Donnellan's distinction. *Philosophical Studies*, 37, 281–8.

— In press: Donnellan's distinctions. *Australasian Journal of Philosophy*.

Black, Max 1962: *Models and Metaphors*. Ithaca, New York: Cornell University Press.

Block, Ned (ed.) 1981: *Readings in Philosophy of Psychology, Vol. 2*. Cambridge, Mass.: Harvard University Press.

— in press: Advertisement for: A semantics for psychology. In Peter A. French, Theodore E. Uehling Jr and Howard K. Wettstein (eds), *Midwest Studies in Philosophy, Vol. X: Studies in the Philosophy of Mind*. Minneapolis: University of Minnesota Press.

Bloomfield, L. 1933: *Language*. New York: Holt, Rinehart and Winston.

Boden, M. A. 1984: Animal perception from an artificial intelligence viewpoint. In C. Hookway (ed.), *Minds, Machines and Evolution*. Cambridge: Cambridge University Press.

Bradley, R. and Schwartz, N. 1979: *Possible Worlds*. Oxford: Basil Blackwell.

Burge, Tyler 1979: Individualism and the mental. In Peter A. French, Theodore E. Uehling Jr and Howard K. Wettstein (eds) *Midwest Studies in Philosophy, Vol. IV: Studies in Metaphysics*, 73–121. Minneapolis: University of Minnesota Press.

Butler, R. J. (ed) 1965: *Analytical Philosophy*, 2nd series. Oxford: Basil Blackwell.

Campbell, Keith 1976: *Metaphysics*. Encio, California: Dickenson Publishing Company.

Canfield, John V. 1977: Donnellan's theory of names. *Dialogue*, 16, 104–27.

Carnap, Rudolf 1932: The elimination of metaphysics through logical analysis of language. [In Ayer 1959: 60–81. 1st publ. in German in *Erkenntnis*, 2.]

— 1950: Empiricism, semantics and ontology. *Review Internationale de Philosophie*, 4, 20–40. [Reprinted in Linsky 1952.]

— 1956: *Meaning and Necessity: A Study in Semantics and Modal Logic*, 2nd edn. Chicago: University of Chicago Press. [1st edn, 1947.]

Carroll, Lewis 1962: *Alice's Adventures in Wonderland and Through the Looking Glass*. New York: Collier Books. [1st edn of *Through the Looking Glass*, 1872.]

Cartwright, R. L. 1960: Negative existentials. *Journal of Philosophy*, 57, 629–39. [Reprinted in Caton 1963.]

Caton, C. E. (ed.) 1963: *Philosophy and Ordinary Language*. Urbana: University of Illinois Press.

Chastain, Charles 1975: Reference and context. [In Gunderson 1975: 194–269.]

Chomsky, Noam 1957: *Syntactic Structures*. The Hague: Mouton.

— 1959: Review of Skinner 1957. *Language*, 35, 26–58. [Reprinted in Fodor and Katz 1964.]

— 1961: On the notion 'Rule of Grammar'. [In Fodor and Katz 1964: 119–36. 1st publ., *Proceedings of the Twelfth Symposium in Applied Mathematics*, XII (1961).]

— 1965: *Aspects of the Theory of Syntax*. Cambridge, Mass.: MIT Press.

— 1966: *Topics in the Theory of Generative Grammar*. The Hague: Mouton. [Excerpts in Searle 1971.]

— 1969a: Linguistics and philosophy. [In Hook 1969: 51–94. Excerpts in Stich 1975.]

— 1969b: Comments on Harman's reply. [In Hook 1969: 152–9.]

— 1971: Deep structure, surface structure, and semantic interpretation. [In Steinberg and Jacobovits 1971: 183–216.]

— 1975: Knowledge of language. [In Gunderson 1975: 299–320.]

— 1980: *Rules and Representations*. New York: Columbia University Press.

Churchland, Patricia 1980: Language, thought and information processing. *Nous*, 14, 147–70.

Churchland, Paul M. 1979: *Scientific Realism and the Plasticity of Mind*. Cambridge: Cambridge University Press.

—— 1984: *Matter and Consciousness*. Cambridge, Mass.: Bradford Books/MIT Press.

Cohen, L. J. 1981: Can human irrationality be experimentally demonstrated? *Behavioral and Brain Sciences*, 4, 317–70. [Includes peer commentaries and response by author.]

Crittenden, C. 1966: Fictional existence. *American Philosophical Quarterly*, 3, 317–21.

Culler, Jonathan 1976. *Saussure*. London: Fontana.

Currie, Gregory 1982: *Frege, an Introduction to his Philosophy*, Totowa, New Jersey: Barns and Noble.

Davidson, Donald 1980: *Essays on Actions and Events*. Oxford: Clarendon Press.

—— 1984: *Inquiries into Truth and Interpretation*. Oxford: Clarendon Press.

—— and Harman, Gilbert (eds) 1972: *Semantics of Natural Language*. Dordrecht: Reidel.

—— and —— (eds) 1976: *The Logic of Grammar*. Encino, Calif.: Dickenson.

—— and Hintikka, Jaakko (eds) 1969: *Words and Objections: Essays on the Work of W. V. Quine*. Dordrecht: Reidel.

De George, Richard and de George, Fernande (eds) 1972: *The Structuralists from Marx to Levi-Strauss*. New York: Doubleday and Company Inc.

Dennett, Daniel 1978: *Brainstorms*. Cambridge, Mass.: Bradford Books.

—— 1981a: Three kinds of intentional psychology. In R. A. Healey (ed.), *Reduction, Time and Reality: Studies in the Philosophy of the Natural Sciences*. Cambridge: Cambridge University Press: 37–62.

—— 1981b: True believers: the intentional strategy and why it works. In A. Heath (ed.), *Scientific Explanation*. Oxford: Oxford University Press.

—— 1983: Intentional systems in cognitive ethology: the 'Panglossian Paradigm' defended. *Behavioral and Brain Sciences*, 6, 343–90. [Includes peer commentaries and response by author.]

—— 1985: *Elbow Room: The Varieties of Free Will Worth Wanting*. Oxford: Basil Blackwell.

Derrida, Jacques 1977a: Signature event context. *Glyph*, 1, 172–97.

—— 1977b: Limited Inc. abc . . . *Glyph*, 2, 162–254.

—— 1986: *The Archaeology of the Frivolous*. Pittsburg: Duquesne University Press.

Devitt, Michael 1979: Against incommensurability. *Australasian Journal of Philosophy* 57, 29–50.

—— 1980a: Brian Loar on singular terms. *Philosophical Studies*, 37, 271–80.

—— 1980b: 'Ostrich nominalism' or 'mirage realism'? *Pacific Philosophical Quarterly*, 61, 433–9.

—— 1981a: *Designation*. New York: Columbia University Press.

—— 1981b: Donnellan's distinction. In Peter A. French, Theodore E. Uehling Jr and Howard K. Wettstein (eds) *Midwest Studies in Philosophy, Volume VI: The Foundations of Analytic Philosophy*: 511–24. Minneapolis: University of Minnesota Press.

—— 1983: Dummett's anti-realism. *Journal of Philosophy*, 80, 73–99.

—— 1984a: *Realism and Truth*. Oxford: Basil Blackwell.

—— 1984b: Thoughts and their ascription. In Peter A. French, Theodore E. Uehling Jr and Howard K. Wettstein (eds), *Midwest Studies in Philosophy, Volume IX: Causation and Causal Theories*: 385–420. Minneapolis: University of Minnesota Press.

—— 1985: Critical notice of Evans 1982. *Australasian Journal of Philosophy*, 63, 216–32.

— and Sterelny, Kim. In preparation a: Linguistics: What's wrong with 'the right view'.

— and— In preparation b: Detoxifying Fodor's paradox.

Dilthey, W. 1976: In H. P. Rickman (ed.), *Selected Writings*. Cambridge: Cambridge University Press.

Donnellan, Keith S. 1966: Reference and definite descriptions. *Philosophical Review*, 75, 281-304. [Reprinted in Steinberg and Jacobovits 1971, Rosenberg and Travis 1971, and Schwartz 1977.]

— 1968: Putting Humpty Dumpty together again. *Philosophical Review*, 77, 203-15.

— 1972: Proper names and identifying descriptions. [In Davidson and Harman 1972: 356-79.]

— 1974: Speaking of nothing. *Philosophical Review*, 83, 3-31. [Reprinted in Schwartz 1977.]

— 1983: Kripke and Putnam on natural kind terms. In Carl Ginet and Sydney Shoemaker (eds), *Knowledge and Mind: Philosophical Essays*. Oxford: Oxford University Press.

Dowty, D. R., Wall, R. E. and Peters, S. 1981: *Introduction to Montague Semantics*. Dordrecht: Reidel.

Dummett, Michael 1973: *Frege: Philosophy of Language*. London: Duckworth.

— 1975: What is a theory of meaning? [In Guttenplan 1975: 97-138.]

— 1976: What is a theory of meaning? (II). In G. Evans and J. McDowell (eds), *Truth and Meaning: Essays in Semantics*, Oxford: Clarendon Press, 67-137.

— 1977: *Elements of Intuitionism*. Oxford: Clarendon Press.

— 1978: *Truth and Other Enigmas*. Cambridge, Mass.: Harvard University Press.

Dupre, J. 1981: Natural kinds and biological taxa. *Philosophical Review*, 90, 66-90.

Eagleton, Terry 1983: *Literary Theory: An Introduction*. Oxford: Basil Blackwell.

Eco, U. 1984: *Semiotics and the Philosophy of Language*. London: Macmillan.

Erwin, E., Kleinman, L. and Zemach, E. 1976: The historical theory of reference. *Australasian Journal of Philosophy*, 54, 50-7.

Evans, Gareth 1983: The causal theory of names. *Proceedings of the Aristotelian Society*, 47, 187-208. [Reprinted in Schwartz 1977.]

— 1982: John McDowell (ed.), *The Varieties of Reference*, Oxford: Clarendon Press.

Feyerabend, Paul 1970a: Consolations for the specialist. [In Lakatos and Musgrave 1970: 197-230.]

— 1970b: Against method: outline of an anarchistic theory of knowledge. In Michael Radner and Stephen Winokur (eds), *Minnesota Studies in the Philosophy of Science, Vol. IV: Analyses of Theories and Methods of Physics and Psychology*, 17-130.

— 1975: *Against Method: An Outline of an Anarchistic Theory of Knowledge*. London: New Left Books.

Field, Hartry 1972: Tarski's theory of truth. *Journal of Philosophy*, 69, 347-75. [Reprinted in Platts 1980.]

— 1973: Theory of change and the indeterminacy of reference. *Journal of Philosophy*, 70, 462-81.

—1978: Mental representation. *Erkenntnis*, 13, 9-61. [Reprinted with postscript in Block 1981: 78-114 (page references are to Block).]

Fine, Arthur 1975: How to compare theories: reference and change. *Nous*, 9, 17-32.

Fishman, J. A. 1960: A systematization of the Whorfian analysis. *Behavioral Science*, 5, 329–39. [Reprinted in J. W. Berry and P. R. Dasen (eds), *Culture and Cognition: Readings in Cross-Cultural Psychology*. London: Methuen, 1974.]

Fitch, F. B. 1949: The problem of the morning star and the evening star. *Philosophy of Science*, 16, 137–41.

Fodor, Janet D. 1977: *Semantics: Theories of Meaning in Generative Grammar*. New York: Thomas Y. Crowell.

Fodor, Jerry A. 1975: *The Language of Thought*. New York: Thomas Y. Crowell.

— 1980: Methodological solipsism considered as a research strategy in cognitive psychology. *Behavioral and Brain Sciences*, 3, 63–109. [Includes peer commentaries and responses by author.] [Reprinted in Fodor 1981a.]

— 1981a: *Representations: Philosophical Essays on the Foundations of Cognitive Science*. Cambridge, Mass.: Bradford Books/MIT Press.

— 1981b: Introduction: some notes on what linguistics is talking about. [In Block 1981: 197–207.]

— 1983: *The Modularity of Mind: An Essay on Faculty Psychology*. Cambridge, Mass.: Bradford Books/MIT Press.

— 1985: Precis of *The Modularity of Mind*. *Behavioral and Brain Sciences*, 8, 1–42 [Includes peer commentaries and response by author].

— and Katz, J. Jerrold (eds) 1964: *The Structure of Language: Readings in the Philosophy of Language*. Englewood Cliffs, N.J.: Prentice-Hall.

Follesdal, D. and Hilpinen, R. 1981: Deontic logic: an introduction. [In Hilpinen 1981: 1–35.]

Frege, G. 1918: The thought. *Mind*, 65 (1956): 289–311. [Reprinted in Klemke 1968, 1st publ. in German, 1918–19.]

— 1952: *Translations from the Philosophical Writings of Gottlob Frege*, 2nd edn, corrected 1960. Peter Geach and Max Black (eds). Oxford: Blackwell.

— 1979: *Posthumous Writings*, trans. P. Long and R. White. Oxford: Basil Blackwell.

Geach, Peter 1962: *Reference and Generality*. Ithaca, New York: Cornell University Press.

Gellner, E. 1959: *Words and Things*. London: Victor Gollanz.

George, Alexander 1984: On Devitt and Dummett. *Journal of Philosophy*, 81, 516–27.

Godfrey-Smith, P. In press: Why semantic properties don't earn their keep. *Philosophical Studies*.

— and Sterelny, Kim. In preparation: Semantic psychology.

Gould, S. J. 1983: *The Panda's Thumb*. Harmondsworth: Penguin.

Graves, Christina, Katz, J. J., Nishiyama, Y., Soames, Scott, Stecker, P. and Tovey, P. 1973: Tacit knowledge. *Journal of Philosophy*, 70, 318–30.

Grice, H. P. 1957: Meaning. *Philosophical Review*, 66, 377–88. [Reprinted in Rosenberg and Travis 1971 and in Steinberg and Jakobovits 1971 (page references are to Rosenberg and Travis).]

— 1968: Utterer's meaning, sentence meaning, and word meaning. *Foundations of Language*, 4, 1–18. [Reprinted in Searle 1971.]

— 1969: Utterer's meaning and intentions. *Philosophical Review*, 78, 147–77.

— 1975: Logic and conversation. In P. Cole and J. Morgan (eds), *Syntax and Semantics, Vol. 3: Speech Acts*. New York: Academic Press: 41–59. [Reprinted in Davidson and Harman 1976.]

Grover, Dorothy L., Camp Jr, Joseph L. and Belnap Jr, Nuel D. 1975: A prosentential theory of truth. *Philosophical Studies*, 27, 73–125.

Gunderson, Keith (ed.) 1975: *Minnesota Studies in the Philosophy of Science, Vol. VII: Language, Mind and Knowledge*. Minneapolis: University of Minnesota Press.

Guttenplan, S. (ed.) 1975: *Mind and Language*. Oxford: Clarendon Press.

Hacking, Ian 1975: *Why Does Language Matter to Philosophy?* Cambridge: Cambridge University Press.

Harman, Gilbert 1967: Psychological aspects of the theory of syntax. *Journal of Philosophy*, 64, 75–87. [Reprinted in Stich 1975.]

— 1968: Three levels of meaning. *Journal of Philosophy*, 65, 590–602. [Reprinted in Steinberg and Jacobovits 1971.]

— 1969: Linguistic competence and empiricism. [In Hook 1969: 143–51.]

— 1973: *Thought*. Princeton: Princeton University Press.

— (ed.) 1974: *On Noam Chomsky: Critical Essays*. Garden City, New York: Anchor Press/Doubleday.

— 1975: Language, thought, and communication. [In Gunderson 1975: 270–98.]

Hawkes, Terence 1977: *Structuralism and Semiotics*. London: Methuen.

Hempel, C. G. 1950: Problems and changes in the empiricist criterion of meaning. *Revue Internationale de Philosophie*, 11, 41–63. [Reprinted in Linsky 1952.]

— 1954: A logical appraisal of operationism. *Scientific Monthly*,1, 215–20.

— 1966: *Philosophy of Natural Science*. Englewood Cliffs, N.J.: Prentice-Hall.

Hilpinen, Risto (ed.) 1981: *Deontic Logic: Introductory and Systematic Readings*, 2nd edn. Dordrecht: Reidel.

Hintikka, Jaakko 1962: *Knowledge and Belief*. Ithaca, New York: Cornell University Press.

Hook, Sidney (ed.) 1969: *Language and Philosophy: A Symposium*. New York: New York University Press.

Horwich, Paul 1982: Three forms of realism. *Synthèse*, 51, 181–202.

Jackendoff, Ray S. 1972: *Semantic Interpretation in Generative Grammar*. Cambridge, Mass.: MIT Press.

Jameson, Frederic 1972: *The Prison-House of Language*. Princeton, New Jersey: Princeton University Press.

Kant, Immanuel 1929: *Critique of Pure Reason*, trans. Norman Kemp Smith. London: Macmillan. [1st German edn, 1781.]

— 1953: *Prolegomena to Any Future Metaphysics*, trans. Peter G. Lucas. Manchester: Manchester University Press. [1st German edn, 1783.]

Kaplan, David 1969: Quantifying in. [In Davidson and Hintikka 1969: 206–42. Reprinted in Linskey 1971 and Davidson and Harman 1976.]

Katz, Jerrold J. 1964: Mentalism in linguistics. *Language*, 40, 124–37.

— 1966: *The Philosophy of Language*. New York: Harper and Row. [Excerpts in Stich 1975 and in Block 1981.]

— 1971. *The Underlying Reality of Language and Its Philosophical Import*. New York: Harper and Row.

— 1972: *Semantic Theory*. New York: Harper and Row.

— 1975: Logic and language: an examination of recent criticisms of intentionalism. [In Gunderson 1975: 36–130.]

Katz, Jerrold J. 1977: The real status of semantic representations. *Linguistic Inquiry*, 8, 559–84. [Reprinted in Block 1981: 253–75 (page references are to Block).]

— and Fodor, Jerry A. 1963: The structure of a semantic theory. *Language*, 39, 170–210. [Reprinted in Fodor and Katz 1964 and in Rosenberg and Travis 1971.]

Kempson, Ruth 1977: *Semantic Theory*. Cambridge: Cambridge University Press.

Kenny, A. 1973: *Wittgenstein*. London: Pelican Books.

Klemke, E. D. (ed.) 1968: *Essays on Frege*. Urbana: University of Illinois Press.

Kornblith, Hilary 1980: Referring to artifacts. *Philosophical Review*, 89, 109–14.

— (ed.) 1985: *Naturalizing Epistemology*. Cambridge, Mass.: Bradford Books/MIT Press.

Kripke, Saul A. 1959: A completeness theorem in modal logic. *Journal of Symbolic Logic*, 24, 1–14.

— 1962: Semantical considerations on modal logic. *Acta Philosophica Fennica*, 16, 83–94. [Reprinted in Linsky 1971.]

— 1971: Identity and necessity. In Milton K. Munitz (ed.), *Identity and Individuation*. New York: New York University Press, 135–64. [Reprinted in Schwartz 1977.]

— 1979: Speaker's reference and semantic reference. In Peter A. French, Theodore E. Uehling Jr and Howard K. Wettstein (eds), *Contemporary Perspectives in the Philosophy of Language*. Minneapolis: University of Minnesota Press, 6–27.

— 1980: *Naming and Necessity*. Cambridge, Mass.: Harvard University Press. [A corrected version of an article on the same name (plus an appendix) in Davidson and Harman 1972, together with a new preface.]

Kroon, Frederick W. 1982: The problem of 'Jonah': how *not* to argue for the causal theory of reference. *Philosophical Studies*, 43, 281–99.

— 1985: Theoretical terms and the causal view of reference. *Australasian Journal of Philosophy*, 63, 143–66.

Kuhn, Thomas S. 1962: *The Structure of Scientific Revolutions*. Chicago: Chicago University Press. [2nd edn, 1970.]

— 1970: Reflections on my critics. [In Lakatos and Musgrave 1970: 231–78.]

Lakatos, Imre and Musgrave, Alan (eds) 1970: *Criticism and the Growth of Knowledge*. Cambridge: Cambridge University Press.

Lakoff, George 1971: On generative semantics. [In Steinberg and Jacobovits 1971: 232–96.]

Leeds, Stephen 1978: Theories of reference and truth. *Erkenntnis*, 13, 111–29.

Lenneberg, E.H. 1953: Cognition in ethnolinguistics. *Language*, 29, 463–71.

— 1964: The capacity for language acquisition. [In Fodor and Katz 1964: 579–603.]

Lewis, David K. 1969: *Convention: A Philosophical Study*. Cambridge, Mass.: Harvard University Press.

— 1972: General semantics. [In Davidson and Harman 1972: 169–218. Reprinted in Lewis 1983.]

— 1973: *Counterfactuals*. Oxford: Basil Blackwell.

— 1974: Languages, language, and grammar. [In Harman 1974: 253–66.]

— 1975: Languages and language. [In Gunderson 1975: 3–35. Reprinted in Lewis 1983.]

— 1983: *Philosophical Papers, Vol. I*. Oxford: Oxford University Press.

— 1986: *On the Plurality of Worlds*. Oxford: Basil Blackwell.

Linsky, Leonard (ed.) 1952: *Semantics and the Philosophy of Language*. Urbana: University of Illinois Press.

—— 1963: Reference and referents. [In Caton 1963: 74–89. Reprinted in Steinberg and Jakobovits 1971.]

—— (ed.) 1971: *Reference and Modality*. Oxford: Oxford University Press.

—— 1977: *Names and Descriptions*. Chicago: Chicago University Press.

Loar, Brian 1976: The semantics of singular terms. *Philosophical Studies*, 30, 353–77.

—— 1981: *Mind and Meaning*. Cambridge: Cambridge University Press.

Loux, M. S. (ed.) 1979: *The Possible and the Actual*. Ithaca, New York: Cornell University Press.

Lycan, W. G. 1979: The trouble with possible worlds. [In Loux 1979: 274–316.]

—— 1981a: Psychological laws. *Philosophical Topics*, 12, 9–38.

—— 1981b: Toward a homuncular theory of believing. *Cognition and Brain Theory*, 4, 139–59.

—— 1984: *Logical Form in Natural Language*. Cambridge, Mass.: Bradford Books/MIT Press.

Lyons, John 1981: *Language and Linguistics: An Introduction*. Cambridge: Cambridge University Press.

McCawley, J. D. 1971: Prelexical syntax. In R. J. O'Brien (ed.), *Report of the 22nd Annual Round Table Meeting of Linguistics and Language Studies*, Washington D.C.: Georgetown University Press. [Reprinted in Seuren 1974.]

—— 1972: A program for logic. [In Davidson and Harman 1972: 498–544.]

McCormack, W. C. and Wurm, S. A. (eds) 1977: *Language and Thought: Anthropological Issues*. The Hague: Mouton.

McDonald, G. and Pettit, P. 1981: *Semantics and Social Science*. London: Routledge and Kegan Paul.

McDowell, John 1977: On the sense and reference of proper names. *Mind*, 86, 159–85. [Reprinted in Platts 1980.]

—— 1978: Physicalism and primitive denotation: Field on Tarski. *Erkenntnis*, 13, 131–52. [Reprinted in Platts 1980.]

McGinn, Colin 1977: Charity, interpretation and belief. *Journal of Philosophy*, 74, 521–35.

—— 1982: The structure of content. [In Woodfield 1982: 207–58.]

McKay, Thomas 1984: Critical study of Devitt 1981a. *Nous*, 18, 357–67.

McKinsey, Michael 1976: Divided reference in causal theories of names. *Philosophical Studies*, 30, 235–42.

—— 1978: Names and intentionality. *Philosophical Review*, 87, 171–200.

Mellor, D. H. 1977: Natural kinds. *British Journal for the Philosophy of Science*, 28, 299–312.

Mill, J. S. 1961: *A System of Logic*, 8th edn. London: Longmans. [1st edn, 1867.]

Millikan, R. 1984: *Language, Thought and Other Biological Categories: New Foundations for Realism*. Cambridge, Mass.: MIT Press.

Montague, R. E. 1974: *Formal Philosophy: Selected Papers of R. E. Montague*, (ed.) R. H. Thomason. New Haven: Yale University Press.

Nagel, Ernst 1961: *The Structure of Science*. London: Routledge and Kegan Paul.

Nagel, Thomas 1969: Linguistics and epistemology. [In Hook 1969: 171–82. Reprinted in Harman 1974.]

Newton-Smith, W. H. 1981: *The Rationality of Science*. London: Routledge and Kegan Paul.

Papineau, David 1979: *Theory and Meaning*. Oxford: Clarendon Press.

Passmore, John 1966: *A Hundred Years of Philosophy*, 2nd edn. London: Penguin Books. [1st edn, 1957.]

Pears, David 1971: *Wittgenstein*. London: Fontana Modern Masters.

Pettit, Philip 1977: *The Concept of Structuralism*. Berkeley: University of California.

— and McDowell, John (eds) 1986: *Subject, Thought and Context*. Oxford: Oxford University Press.

Piatelli-Palmarini, M. (ed.) 1980: *Language and Learning: The Debate between Jean Piaget and Noam Chomsky*. Cambridge: Cambridge University Press.

Plantinga, Alvin 1974: *The Nature of Necessity*. Oxford: Oxford University Press.

Platts, Mark 1979: *The Ways of Meaning*. London: Routledge and Kegan Paul.

— (ed.) 1980: *Reference, Truth and Reality: Essays on the Philosophy of Language*. London: Routledge and Kegan Paul.

Popper, Karl 1959: *The Logic of Scientific Discovery*. London: Hutchinson. [1st German edn, 1934.]

Putnam, Hilary 1967: The 'innateness hypothesis' and explanatory models in linguistics. *Synthèse*, 17, 12–22. [Reprinted in Searle 1971, in Stich 1975, and in Block 1981: 292–99 (page reference is to Block).]

— 1973: Meaning and reference. *Journal of Philosophy*, 70, 699–711. [Reprinted in Schwartz 1977.]

— 1975: *Mind, Language and Reality: Philosophical Papers, Vol. 2*. Cambridge: Cambridge University Press.

— 1978: *Meaning and the Moral Sciences*. London: Routledge and Kegan Paul.

— 1981: *Reason, Truth and History*. Cambridge: Cambridge University Press.

Pylyshyn, Z. 1973: What the mind's eye tells the mind's brain: a critique of mental imagery. *Psychological Bulletin*, 80, 1–24.

— 1980: Computation and cognition: issues in the foundations of cognitive science. *Behavioral and Brain Sciences*, 3, 111–69. [Includes peer commentaries and response by author.]

— 1984: *Computation and Cognition*. Cambridge, Mass.: Bradford Books/MIT Press.

Quine, W. V. 1940: *Mathematical Logic*. New York: W. W. Norton.

— 1960: *Word and Object*. Cambridge, Mass.: MIT Press.

— 1961: *From a Logical Point of view*, 2nd edn. Cambridge Mass.: Harvard University Press. [1st edn, 1953.]

— 1966: *The Ways of Paradox and Other Essays*. New York: Random House.

— 1969: *Ontological Relativity and Other Essays*. New York: Columbia University Press.

— 1970: *Philosophy of Logic*. Englewood Cliffs, New Jersey: Prentice-Hall.

— 1975: The nature of natural knowledge. [In Guttenplan 1975: 67–81.]

— 1980: Soft impeachment disowned. *Pacific Philosophical Quarterly*, 61, 450–1.

Romanos, G. D. 1983: *Quine and Analytic Philosophy: The Language of Language*. Cambridge, Mass.: Bradford Books/MIT Press.

Rorty, R. (ed.) 1967: *The Linguistic Turn*. Chicago: Chicago University Press.

Rosch, Eleanor 1977: Linguistic relativity. In P. N. Johnson-Laird and P. C. Wason (eds), *Thinking: Readings in Cognitive Science*. Cambridge: Cambridge University Press, 501–19.

Rosenberg, J. F. and Travis, C. (eds) 1971: *Readings in the Philosophy of Language*. Englewood Cliffs, New Jersey: Prentice-Hall.

Russell, Bertrand 1967: *The Problems of Philosophy*. London: Oxford Paperbacks. [1st publ. 1912.]

—— 1957: *Mysticism and Logic*. New York: Doubleday Anchor. [1st publ. 1917.]

—— 1919: *Introduction to Mathematical Logic*. London: George Allen and Unwin.

—— 1956: *Logic and Knowlege*. ed. R. C. Marsh. London: George Allen and Unwin.

Ryle, Gilbert 1949: *The Concept of Mind*. London: Hutchinson.

—— 1979: *On Thinking*. Oxford: Basil Blackwell.

Salmon, Nathan U. 1982: *Reference and Essence*. Princeton: Princeton University Press.

Sampson, C. 1975: *The Form of Language*. London: Weidenfield and Nicholson.

Sapir, Edward 1931: Conceptual categories in primitive languages. *Science*, 74, 578. [Reprinted in D. Hymes (ed.), *Language in Culture and Society: A Reader in Linguistics and Anthropology*. New York: Harper and Row, 1964: 128 (page references are to Hymes).]

—— 1949: *Selected Writings in Language, Culture and Personality*, ed. David G. Mandelbaum. Berkeley: University of California Press.

Saussure, Ferdinand de 1966: *Course in General Linguistics*, eds Charles Bally and Albert Sechehaye, trans. Wade Baskin. New York: McGraw-Hill Book Co. [1st French edn, 1916.]

Scheffler, I. 1967: *Science and Subjectivity*. New York: Bobbs Merrill.

Schiffer, Stephen 1972: *Meaning*. Oxford: Clarendon Press.

—— 1978: The basis of reference. *Erkenntnis*, 13, 171–206.

—— 1981: Truth and theory of content. In Herman Parrett and Jacques Bouveresse (eds), *Meaning and Understanding*, Berlin: Walter de Gruyter.

Schlick, Moritz 1932–33: Positivism and realism. [In Ayer 1959: 82–107. 1st publ. in German in *Erkenntnis*, 3.]

Schwartz, Robert 1969: On knowing a grammar. [In Hook 1969: 183–909.]

Schwartz, Stephen P. (ed.) 1977: *Naming, Necessity, and Natural Kinds*. Ithaca, New York: Cornell University Press.

—— 1978: Putnam on artifacts. *Philosophical Review*, 87, 566–74.

—— 1980: Natural kinds and nominal kinds. *Mind*, 89, 182–95.

Searle, J. R. 1958: Proper names. *Mind*, 67, 166–73. [Reprinted in Caton 1963.]

—— 1969: *Speech Acts: An Essay in the Philosophy of Language*. Cambridge: Cambridge University Press.

—— (ed.) 1971: *The Philosophy of Language*. London: Oxford University Press.

—— 1972: Chomsky's revolution in linguistics. *New York Review of Books*, 18, 16–24. [Reprinted in Harman 1974: 2–33.]

—— 1977: Reiterating the differences: a reply to Derrida. *Glyph*, 1, 198–209.

—— 1983a: *Intentionality: An Essay in the Philosophy of Mind*. Cambridge: Cambridge University Press.

—— 1983b: The world turned upside down. *New York Review of Books*, 30, 74–9.

Searle, J. R. and Mackey, L. H. 1984: An exchange on deconstruction. *New York Review of Books*, 31, 47–8.

Seuren, P. A. 1972: Autonomous *versus* semantic syntax. *Foundations of Language*, 8, 237–65. [Reprinted in Seuren 1974.]

— (ed.) 1974: *Semantic Syntax*. London: Oxford University Press.

Shwayder D. S. 1956: '='. *Mind*, 65,16–37.

Skinner, B. F. 1957: *Verbal Behaviour*. New York: Appleton-Century-Crofts.

Smart, J. J. C. 1984: *Ethics, Persuasion and Truth*. London: Routledge and Kegan Paul.

Soames, Scott 1984: Linguistics and psychology. *Linguistics and Philosophy*, 7, 155–79.

Steinberg, Danny D. and Jakobovits, Leon A. (eds) 1971: *Semantics: An Interdisciplinary Reader in Philosophy, Linguistics and Psychology*. Cambridge: Cambridge University Press.

Sterelny, Kim 1981: Critical notice of Dennett 1978. *Australasian Journal of Philosophy*, 59, 442–53.

— 1982: Against conversational implicature. *Journal of Semantics*, 1, 187–94.

— 1983a: Natural kind terms. *Pacific Philosophical Quarterly*, 64, 110–25.

— 1983b: Mental representation: what language is Brainese. *Philosophical Studies*, 43, 365–82.

— 1984: Critical review of Woodfield 1982. *Journal of Semantics*, 3, 277–94.

Stich, Stephen P. 1971: What every speaker knows. *Philosophical Review*, 80, 476–96.

— 1972: Grammar, psychology, and indeterminacy. *Journal of Philosophy*, 69, 799–818. [Reprinted in Block 1981.]

— (ed.) 1975: *Innate Ideas*. Berkeley: University of California Press.

— 1978a: Empiricism, innateness, and linguistic universals. *Philosophical Studies*, 33, 273–86.

— 1978b: Beliefs and subdoxastic states. *Philosophy of Science*, 45, 499–518.

— 1982: On the ascription of content. [In Woodfield 1982: 153–206.]

— 1983: *From Folk Psychology to Cognitive Science*. Cambridge, Mass.: Bradford/MIT Press.

— 1985: Could man be an irrational animal? Some notes on the epistemology of rationality. [In Kornblith 1985: 249–67.]

Strawson, P. F. 1950: On referring. *Mind*, 59, 320–44. [Reprinted in Caton 1963 and Rosenberg and Travis 1971.]

— 1959: *Individuals: An Essay in Descriptive Metaphysics*. London: Methuen.

— *The Bounds of Sense*. London: Menthuen.

Sturrock, J. 1979: *Structuralism and Since*. Oxford: Oxford University Press.

Suppe, F. (ed.) 1977: *The Structure of Scientific Theories*, 2nd edn. Urbana: University of Illinois. [1st edn, 1973.]

Tarski, Alfred 1956: *Logic, Semantics, Metamathematics*, trans. J. H. Woodger. Oxford: Clarendon Press.

Unger, Peter 1983: The causal theory of reference. *Philosophical Studies*, 43, 1–45.

Walker, R. 1975: Conversational implicatures. In S. Blackburn (ed.), *Meaning, Reference and Necessity*. Cambridge: Cambridge University Press.

Warnock, G. J. 1958: *English Philosophy Since 1900*. London: Oxford University Press.

Weber, Max 1949: *The Methodology of the Social Sciences*, trans. and eds, E. A. Shils and H. A. Finch. Chicago: Free Press.

Wettstein, Howard 1981: Demonstrative reference and definite descriptions. *Philosophical Studies*, 40, 241–57.

Whorf, Benjamin Lee 1956: *Language, Thought, and Reality*, ed. and intro. John B. Carroll. Cambridge, Mass.: MIT Press.

Wiggins, D. 1965: Identity-statements. [In Butler 1965: 40–71.]

Wilson, N. L. 1959: Substances without substrata. *Review of Metaphysics*, 12, 521–39.

Wittgenstein, Ludwig 1953: *Philosophical Investigations*, trans. G. E. M. Anscombe. Oxford: Basil Blackwell.

Woodfield, A. (ed.) 1982: *Thought and Object*. Oxford: Clarendon Press.

Zemach, Eddy 1976: Putnam's theory on the reference of substance terms. *Journal of Philosophy*, 73, 116–27.

Index